Wittgenstein and Literary Studies

Wittgenstein is often regarded as the most important philosopher of the twentieth century and, in recent decades, his work has begun to play a prominent role in literary studies, particularly in debates over language, interpretation, and critical judgment. *Wittgenstein and Literary Studies* solidifies this critical movement, assembling recent critics and philosophers who understand Wittgenstein as a counterweight to long-standing tendencies in both literary studies and philosophical aesthetics. The chapters here cover a wide range of topics. Why have contemporary writers been so drawn to Wittgenstein? What is a Wittgensteinian response to New Historicism, Post-Critique, and other major critical movements? How does Wittgenstein help us understand the nature of style, fiction, and poetry, and the link between ethics and aesthetics? As the volume makes clear, Wittgenstein's work provides a rare bridge between professional philosophy and literary studies, offering us a way out of entrenched positions and their denials – what Wittgenstein himself called "pictures ... that held us captive."

Robert Chodat is Professor of English at Boston University. He is the author of *The Matter of High Words: Naturalism, Normativity, and the Postwar Sage* (2017) and *Worldly Acts and Sentient Things: The Persistence of Agency from Stein to DeLillo* (2008).

John Gibson is Professor of Philosophy at the University of Louisville. He is the author of *Fiction and the Weave of Life* (2008), editor of *The Philosophy of Poetry* (2015), and coeditor of *The Routledge Companion to the Philosophy of Literature* (2015), *Narrative, Emotion, and Insight* (2011), and *The Literary Wittgenstein* (2004).

Cambridge Studies in Literature and Philosophy

Editor

Anthony J. Cascardi, *University of California, Berkeley*

Tracing the impact of philosophy on literature in both content and form, this series shows how a philosopher's thinking filtered thematically and substantively into literature, as well as into the generic evolution of creative writing. Cambridge Studies in Literature and Philosophy also provides a summation of the state of twenty-first-century knowledge on what impact a philosopher or theme has had on literature.

Forthcoming Books in this Series:

Andrew Benjamin *Heidegger and Literary Studies*

James I. Porter *Nietzsche and Literary Studies*

Claudia Brodsky *Kant and Literary Studies*

Kate Stanley and Kirsten Case *William James and Literary Studies*

Wittgenstein and Literary Studies

Edited by

Robert Chodat
Boston University

John Gibson
University of Louisville

Shaftesbury Road, Cambridge CB2 8EA, United Kingdom

One Liberty Plaza, 20th Floor, New York, NY 10006, USA

477 Williamstown Road, Port Melbourne, VIC 3207, Australia

314–321, 3rd Floor, Plot 3, Splendor Forum, Jasola District Centre, New Delhi – 110025, India

103 Penang Road, #05–06/07, Visioncrest Commercial, Singapore 238467

Cambridge University Press is part of Cambridge University Press & Assessment, a department of the University of Cambridge.

We share the University's mission to contribute to society through the pursuit of education, learning and research at the highest international levels of excellence.

www.cambridge.org
Information on this title: www.cambridge.org/9781108833219

DOI: 10.1017/9781108973687

© Cambridge University Press & Assessment 2022

This publication is in copyright. Subject to statutory exception and to the provisions of relevant collective licensing agreements, no reproduction of any part may take place without the written permission of Cambridge University Press & Assessment.

First published 2022

Printed in the United Kingdom by TJ Books Ltd, Padstow Cornwall

A catalogue record for this publication is available from the British Library.

Library of Congress Cataloging-in-Publication Data
Names: Chodat, Robert, 1970- editor. | Gibson, John, 1969- editor.
Title: Wittgenstein and literary studies / edited by Robert Chodat, John Gibson.
Description: Cambridge ; New York, NY : Cambridge University Press, 2022. | Series: Cambridge studies in literature and philosophy | Includes bibliographical references and index.
Identifiers: LCCN 2022017658 (print) | LCCN 2022017659 (ebook) | ISBN 9781108833219 (hardback) | ISBN 9781108978163 (paperback) | ISBN 9781108973687 (epub)
Subjects: LCSH: Wittgenstein, Ludwig, 1889-1951. | Criticism. | Literature–Philosophy. | BISAC: LITERARY CRITICISM / Semiotics & Theory
Classification: LCC B3376.W564 W521346 2022 (print) | LCC B3376.W564 (ebook) | DDC 192–dc23/eng/20220705
LC record available at https://lccn.loc.gov/2022017658
LC ebook record available at https://lccn.loc.gov/2022017659

ISBN 978-1-108-83321-9 Hardback

Cambridge University Press & Assessment has no responsibility for the persistence or accuracy of URLs for external or third-party internet websites referred to in this publication and does not guarantee that any content on such websites is, or will remain, accurate or appropriate.

Contents

List of Contributors	page	ix
Abbreviations of Wittgenstein's Major Works		xii

Introduction: Why Wittgenstein and Literary Studies?   1
John Gibson

1 Writing after Wittgenstein   16
Michael LeMahieu

2 A Wittgensteinian Phenomenology of Criticism   41
Toril Moi

3 Appreciating Material: Criticism, Science, and the Very Idea of Method   62
Robert Chodat

4 A Vision of Language for Literary Historians: Forms of Life, Context, Use   82
Sarah Beckwith

5 Wittgenstein and the Prospects for a Contemporary Literary Humanism   104
Espen Hammer

6 Storied Thoughts: Wittgenstein and the Reaches of Fiction   126
Magdalena Ostas

7 Wittgenstein and Lyric   146
Hannah Vandegrift Eldridge

8	**Life, Logic, Style: On Late Wittgenstein** *Henry W. Pickford*	168
9	**Wittgenstein's Apocalyptic Subjectivity** *Ben Ware*	194
	Index	214

Contributors

Sarah Beckwith is the Katherine Everett Gilbert Professor of English at Duke University. She is the author most recently of *Shakespeare and the Grammar of Forgiveness* (Cornell University Press, 2011), and of numerous essays on literature and ordinary language philosophy in the tradition of Austin, Wittgenstein, and Cavell. She is a coeditor of *The Journal of Medieval and Early Modern Studies*, and the book series, *Re-Formations*, with the University of Notre Dame Press. She is currently completing a book on Shakespeare and the ethics of tragedy and working on another project, *The Book of Second Chances*, on versions of Shakespeare's *The Winter's Tale*.

Robert Chodat is Professor of English at Boston University, where he teaches courses on post-World War II American fiction, literary theory, and the relationship between literature and philosophy. He is the author of *The Matter of High Words: Naturalism, Normativity, and the Postwar Sage* (Oxford University Press, 2017) and *Worldly Acts and Sentient Things: The Persistence of Agency from Stein to DeLillo* (Cornell University Press, 2008). He has published articles on Philip Roth, Lorrie Moore, Stanley Cavell, narrative theory, evolutionary aesthetics, cognitivist accounts of style, and other topics.

Hannah Vandegrift Eldridge is Professor of German in the Department of German, Nordic, and Slavic+ at the University of Wisconsin–Madison. She works on German literature from the eighteenth to twenty-first centuries, especially lyric poetry, philosophy, and prosody. Her first book, *Lyric Orientations: Hölderlin, Rilke, and the Poetics of Community*, appeared with Cornell University Press in 2015. She has published articles on Hölderlin, Rilke, Cavell, Wittgenstein, Klopstock, Nietzsche, and Grünbein. She coedited *Rilke's Sonnets to Orpheus: Critical and Philosophical*

Perspectives (Oxford University Press, 2019); a monograph on metrical theory and practice in Klopstock, Nietzsche, and Grünbein is forthcoming in October, 2022.

John Gibson is Professor of Philosophy at the University of Louisville. His research focuses on topics in aesthetics, the philosophy of literature, and the philosophy of the self. He is the author of *Fiction and the Weave of Life* (Oxford 2007), editor of *The Philosophy of Poetry* (Oxford University Press, 2015), and coeditor of *The Literary Wittgenstein* (Routledge, 2004), *The Routledge Companion to Philosophy of Literature* (Routledge, 2015), and *A Sense of the World* (Routledge, 2009). He is currently writing a book on poetry, metaphor, and meaning.

Espen Hammer is Professor of Philosophy at Temple University, Philadelphia. He is the author of *Stanley Cavell: Skepticism, Subjectivity, and the Ordinary* (Polity Press, 2002), *Adorno and the Political* (Routledge, 2006), *Philosophy and Temporality from Kant to Critical Theory* (Cambridge University Press, 2011), and *Adorno's Modernism: Art, Experience, and Catastrophe* (Cambridge University Press, 2015). He has been an editor of *German Idealism: Contemporary Perspectives* (Routledge, 2007) and *Kafka's The Trial: Philosophical Perspectives* (Oxford University Press, 2018). He has coedited *The Routledge Companion to the Frankfurt School* (Routledge, 2018) and *A Companion to Adorno* (Wiley Blackwell, 2020).

Michael LeMahieu is Professor of English at Clemson University and editor of the journal *Contemporary Literature*. He is the author of *Fictions of Fact and Value: The Erasure of Logical Positivism in American Literature, 1945–1975* (Oxford University Press, 2013) and coeditor of the volume *Wittgenstein and Modernism* (University of Chicago, 2017). His articles and reviews have appeared in journals including *African American Review*, *American Literary History*, *American Studies*, *College Literature*, and *Poetics Today*. He has been awarded fellowships from the American Council of Learned Societies and the National Endowment for the Humanities.

Toril Moi is James B. Duke Professor in Literature and Romance Studies, and Professor of English, Philosophy, and Theater Studies at Duke University. Among her books are *Simone de Beauvoir: The Making of an Intellectual Woman* (Oxford University Press, 1994), *What Is a Woman?* (Oxford University Press, 1999), *Henrik Ibsen and the Birth of Modernism* (Oxford University Press, 2006), and *Revolution of the Ordinary: Literary Studies after Wittgenstein, Austin, and Cavell* (University of Chicago Press, 2017). She has also written extensively on Norwegian literature, including Karl Ove Knausgaard's *My Struggle*, and regularly contributes to the Norwegian weekly *Morgenbladet*. She is currently interested in the question of formalism in literary criticism.

Magdalena Ostas works at the crossroads of literature, philosophy, and the arts. She has written on a range of figures at this intersection, and her essays have appeared in *symplokē*, *Studies in Romanticism*, and *nonsite*, and in the collections *Michael Fried and Philosophy* (Routledge, 2018), *Approaches to Teaching Jane Austen's Persuasion* (MLA, 2020), and *The Poetry of Emily Dickinson: Philosophical Perspectives* (Oxford University Press, 2021). She is working on a study about literature, philosophy, and the interior lives of persons in the nineteenth century and after. She has taught at Rhode Island College, Boston University, and Florida Atlantic University.

Henry W. Pickford is Professor of German and Philosophy at Duke University. He is the author of *The Sense of Semblance: Philosophical Analyses of Holocaust Art* (Fordham University Press, 2013) and *Thinking with Tolstoy and Wittgenstein: Expression, Emotion, and Art* (Northwestern University Press, 2015), and is coauthor of *In Defense of Intuitions: A New Rationalist Manifesto* (Palgrave Macmillan, 2013). He is coeditor of *Der aufrechte Gang im windschiefen Kapitalismus* (Springer, 2018), and is editor and translator from the German of Theodor W. Adorno, *Critical Models: Interventions and Catchwords* (Columbia University Press, 2005) and from the Russian of Lev Loseff, *Selected Early Poems* (Spuyten Duyvil, 2013).

Ben Ware is the Co-Director of the Centre for Philosophy and the Visual Arts at King's College, London. He is the author of *Dialectic of the Ladder: Wittgenstein, the "Tractatus" and Modernism* (Bloomsbury, 2015) and *Living Wrong Life Rightly: Modernism, Ethics and the Political Imagination* (Palgrave, 2017), and is editor of *Francis Bacon: Painting, Philosophy, Psychoanalysis* (Thames & Hudson, 2019). He is currently completing a new book on extinction and philosophy for the publisher Verso.

Abbreviations of Wittgenstein's Major Works

BB	*The Blue and Brown Books.* Ed. R. Rhees. Second edition. Oxford: Blackwell, 1969.
CV	*Culture and Value: A Selection from the Posthumous Remains.* Revised edition by A. Pichler. Trans. P. Winch. Oxford: Blackwell, 1977/1998.
LC	*Lectures and Conversations on Aesthetics, Psychology and Religious Belief* [1938–1946]. Ed. C. Barrett. Oxford: Blackwell, 1966.
LWPP I	*Last Writings on the Philosophy of Psychology* (Vol. I). Ed. G. Wright and H. Nyman. Trans. C. G. Luckhardt and M. A. E. Aue. Oxford: Blackwell, 1982.
LWPP II	*Last Writings on the Philosophy of Psychology* (Vol. II). Ed. G. Wright and H. Nyman. Trans. C. G. Luckhardt and M. A. E. Aue. Oxford: Blackwell, 1992.
OC	*On Certainty* [1951]. Ed. G. E. M. Anscombe and G. H. von Wright. Trans. D. Paul and G. E. M. Anscombe. Oxford: Blackwell, 1974.
PI	*Philosophical Investigations* [1938–1945]. Ed. G. E. M. Anscombe and R. Rhees. Fourth, revised edition by P. M. S. Hacker and J. Schulte. Trans. G. E. M. Anscombe, P. M. S. Hacker, and J. Schulte. Oxford: Wiley Blackwell, 1953/2009.
PPF	*Philosophy of Psychology – A Fragment* [1946–1949]. In PI (1953/2009, pp. 183–243). Ed. P. M. S. Hacker and J. Schulte. Trans. G. E. M. Anscombe, P. M. S. Hacker, and J. Schulte. [Previously known as PI Part ii]
RFM	*Remarks on the Foundations of Mathematics.* Ed. G. H. von Wright, Rush Rhees, and G. E. M. Anscombe. Trans. G. E. M. Anscombe. Oxford: Blackwell, 1978.

RPPI	*Remarks on the Philosophy of Psychology* (Vol. 1). [1945–1947]. Ed. G. E. M. Anscombe and G. H. von Wright. Trans. G. E. M. Anscombe. Oxford: Blackwell, 1980.
TLP	*Tractatus Logico-Philosophicus* [1922]. Trans. D. F. Pears and B. F. McGuinness. London: Routledge, 1961.
Z	*Zettel* [1945–1948]. (1967). Ed. G. E. M. Anscombe and G. H. von Wright. Trans. G. E. M. Anscombe. Oxford: Blackwell, 1984.

Introduction
Why Wittgenstein and Literary Studies?
John Gibson

Abstract: The Introduction offers a brief overview of why Wittgenstein has come to matter to contemporary literary studies and philosophical work on literature. In addition to explaining what literary Wittgensteinianism is, it provides a point of entry into the chapters of this volume by explaining the basic difference between the early and late Wittgenstein and how each has opened up novel ways of thinking about the relationship between philosophy and literature.

Keywords: Literary Wittgensteinianism, Philosophy and Literature, Skepticism, Sense/Nonsense distinction, Resolute versus Irresolute Readings, Perspicuous Representations, Antitheory, Picture Theory of Meaning, Early versus Late Wittgenstein.

Wittgenstein was not a literary scholar. Nor was he a philosopher of literature. And he clearly was not a critic, though he frequently expressed intense judgments about art and culture.[1] He was perhaps an aesthetician, but never to the extent that he was a philosopher of language, logic, and mind. In short, Wittgenstein was none of the things that would explain the existence of a book titled *Wittgenstein and Literary Studies*. The conjunction in the title is not the sort that could just as well be replaced with "on," as it could be if the title were *Wittgenstein and Skepticism*, *Wittgenstein and Ordinary Language*, or *Wittgenstein and Self-Expression*. What the title of this book conjoins is not a philosopher and his subject matter but a community, composed chiefly of literary scholars and philosophers who labor over central questions about the

---

[1] See, for example, CV for an excellent sense of Wittgenstein's view on culture and the tenor of his critical comments about artistic culture. See LC for his contributions to debates in the philosophy of art and, chiefly, his original views on the logical behavior of aesthetic predicates.

nature and point of literature and who enlist Wittgenstein for thinking these questions through. It is in the work of these "literary Wittgensteinians" that the conjunction is given sense, and this volume exists to showcase their work and the unique possibilities it has opened for thinking about the relationship between philosophy and literature.

Wittgenstein's work has come to play a distinctive role in creating a site of rapprochement between philosophers and literary scholars and, if one is to understand this role, it is important first to say a few general things about their institutional relationship. It will be a surprise to no one to hear that the sensibilities characteristic of professional philosophy and literary studies – certainly in the Anglophone world – are very different, even if they often share an interest in many of the same theoretical questions about language, affect, selves, politics, and the like. The relationship between the two became both more intimate and more fraught in the late 1960s, when literary studies began to absorb the thought of largely poststructural and postmodern thinkers that English-language academic philosophy tended to ignore. It would be wrong to think that the rise of "theory" made literature departments appear in part to be centers of a certain kind of philosophy, but it would be an honest mistake. Those of us who work in a philosophy department know that for many years a common reason for our students to migrate to English or Comparative Literature was simply that they wished to study postwar French and German philosophy (and more radical ways of thinking about culture and politics than one finds in the work of John Rawls and Martha Nussbaum, but that's another story). Here is the important point. This partial philosophicalization of literature departments reproduced, now in institutional terms, an altogether basic distinction between two kinds of twentieth-century philosophy: analytic and continental. Part of what philosophy and literary studies reproduced institutionally when they took their respective analytic and continental turns was a form of mutual suspicion about the styles of thought and writing associated with each. In this sense, a presumed philosophical divide came in part to explain a very real divide between the two disciplines at the heart of the humanities.

This suspicion, it must be said, was never in great evidence in philosophy prior to this, occasional Hegel and Heidegger jokes notwithstanding. And those in the know usually find this distinction between analytic and continental kinds of philosophy to be misleading and a tad crude. But most people know the stereotypes and how much they influence our sense of what scholars on either side of the disciplinary divide do for a living. To the literary scholar, analytic philosophy can seem to have missed not only the 1960s but the entire rise of modernity, pursuing its projects in an abstracted logical space – its method of conceptual analysis – in such a way that it finds itself without resources for speaking interestingly about products of culture and history, for instance all literature. Literary theory, the philosophical bias goes, takes great interest in simplistic forms of skepticism and cynicism, and it tends to have a derisibly uncritical relationship to the very forms of critical theory it celebrates, citing its favored German and French philosophers in a manner that often resembles hagiography. Both characterizations are hugely unfair, but anyone who works in either of these disciplines can attest to their presence and the role they have played in alienating us from certain of our colleagues down the hall.

One way of answering the "Why Wittgenstein and Literary Studies?" question is the following. Wittgenstein has come to matter to philosophers and literary theorists who wish to speak to one another because his work functions extremely well as a bridge between the two disciplines, at any rate, between those regions of each discipline that concern themselves with the entanglement of meaning, mind, and culture. When speaking in a Wittgensteinian register, the philosopher and literary theorist often seem suddenly intelligible to one another yet without sacrificing what is distinctive about their unique disciplinary perspectives, interests, and anxieties. Wittgenstein's work has come to offer both parties to the not-so-ancient debate a space that seems to excise from analytic philosophy its perceived cultural illiteracy and from literary studies its supposedly hip but thin reliance on wholly negative and skeptical forms of criticism (its "hermeneutics of suspicion").[2] Wittgenstein is especially appealing to scholars who find a grain of truth in these unflattering descriptions of their own fields. For many academic philosophers, Wittgenstein is a thinker who has helped us see how to employ the resources of our broadly analytic education in culturally and aesthetically productive ways, and his work can position us to enter the debates that animate literary studies and hence a much larger region of the humanities. It is much the same with why many literary scholars

---

[2] For discussion, see Timothy Aubry, *Guilty Aesthetic Pleasures* (Cambridge, MA: Harvard University Press, 2018), Rita Felski, *The Limits of Critique* (Chicago, IL: University of Chicago Press, 2015), Richard Eldridge and Bernard Rhie, *Stanley Cavell and Literary Studies: Consequences of Skepticism* (New York: Continuum, 2011), and Toril Moi, *Revolution of the Ordinary: Literary Studies after Wittgenstein, Austin, and Cavell* (Chicago, IL: The University of Chicago Press, 2017). Also see Espen Hammer's chapter in this volume (Chapter 5).

come to Wittgenstein, as his work can seem to offer constructive nuance to ways of thinking about criticality and the limits of language[3] as well to grant access to the broader debates on meaning and mind that define much philosophy of the past hundred years (philosophical debates tend not to spoil quickly so this expanse of time is manageable). Moreover, Wittgenstein has proven to be useful in bringing both philosopher and literary theorist together in manner that is neither reactionary nor adversarial and that allows us to go on talking to our colleagues who are content with business as usual in academic philosophy and literary studies. There are many philosophers who matter much more to contemporary literary theory than Wittgenstein, but few have quite this power of rapprochement.

Wittgenstein's early work on logic and nonsense and later turn to the rough ground of ordinary language and *Lebensform* (a form of life) revolutionized the way many philosophers think about interpretation, expression, agency, truth, doubt, skepticism, and, crucially, the nature and limits of language. These are, of course, issues that in one way or another are implicated in many of the central debates of literary theory.[4]

---

[3] In Charles Altieri's words, "Wittgenstein understands better than any other philosopher how to frame the limits of discourse without resorting to any kind of skepticism." Charles Altieri, *Reckoning with the Imagination: Wittgenstein and the Aesthetics of Literary Experience* (Ithaca, NY: Cornell University Press, 2015), viii. Altieri's claim gestures toward what many literary theorists find so unique (or detestable, depending) in Wittgenstein's work and how it distinguishes itself from kinds of philosophy on which theory habitually draws. The concern with the limits of discourse unites all parties; their respective attitudes toward the reach of skepticism will be what divides them. Wittgensteinians tend to be interested in *diagnosing* the sources of skepticism rather than defending or dismissing skepticism, and it is important to keep this in mind, since it explains the sense that his work offers nuance to, not a cranky rejection of, the forms of cynicism and skepticism with which theory is often, if at times unfairly, associated.

[4] Most studies of Wittgenstein and literature are concerned with his work on language, knowledge, mind, and value theory, which is little surprise since these are the topics on which he wrote and lectured. There is less on the relevance of his work to current cultural debates regarding gender, race, class, and other issues of a broadly political sort, though this is beginning to change. The articles in a special issue of *New Literary History* (46.2. [2016]) titled "Feminist Investigations" are broadly Wittgensteinianism in scope and showcase the work of leading feminist philosophers and literary critics. Beyond this, the work of Nancy Bauer, Naomi Sheman, and Toril Moi are essential reading for those with an interest in Wittgensteinianism approaches to feminism and gender. There is also something of a cottage industry of work on Wittgenstein and Marx, and at the very least this shows that it is possible to make Wittgenstein, a logician at heart, a fruitful participant in political discourse. See, for example, the essays collected in *Marx and Wittgenstein: Knowledge, Morality and Politics*, eds. Gavin Kitching and Nigel Pleasants (London: Routledge, 2002).

Each of the chapters of this volume deals with some and not others of them. And while the volume presupposes no prior familiarity with Wittgenstein, it will prove helpful to have a serviceable sense of what this passage from the early to late Wittgenstein consists in.[5] Many of the chapters here begin their discussion somewhere on the spectrum that runs from the early to late Wittgenstein, and I will try to explain the distinction briefly and painlessly. Bear in mind that everything I say here is subject to intense and principled critical disagreement, and I shall leave many important details to the side. Since the chapters of this volume introduce readers to Wittgenstein's reception in literary studies (see especially the first four chapters), I will not attempt to tell *that* story here. I will limit my overview to core features of Wittgenstein's work, and my hope is that what I say here will provide a philosophical point of entry into the chapters of this volume.

An interest that runs throughout the entire chord of Wittgenstein's career is the distinction between sense and nonsense, and much of his work is dedicated to identifying the conditions that lead us to speak on the unflattering side of it. His radical point is that philosophy is often one such condition, especially in its grander metaphysical moments. One detects this line between sense and nonsense when juxtaposing everyday questions with their recognizably philosophical counterparts. It is easy to prepare one's ear for this. Consider the passage from questions like:

> What time is it?
> How much time has passed since his last visit?
> How does time work in the novel?

to the philosophical bluntness of:

> What is time?

Unlike the first three questions, the blunt fourth one turns an abstraction into a subject, and, importantly, asks us to consider "time" shorn of context − linguistic, practical, agential, or, to use a term Wittgensteinians favor, *everyday* context. Nothing is as of yet wrong with this, and surely many philosophers have posed abstract questions about time in meaningful ways. But there is a good chance that one might be a

---

[5] I offer a more elaborate account of the passage from early to late Wittgenstein and its relevance to philosophy of literature in "What Makes a Poem Philosophical?," in *Wittgenstein and Modernism*, eds. Michael LeMahieu and Karen Zumhagen-Yekplè (Chicago, IL: University of Chicago Press, 2016), 130–152. The following is a much-condensed version of the argument I offer there.

Wittgensteinian if one is struck by the oddness (*seltsam*) of the philosophical question. The term *time* here will strike Wittgensteinians as uncanny, as though homeless (*unheimlich*), and they will sense both the risk of reification and an invitation to conceptual confusion. For Wittgenstein, "philosophical problems arise when language goes on holiday" (PI §38). When on holiday, philosophical language idles in a particularly deceptive way, producing a veneer of depth while really saying nothing at all. Friedrich Nietzsche once joked that "mystical explanations are considered deep; the truth is, they are not even shallow."[6] It is fair to see Wittgenstein's project to be that of showing that much the same is true of standard forms of philosophical explanation.

Take a different example, now epistemic rather than metaphysical. Consider the movement from questions like:

> How do you know Marcus?
> What does Marcus know? (asked dismissively)
> How do you know that what Marcus said is true?
> Doesn't Marcus's past give us good reason to doubt everything he says?

to, again bluntly:

> What is knowledge?
> What is truth?
> Can we ever know anything?

Note that answers to the first four questions will clearly represent a state of affairs in such a way that it will be sensible to ask whether they do so *accurately, correctly, misleadingly, falsely*, and so on. But it is entirely unclear whether answers to the final three philosophical questions represent, picture, or mirror anything at all. If not, then what are we imagining when we imagine the answers to these questions to be true or false? True or false of precisely what? The motion in the above questions is from intelligible *local* doubts and questions to *global* ones – this will greatly increase the risk of slippage into nonsense – that fancy themselves as inviting a philosophical account of something like "our epistemic situation." We know the crude form they can take when presented as incautious answers, often comical in the performative contradictions they embody: Knowledge is impossible! Skepticism is justified! Note immediately that if there is a problem with the meaning of these

---

[6] Friedrich Nietzsche, *The Gay Science*. ed. Bernard Williams, trans. *Josefine Nauckhoff, and Adrian Del Caro* (Cambridge: Cambridge University Press, 2001), §126.

statements, then the denial of them will invite the very same problems, and this is a point that is easily overlooked. Wittgenstein's critical project places under suspicion any attempt – both radical and conservative alike – to speak so abstractly and categorically about the nature and limits of human knowledge. His work helps us to see that fashionable forms of skepticism, realism, idealism, and relativism in fact rotate around the same axis, and he wishes to expose this and unsettle our sense that the motion between them is natural.

Before one draws the entirely wrong conclusion, note that none of these observations targets the range of linguistic acts running from deeply imaginative metaphors to radical poetic experimentation, all of which at times might succeed, depending on one's theory, in sprinting past the limits of sense and, in doing so, produce beautiful, sublime, or liberating uses of language – in short, literature. The idea is rather that there are pernicious cases and that the risk of them is endemic to philosophy, with "philosophy" here of course intended broadly to include what today we would call "theory." It is the way that Wittgenstein's work both helps us to see something extraordinary about literary and poetic uses of language *and* casts suspicion on the kinds of theory we have woven to explain this that has come to matter to literary Wittgensteinianism.

All this sets up a straightforward way of explaining the difference between the early and late Wittgenstein. As a first pass, one can say that in his early works representational worries guide his critique of philosophical nonsensicality; in the later works, he turns to the everyday to establish the boundaries of sense. It is, if you will, a matter of privileging either logic or a *Lebensform* in delineating these boundaries. Let me explain.

The central text of Wittgenstein's early period is the *Tractatus Logico-Philosophicus* (1922), which is the only book he published during his lifetime, the rest being edited editions of his copious notebooks or transcriptions of his lectures. The *Tractatus* itself is a series of tersely – often gnomically – formulated propositions that jointly yield an account of how language and thought can picture reality in a manner that will allow us to explain how a sentence or a thought can be true (or false). It does this by developing a "picture theory" of meaning that explains how sentences, as vehicles of propositions, can have cognitive content, that is, succeed in saying something that is informative of the world. The *Tractatus* shows this to be a matter of how the logical structure of certain empirical propositions can mirror the structure of reality: can represent it and thereby overstep the space between word and world, thought and reality.

Here's the rub. The *Tractatus* specifies the conditions under which a use of language can be meaningful. It shows this to consist in how a sentence conveys a proposition in such a way that it can picture reality. Thus, the *Tractatus*, as a statement of this theory, will necessarily fail to satisfy the very conditions of meaningfulness it elaborates. The *Tractatus*, as a philosophical work, traffics in theoretical explanations of what must be the case rather than empirical statements of what actually is the case. But only the latter use of language can satisfy the conditions of meaningfulness the *Tractatus* articulates. By the letter of its own theory, the propositions of the *Tractatus* are without cognitive content, empty. Thus, the text embodies a great paradox: if its theory is sound, then the attempt to offer a philosophical statement of it is impossible. Wittgenstein, of course, knows this well and concludes the *Tractatus* with a remarkable admission:

My propositions serve as elucidations in the following way: anyone who understands me eventually recognizes them as nonsensical, when he has used them – as steps – to climb up beyond them. (He must, so to speak, throw away the ladder after he has climbed up it.)

He must transcend these propositions, and then he will see the world aright.

What we cannot speak about we must pass over in silence. (TLP 6.54–57)

The *Tractatus*, then, is a work of nonsense. But it is apparently a philosophically significant sort of nonsense. The great interpretive problem is that of explaining its philosophical significance, which becomes the question of how Tractarian nonsense succeeds in getting us to see the "the world aright." What we have come to call "irresolute" readings take Tractarian nonsense to be a technical notion. It reads it as a form of nonsense that permits us to make manifest what one necessarily cannot say, presumably in a manner that yields a philosophical insight that is along the lines of, but certainly not identical to, the theory the work wears on its sleeve.[7] The so-called "resolute" reading, which has been much more important to literary Wittgensteinians, takes Wittgenstein's final words at face value and leans into its paradox much as one would with any great modernist poet: nonsense is just that, and thus the *Tractatus*

---

[7] For discussion of the resolute and irresolute readings, see James Conant, "Elucidation and Nonsense in Frege and the Early Wittgenstein," in *The New Wittgenstein*, eds. Alice Crary and Rupert Read (London: Routledge, 2000), 174–217; Cora Diamond, "Ethics, Imagination and the Method of Wittgenstein's Tractatus," in *The New Wittgenstein*, eds. Crary and Read, 149–173; and Michael Kremer, "The Purpose of Tractarian Nonsense," *NOÛS* 35(1): 39–73 (2001).

fails to express anything positive at all about its great topic. The irresolute reading argues that the *Tractatus* uses nonsense to establish its apparent thesis obliquely; the resolute reading urges that the confession of nonsense shows its apparent thesis to be thoroughly nonsensical, too. According to the irresolute reading, the *Tractatus* opens up ways of thinking about the ineffable and how certain employments of language can, perhaps like metaphors, produce surface nonsense while sneaking a great insight in through the back door. By the lights of the resolute reading, Wittgenstein's status as an author is made paramount and his rhetorical strategy is the object of focus. It asks us to think not of what the text shows us but how Wittgenstein wishes it to work upon the expectations of a certain kind of reader. This reader will be a philosopher who wants to have a theory of the relationship between language, meaning, and reality. As such, the confession of nonsense at the conclusion of the work is utterly destructive since it functions to show this reader that the entire enterprise is itself nonsensical and that their craving for a theory is philosophically naïve. This, too, brings a kind a philosophical clarity, though likely not of the sort that the earnest reader expected from the *Tractatus*.

Regardless of what Wittgenstein meant to accomplish with his brilliant and maddening early work, scholars typically think that the final confession paved the way for his later turn, starting in the 1930s, away from the structure of propositions and toward the structure of everyday language use: to "language-games" and the manner in which they show how a word is given a point and purpose – meaning – in a form of life. In the posthumously published *Philosophical Investigations*, which is generally taken to be the central text of the later Wittgenstein, the realm of sense becomes coextensive with these language-games and the *Lebensform* that gives them domicile. This is an important difference from the *Tractatus*, but it also shows the continuity of his philosophical project across his early and late periods, since it will offer just a new way of accounting for his standing interest in nonsense and the peculiar condition of philosophical language. Context, history, culture, and public linguistic behavior now become decisive, and the logical abstraction of his early work gives way to what one can think of as a kind of sociology of meaning.

A common thread of argumentation in the *Investigations* is that philosophical problems – problems concerning the mind, the self, meaning, knowledge, reality, and so on – are typically made, not discovered, *by* philosophy. They are created precisely by engaging language beyond the limits of sense. In this respect, the *forms* of philosophical expression used to articulate these problems are constitutive of the problems themselves. This is generally not a good thing. Wittgenstein sees much philosophical language as a flight from everyday contexts of speech and so the very grounds for meaningful uses of language: for *making* sense. Many philosophical employments of language remove words from their everyday contexts and place them in a space in which they are bound to feel *unheimlich* – recall the use of "time" earlier in this Introduction – and so prompt in us a sense of philosophical wonder, usually unwarranted. The *Investigations* urges us to respond to this urge by finding an example of language use that undoes the sense of puzzlement and quiets our urge to devise philosophical explanations to furnish us with the intellectual clarity we desire. Clarity is furnished elsewhere.

For Wittgenstein, philosophy, when done properly, in fact explains nothing:

Philosophy simply puts everything before us, and neither explains nor deduces anything. – Since everything lies open to view, there is nothing to explain. For what is hidden, for example, is of no interest to us. (PI §126)

The "hidden" designates what Wittgenstein thinks are the noxious theoretical items philosophers invent to explain the worldly phenomena that perplex them, for instance a metaphysically "private" psychological interior that houses a will, intentions, a self, an immaterial mind, or the meaning of a poem. This is not to dismiss the existence of these things, though it is a call to demystify our sense of their status. And note what Wittgenstein offers us to make manifest that which unreformed philosophers think we need a metaphysical thesis to explain:

A main source of our failure to understand is that we do not command a clear view of the use of our words. – Our grammar is lacking in this sort of perspicuity. A perspicuous presentation produces just that understanding which consists in "seeing connections". Hence the importance of finding and inventing intermediate cases. The concept of a perspicuous representation is of fundamental importance for us. It earmarks the form of the account we give, the way we look at things. (PI §122)

Wittgenstein scholars are divided on the importance and meaning of this passage, but it brings into relief three things that all will agree are important to the work of his later period. The first is that Wittgenstein sees "perspicuous presentations" as what the philosopher devises in order to "lead words back from their metaphysical to their everyday use" (PI §116). They are *examples*, not explanations, and in them we see language used in a manner that dispels our sense that there is a philosophical itch that only a theory can scratch. They, and not theories, quiet our fits of philosophical wonderment. Second, the passage reveals Wittgenstein's commitments to a kind of philosophical *particularism*. He effectively redirects the philosophical imagination away from the general and abstract and toward the fine-grainedness of, to steal Fredric Jameson's phrase, "the here and now of this unique situation and this unique expression."[8] It is hard to overstate the philosophical novelty of this move and the extent to which it runs up against many of the standing habits of thought in philosophy, even the form of "high" analytic philosophy of which Wittgenstein was a chief architect. It also does much to give one a nuanced sense of what it means to call the later Wittgenstein an *ordinary* language philosopher. Finally, these perspicuous presentations are, in Wittgenstein's work, typically not representations of anything real at all. They are deeply creative, often fictional, and draw attention to their artificiality, so much so that his examples of them in the *Investigations* often collapse the distinction between philosophical and literary employments of the imagination. The *Investigations* is full of talking kettles (PI §297), workers whose language consists of just five masonry terms (PI §§2–21), and an odd thing called a beetle box (PI §293). In other words, Wittgenstein's later philosophy is not concerned with tediously documenting "what we say when." Perspicuous presentations act as "intermediate cases" that function to lead the mind *back* to the rough ground of the everyday, now with the sense of rightness with the world in thought and language that the *Tractatus* had promised.

The chapters of this volume provide a fuller reckoning with these features of Wittgenstein's early and later philosophy, but this brief overview furnishes an initial sense of the work they can do in literary theory and related fields. Most generally, Wittgenstein's philosophy has proven to be of great help in getting us beyond entrenched positions and their denials, that is, in charting a course in a debate that reconfigures our sense of both what the problem is and the range of theoretical moves available for responding to it. The familiar pendulum swing between forms of intentionalism and anti-intentionalism, positions that privilege authors, impersonal texts, or readers in the production meaning, common ways of drawing the line between what is "inside" and "outside" a work, a subject, or language itself, between theories that claim that we project affect onto a work and those that insist that we discover

---

[8] Fredric Jameson, *Postmodernism, or, the Cultural Logic of Late Capitalism* (Durham, NC: Duke University Press, 1991), 152.

it in it, those which argue about whether to interpret to notions of expression, style, and voice in purely material or irreducibly humanistic terms—these and similar issues are all subject to Wittgensteinian forms of critique and transformation. A good part of the labor of "literary Wittgensteinianism" is just this: questioning our sense of what the problems of literary studies are and exposing the assumptions—the pictures "that held us captive" (PI §115)—that make them appear intuitive or natural. After Wittgenstein, how do we understand what it means to see literary works as "minded" objects, that is, as shot through with psychological life and purposiveness? After Wittgenstein, how do we reimagine the constellation of problems that concern authorial agency and readerly reception: of what it means to create and respond to such minded objects, to see them as expressive of subjective life, and to acknowledge the ways in which they align us with or alienate us from one another and a common world, establish or disrupt forms of ethical community, or express a mood, passion, or thought in which we can share?

All of these questions are taken up in the following chapters. Since each chapter is intended to introduce readers to a region of contemporary literary Wittgensteinianism, it would be odd to introduce the chapters themselves, apart from explaining the point of their inclusion and alerting the reader to what they will find there. While the volume is not divided into parts, there is a natural progression of topics.

The first half of the volume explores issue directly related to understanding Wittgenstein's influence, actual or desired, on both literature and contemporary critical practices, and so these chapters each tell a part of the story of Wittgenstein's reception in literary studies. We open with Michael LeMahieu's "Writing after Wittgenstein." LeMahieu's chapter is a wide-ranging study of the fascination that Wittgenstein's work, both early and late, has held for many poets and novelists working in his wake. He traces Wittgenstein's influence through postwar literature and the various ways writers have taken interest in his distinctive sense of writing as a mode of discovery (as well as in his person, which itself is a subject of great interest). Toril Moi's "A Wittgensteinian Phenomenology of Criticism" demonstrates how Wittgenstein opens up possibilities for thinking about the point and purpose of criticism, indeed of reading. Moi's discussion offers a rich account of the present culture of literary theory, and she elaborates a highly original way of thinking about what a Wittgensteinianism intervention in it should look like. Her notion of reading as acknowledgment is of special significance. Robert Chodat's "Appreciating Material: Criticism, Science, and the Very Idea of Method" uses as case studies recent empirical turns in criticism to

Big Data and neuroscience to explain literature and its aesthetic affordances, and he enlists Wittgenstein to diagnosis this. He argues that it suffers from the very craving for generality and theoretical depth that the *Investigations* warns us against. In its place, Chodat argues for a reformed vision of criticism and aesthetic experience that draws inspiration from the particularism of Wittgenstein's later work. The final chapter that develops this general line of discussion is Sarah Beckwith's "A Vision of Language for Literary Historians: Forms of Life, Context, Use." Beckwith offers a dazzling reading of Wittgenstein's notions of *Lebensform*, context, and linguistic usage, and she shows how they enrich our understanding of what a commitment to historicist principles amounts to. Along the way, she has much to say about William Empson and the Oxford English Dictionary, as an opportunity to tease out what it means to make examples of actual linguistic usage philosophically and critically productive.

The remaining chapters are less interested in making sense of writers and particular kinds of criticism and more aligned with debates about general philosophical problems of literature. Espen Hammer's "Wittgenstein and the Prospects for a Contemporary Literary Humanism" explores the tension between the "hermeneutics of suspicion" and the longing for a modernized literary humanism, and he argues that our sense of their mutual antagonism is entirely too simple. His chapter offers a nuanced account of Wittgenstein's writings on aesthetics and aspect-perception, and it concludes with a vision of the value of literature that indicates a way of moving beyond the opposition between suspicion and affirmation/cynicism and humanism. Magdalena Ostas's "Storied Thoughts: Wittgenstein and the Reaches of Fiction" explores an issue that is clearly essential to a volume such as this: the literary and imaginative form of Wittgenstein's writing. Her argument reveals fascinating points of continuity in how both philosophical and literary forms allow us to "sound out actualities and realities" and, in this way, illuminate that elusive but crucial bridge between language – in fiction or philosophy – and life. We turn from fiction to poetry with Hannah Vandegrift Eldridge's "Wittgenstein and Lyric." Eldridge uses Wittgenstein to illuminate both the philosophical prospects of the lyric and the poetic potential of philosophy. Central to her account is the manner in which poetry, just as language itself, emerges from a *Lebensform* yet also constitutes it, and this brings clarity to basic features of the cultural and philosophical promise of the lyric. Henry W. Pickford's "Life, Logic, Style: On Late Wittgenstein" shows something remarkable: that Wittgenstein's work on logic offers a model for making sense of the literary style. Wittgenstein's work on *Lebensform* provides the middle term that allows Pickford to move so improbably yet convincingly from logic to literary expression. Pickford's argument shows that, contrary to what I said earlier in this Introduction, logic remains a central concern of Wittgenstein and his interest in it is everywhere present in his later work. The volume concludes with Ben Ware's "Wittgenstein's Apocalyptic Subjectivity." Ware makes a strong case not only for seeing Wittgenstein as a modernist writer but as developing a distinct form of modernist philosophy, significant enough to place him in the company of both Gertrude Stein and Theodor Adorno. This volume thus ends with a novel conception of Wittgenstein, one that runs powerfully counter to the entrenched image of him as fundamentally analytic in significance and orientation.

Before concluding this Introduction, a few words of acknowledgment are in order. This volume attempts to answer the "Why Wittgenstein and Literary Studies?" question by highlighting a very specific community of scholars, namely, those whose work is, at the present moment, particularly visible, novel, and important. But this community has a history, and we are hardly at the beginning of it.[9] The importance of

---

[9] A list of works, classic and contemporary, that are essential to the answering the "Why Wittgenstein and Literary Studies?" question would – in addition to the work of the contributors to this volume – include: Charles Altieri, *Reckoning with the Imagination*; Kristin Boyce, "Literature, Logic and the Liberating Word: The Elucidation of Confusion in Henry James," *Journal of Philosophical Research* 35 (2010): 43–88; Anthony J. Cascardi, *The Bounds of Reason: Cervantes, Dostoevsky, Flaubert* (New York: Columbia University Press, 1986); Stanley Cavell, *Disowning Knowledge in Six Plays of Shakespeare* (Cambridge: Cambridge University Press, 1987); Alice Crary, *Beyond Moral Judgment* (Cambridge, MA: Harvard University Press, 2007); Cora Diamond, "Having a Rough Story about What Moral Philosophy Is," *New Literary History* 15: 155–170) (1983); Richard Eldridge, *Leading a Human Life: Wittgenstein, Intentionality, and Romanticism* (Chicago, IL: University of Chicago Press, 1997); Garry Hagberg, *Meaning & Interpretation: Wittgenstein, Henry James, and Literary Knowledge* (Ithaca, NY: Cornell University Press, 1994); Sandra Laugier, "Voice as Form of Life and Life Form," *Nordic Wittgenstein Review* 4: 63–82 (2015); Yi-Ping Ong, "Lectures on Ethics: Kafka and Wittgenstein," in *Wittgenstein and Modernism*, eds. Michael LeMahieu and Karen Zumhagen-Yekplé (Chicago, IL: University of Chicago Press, 2016); Marjorie Perloff, *Wittgenstein's Ladder: Poetic Language and the Strangeness of the Ordinary* (Chicago, IL: University of Chicago Press, 1996); Rupert Read, *Applying Wittgenstein* (London: Continuum, 2007); David Schalkwyk, *Literature and the Touch of the Real* (Newark, DE: University of Delaware Press, 2004); Ben Tilghman, "Wittgenstein and Poetic Language," *Philosophy and Literature* 27 (1): 188–185 (2003); and Karen Zumhagen-Yekplé, *A Different Order of Difficulty: Literature After Wittgenstein* (Chicago, IL: The University of Chicago Press, 2020). Sascha Bru, Wolfgang Huemer, and Daniel Steuer, *Wittgenstein Reading* (Boston: De Gruyter, 2013); John Gibson and Wolfgang Huemer, *The Literary Wittgenstein* (London: Routledge, 2004), and *Wittgenstein and Modernism*, eds. Michael LeMahieu and Karen Zumhagen-Yekplè (Chicago, IL: University of Chicago Press, 2016).

the work that has come before us was made especially clear at the 2019 meeting of the *Boston University Colloquium on Literature, Philosophy, and Aesthetics* on the topic of Wittgenstein and literature. All the chapters published here had their first airing there. As one would expect, the discussion took stock of the nature of literary Wittgensteinianism, explored its past, and spent a good amount of time imagining its possible futures. Traces of that wonderful and productive discussion survive here, and we would like to thank the participants whose comments and criticisms shaped these chapters and our sense of what a volume such as this should try to accomplish: Richard Eldridge, Theo Davis, Abigail Gillman, Kristin Boyce, Will Waters, Nancy Bauer, Avner Baz, Ben Roth, Naomi Scheman, Samia Hesni, Garry Hagberg, and Laura Quinney.

1 Writing after Wittgenstein
Michael LeMahieu

Abstract: Since his death in 1951 and the posthumous publication of the *Philosophical Investigations* in 1953, Ludwig Wittgenstein's life and work have been a subject of intense fascination for poets, novelists, and playwrights. Wittgenstein's signature approach to writing as a mode of discovery – of writing as philosophical investigation – factors into and emerges out of the literary response to his life and work. That response takes many forms, from a quick reference or veiled allusion to parodic imitation to more extended, complex, or subtle forms of inspiration, influence, or acknowledgment. After examining a number of uses of Wittgenstein's work in texts by mid-twentieth-century authors (Thomas Pynchon, Vladimir Nabokov, Angela Carter, Don DeLillo, Thomas Bernhard, David Markson), ones that construe the philosopher as alternately a logical positivist or a silent mystic, the chapter turns to more contemporary, twenty-first-century responses to Wittgenstein by authors including Maggie Nelson, Kathy Acker, Lydia Davis, Ben Lerner, Nicholas Mosley, W. G. Sebald, David Foster Wallace, and Amiri Baraka. These more contemporary literary responses to Wittgenstein are less uniform in their references to the man and his work but more diverse in their use of Wittgenstein's concepts, arguments, or writings, particularly from the later philosophy.

Keywords: Thomas Pynchon, Thomas Bernard, W. G. Sebald, David Foster Wallace, Ben Lerner, Writing as Philosophical Investigation, Wittgenstein's Influence on Literature.

The idea of "writing after Wittgenstein" runs in multiple directions. When "writing" is understood as a substantive, it stands out as distinct from more specific concepts of poetry or even literature. One might be reminded in this respect of Wittgenstein's frequently cited remark that "philosophy ought really to be written as a form of poetry (*dichten*)" (CV 24) and also of the commonly appended disclaimers explaining that the

German term Wittgenstein uses refers much more expansively than would be suggested by English usage's more limited sense of "poetry" as "lyric poetry."[1] Indeed, one might metaphorically understand Wittgenstein's remark as "philosophy ought really to be written as a form of writing," thereby calling attention to Wittgenstein's self-consciousness about the materiality as opposed to the transparency of the medium in which philosophers work. For it is precisely when Wittgenstein uses symbolic logic that we are reminded that his concern is natural language; it is precisely when he turns to an image that we are reminded that his textual practice extends beyond the verbal. Think here of the duck-rabbit sketch in the *Investigations* and also of the visual field drawing in the *Tractatus*. Wittgenstein literally cut and pasted remarks from one notebook to another, working with the material of his medium to design, construct, and build as with so many blocks, pillars, and slabs.

"Writing after Wittgenstein" also allows us to read "writing" as a gerund, as the nominal form of the act of writing. And as such, "writing" activates two senses of "after." In a first, one writes after Wittgenstein in chronological terms. Wittgenstein himself was famously indifferent to those after whom he came and wrote. "Indeed, what I have written here makes no claim to novelty in detail," he writes in the Preface to the *Tractatus*, "and the reason why I give no sources is that it is a matter of indifference to me whether the thoughts that I have had have been anticipated by someone else" (TLP 3). Wittgenstein's modernist disregard for the past immediately follows his apparently antimodernist indifference to novelty and is followed in turn by an acknowledgment of an indebtedness, implicitly denied, "to Frege's great work and to the writings of my friend Bertrand Russell" (TLP 3). Understanding "writing" as a gerund also activates a second sense of "after." What would it mean to write "after Wittgenstein" in the sense that one might say *to chase after* Wittgenstein, to pursue or to hound him? Or maybe even in the sense *to look after* Wittgenstein, to mind or to monitor him? To write after Wittgenstein is both to come after him and to come for him. These alternate senses of "after" recall a remark by Stanley Cavell about Wittgenstein's style of writing: "The first thing to be said in accounting

---

[1] Allan Janik warns against the mistake of mistranslating *Dichtung* "as lyric poetry (as opposed simply to the genus fiction of which lyric, drama, and epic are the species, according to traditional German classification)." Allan Janik, "Wittgenstein, Loos, and Critical Modernism: Style and Idea in Architecture and Philosophy," in *Wittgenstein and Modernism*, eds. Michael LeMahieu and Karen Zumhagen-Yekplé (Chicago, IL: University of Chicago Press, 2017), 84.

for his style is that he *writes*: he does not report, he does not write up results."[2] In light of Cavell's distinction between "writing" and "writing up," we might draw another between "writing up" and "writing after." On the face of it, to write up results is a form of writing that takes place after something, typically an experiment, has been concluded. When all the actual work is finished, the thinking goes, when the data has been collected, all that is left to do is to write up the results. According to this line of thought, writing up is a form of writing that takes place afterward, and it is a conception of writing that aspires to be transparently communicative: the act of writing up in no way alters the nature of the results, which preexist the act of communicating them. Writing up, however, is what Cavell rightly claims that Wittgenstein does not do; rather, he *writes*. His works do not report the results of experiments; they are, instead, ongoing investigations. Wittgenstein himself is constantly writing after something, seeking out and searching for a clearer formulation, a more perspicuous representation, the method of showing "the fly the way out of the fly-bottle" (PI § 309). Wittgenstein's form of "writing after" is not at all the same as "writing up."

This general sense of writing as a mode of discovery – of writing as philosophical investigation – factors into and emerges out of the literary response to Wittgenstein. That response takes many forms, from a quick reference or veiled allusion to parodic imitation to more extended, complex, or subtle forms of inspiration, influence, or acknowledgment. This last term, one central to Cavell's thinking, hints at a sense of looking after Wittgenstein, of paying attention to Wittgenstein's work and being mindful of its ongoing effects. Since his death in 1951 and the posthumous publication of the *Philosophical Investigations* in 1953, Wittgenstein's life and work have been a subject of intense fascination for poets, novelists, and playwrights, many of whom continue to write after Wittgenstein.

I. Early Wittgenstein in Postmodern Literature

"How many times," Italo Calvino asks in his essay "Philosophy and Literature" (1977), "has the name of Wittgenstein been invoked in discussing writers who have nothing in common except the fact that they have nothing in common with Wittgenstein! To decide who is the writer

---

[2] Stanley Cavell, *Must We Mean What We Say?* (1969; Cambridge, MA: Harvard University Press, 2002), 70.

of logical positivism would be a perfect theme for an international conference of the PEN Club."[3] In addition to the literary critics who Calvino suggests uniformly invoke Wittgenstein's name when discussing rather different writers, those writers themselves also invoke Wittgenstein's name As Calvino's phrase suggests, there's something captivating about "the name of Wittgenstein" itself, which frequently appears in titles of works, from *Wittgenstein, Jr.* to *Wittgenstein's Mistress* to *Wittgenstein's Nephew*; from *Wittgenstein's Vienna* to *Wittgenstein's Poker*; from *Wittgenstein's House* to *The House of Wittgenstein*. Two years after Calvino made his remark, Philip Roth invokes the name of Wittgenstein in *The Ghost Writer* (1979). The protagonist of that novel is modeled on Saul Bellow, who himself invokes Wittgenstein's name in *Mr. Sammler's Planet* (1970) and also in "Zetland: By a Character Witness" (1974), in which the protagonist fancies himself "the Wittgenstein of the West Side."[4] The name of Wittgenstein rings and rhymes.

A foremost postmodern fabulist, Calvino is typical of his post-1945 generation in associating Wittgenstein with logical positivism. And the most representative line of text for this line of thinking is the first proposition of the *Tractatus* – "The world is all that is the case" (TLP 5) – which David Foster Wallace might or might not have considered "the most beautiful opening line in Western lit."[5] The narrator in David Markson's *Wittgenstein's Mistress* (1988) refers to it as "the whole sentence that I also must have said to myself a hundred times, a little later on, about the world being everything that is the case."[6] The Doctor in John Barth's *The End of the Road* (1958) refers to the same line, claiming that "*The world is everything that is the case*, and what the case is is not a

---

[3] Italo Calvino, "Philosophy and Literature," in *The Uses of Literature*, trans. Patrick Creagh (San Diego, CA: Harcourt Brace, 1986), 42.
[4] Saul Bellow, "Zetland: By a Character Witness," in *Him with His Foot in His Mouth and Other Stories*, ed. Saul Bellow (1984; New York: Penguin, 1998), 183. Roth's character Zuckerman finds books by "Heidegger and Wittgenstein" in Lonoff's library. Philip Roth, *The Ghost Writer* (1979; New York: Vintage, 1995), 51. Although apparently no more than a passing remark, it might nevertheless allude to Bellow's Sammler, who refers to "*Kulturny* physicians who wanted to discuss Heidegger and Wittgenstein." Saul Bellow, *Mr. Sammler's Planet* (1970; New York: Penguin, 1996), 79.
[5] In an essay on "Wallace's Wittgenstein," based in large part on a letter he received from Wallace, Lance Olsen writes: "Even if Wallace's mind tells him the first sentence of the *Tractatus* is the most beautiful opening line in Western lit, his gut tells him otherwise: that the world is an enigma, the universe a perplexity." Lance Olsen, "Termite Art, or Wallace's Wittgenstein," *Review of Contemporary Fiction* 13 (2): 206 (Summer 1993).
[6] David Markson, *Wittgenstein's Mistress* (Normal, IL: Dalkey Archive Press, 1988), 170. Hereinafter cited parenthetically.

matter of logic."[7] "Technology," a character in John Updike's novel *Villages* (2004), similarly remarks, "works with what, as Wittgenstein said, is the case."[8] The line appears perhaps most memorably in Thomas Pynchon's first novel, *V.* (1963). As the character Charisma propositions the married Mafia Winsome, he draws explicitly from the *Tractatus*:

> It is something less than heaven
> To be quoted Thesis 1.7
> Every time I make an advance;
> If the world is all that the case is
> That's a pretty discouraging basis
> On which to pursue
> Any kind of romance.[9]

The fabricated Thesis 1.7 conjoins the first proposition of the *Tractatus* with the seventh and final proposition – "What we cannot speak about we must pass over in silence" (TLP 74) – and thus introduces the other most commonly quoted Wittgenstein line in contemporary literature. "I shall have to speak of things," Samuel Beckett writes in *The Unnamable* (1953), "of which I cannot speak."[10] "The novelist says in words," Ursula Le Guin writes with reference to the "linguistic positivists," "what cannot be said in words."[11] "Did you ever read the great philosopher Wittgenstein?" – one character asks another in Walker Percy's novel *The Last Gentleman* (1966) – "After his last work he announced the dictum which summarized his philosophy. He said: Whereof one cannot speak, thereof one should keep silent. And he did. He stopped teaching and went to live in a hut and said no more."[12] The conclusion of John Banville's novel *Birchwood* (1973) echoes the conclusion of the *Tractatus*: "whereof I cannot speak, thereof I must be silent."[13] Not all writers were

---

[7] John Barth, *The Floating Opera and the End of the Road* (1967; New York: Anchor, 1988), 330.
[8] John Updike, *Villages* (New York: Knopf, 2004), 198.
[9] Thomas Pynchon, *V.* (1963; New York: Harper Perennial Modern Classics, 2005), 314–315.
[10] *Samuel Beckett: The Grove Centenary Edition, Vol. II, Novels* (New York: Grove, 2006), 285. Richard Begam discusses the connections between Wittgenstein's conception of language and Beckett's conception of performativity in "How to Do Nothing with Words, or Waiting for Godot as Performativity," *Modern Drama* 50 (2): 138–167 (Summer 2007).
[11] Ursula Le Guin, "Introduction" (1976), in Ursula Le Guin, *The Left Hand of Darkness* (New York: Ace, 1969), np.
[12] Walker Percy, *The Last Gentleman* (1966; New York: Picador, 1999), 376.
[13] John Banville, *Birchwood* (1973; New York: Vintage, 2007), 171. In his interview with the *Paris Review*, Banville confessed, "As a young man I considered myself a Wittgensteinian, but for the little that I read of Wittgenstein, I understood even less." "John Banville: The

as reverential. T. W. Adorno frequently alludes to and denigrates the first proposition of the *Tractatus* and explicitly takes issue with the final proposition, claiming that in it "the extreme of positivism spills over into the gesture of authoritarian authenticity." For Adorno, Wittgenstein's maxim is "utterly antiphilosophical."[14] Irrespective of any given valuation, the combination of these two lines – the positivist emphasis on what is the case and the mystical regard for that which cannot be spoken – encapsulates the fascinating and somewhat contradictory appeal that Wittgenstein's early philosophy holds for writers and artists.[15]

For Calvino's postmodern generation of writers, the name of Wittgenstein served as common currency. Pynchon likely first read the *Tractatus* while an undergraduate at Cornell in the 1950s, a time when Cornell's philosophy faculty included Max Black, translator of Gottlob Frege and Rudolf Carnap as well as author of *A Companion to Wittgenstein's Tractatus*, and also Norman Malcolm, Wittgenstein's former student, commentator, and host during the philosopher's one visit to the United States. While visiting Cornell in the fall of 1949, Wittgenstein attended one of Malcolm's seminars, an appearance witnessed by a young William Gass, who was then studying philosophy with Black. Gass would recall that visit in future years, when Wittgenstein would appear frequently in his writing. One of Pynchon's English teachers at Cornell also refers to Wittgenstein with characteristic wit and insight. Near the end of *Transparent Things* (1972), Vladimir Nabokov slips in an obscure reference:

Days like this give sight a rest and allow other senses to function more freely. Earth and sky were drained of all color. It was either raining or pretending to rain or not raining at all, yet still appearing to rain in a sense that only certain old Northern dialects can either express verbally or not express, but *versionize* as it were, through the ghost of a sound produced by a drizzle in a haze of grateful rose shrubs. "Raining in Wittenberg, but not in Wittgenstein." An obscure joke in *Tralatitions*.[16]

Art of Fiction No. 200," interview with Belinda McKeon, *The Paris Review* 188 (Spring 2009), 145.

[14] Theodor W. Adorno, *Hegel: Three Studies*, trans. Shierry W. Nicholson (1971; Cambridge, MA: MIT Press, 1993), 101–102.

[15] I expand upon this point in terms of Wittgenstein's logical positivism and "aesthetic negativism" in *Fictions of Fact and Value: The Erasure of Logical Positivism in American Literature, 1945–1975* (New York: Oxford University Press, 2013).

[16] Vladimir Nabokov, *Transparent Things* (1972; New York: Vintage, 1989), 91.

Tralatitions is the fictional work of the fictional writer R. The name of Wittgenstein at the end of the passage makes explicit the allusion in the beginning of the passage to the *Tractatus*'s claim that "I know nothing about the weather when I know that it is either raining or not raining" (TLP 34, 4.461). Nabokov's playfulness is perspicacious, for his pithy remark calls attention to how semantic indeterminacy troubles the law of excluded middles. The idea that, in addition to raining or not raining, the weather might be "pretending to rain" or "not raining at all, yet still appearing to rain," a state of affairs perhaps represented by a fog or a mist, or "a drizzle in a haze," suggests an understanding of the world that is scalar and fluid rather than binary and rigid. "She had heard all about excluded middles," Nabokov's student wrote of Oedipa Maas, "they were bad shit, to be avoided."[17] And the idea that such a state of affairs presents something that one cannot express but rather only "versionize" recalls both the final proposition of the *Tractatus* – and Frank Ramsey's attendant question, "Can we whistle it?" – as well as the *Investigations*' persistent interest in forms of expression other than declarative sentences and propositional form. The line is quintessential Nabokov inasmuch as it creates the impression that the author did not have to spend a lot of time studying Wittgenstein's philosophy in order to encapsulate it succinctly in a passage as suggestive as it is humorous.

In her notes for the novel *The Infernal Desire Machines of Doctor Hoffman* (1972), published the same year as *Transparent Things*, Angela Carter likewise refers to the raining or not raining passage from the *Tractatus*. Heidi Yeandle notes that Carter planned to have Doctor Hoffman accuse his Tractarian nemesis – the Minister of Determination (he who attempts "to draw a limit to thought") – of attempting to make "a tautologous city where everything is true because it makes no demands upon the world and everybody will always be satisfied, no matter what the circumstances, since all sentences will be constructed on the model of 'Either it is raining or it is not raining' and so offer absolutely unequivocal alternatives that nobody can quarrel with."[18] Carter, who read Max Black's book on the *Tractatus*, draws widely on Wittgenstein's thought throughout her depiction of the Reality War pitting the Doctor against the Minister, to such an extent that the latter not only voices arguments that draw on the *Tractatus* but even those that draw on the voice of the

---

[17] Thomas Pynchon, *The Crying of Lot 49* (1966; New York: HarperCollins, 1999), 150.
[18] Quoted in Heidi Yeandle, *Angela Carter and Western Philosophy* (London: Palgrave Macmillan, 2017), 137–138.

interlocutor from the *Investigations* who ventriloquizes arguments from the *Tractatus*.

That same year, Don DeLillo ended his second novel *End Zone* (1972) with an image of Wittgenstein as a negative presence. As Gary Harkness looks at the wall of his teammate's dorm room, he focuses on remnants of tape that once affixed a poster to the wall: "Poster of Wittgenstein, I thought. ... Dollar ninety-eight poster of philosopher surrounded by Vienna Circle. Two parts to that man's work. What is written. What is not written. The man himself seemed to favor second part."[19] DeLillo draws on Wittgenstein's distinction between the written and unwritten parts of his work, as well as that between what can be said and what can (only) be shown within the work, to probe in his fiction the possibility of generating meaning before, beyond, or in between words. Both in DeLillo's early fiction – in addition to *End Zone* he also refers to Wittgenstein in *Great Jones Street* (1973) and *Ratner's Star* (1976) – and in Wittgenstein's early philosophy there is a preoccupation with that which lies beyond the limits of language: with the unthinkable, the untellable, the unwritten.

That DeLillo, Carter, and Nabokov were all turning to Wittgenstein in novels published in 1972 is indicative of a moment in which a burgeoning postmodernism – not yet a tired set of metafictional conventions but rather a spirit of innovation and exploration – confronted Wittgenstein as a figure of logical positivism but also of something additional and perhaps critical of that same positivism out of which it issued. That same year saw the debut of Tom Stoppard's *Jumpers*, which lampoons logical positivism. Although the main character is based primarily on A. J. Ayer, in his lines one can hear echoes of the early Wittgenstein: "The fact that I cut a ludicrous figure in the academic world," the protagonist reflects, "is largely due to my aptitude for traducing a complex and logical thesis to a mysticism of staggering banality."[20] Stoppard followed *Jumpers* with another Wittgenstein-inspired effort, 1979's *Dogg's Hamlet*, which is in

---

[19] Don DeLillo, *End Zone* (1972; New York: Penguin, 1986), 233. DeLillo displays his familiarity with Wittgenstein's work beyond simply the primary texts, for this passage refers to a letter Wittgenstein wrote to Ludwig von Ficker in which he describes the *Tractatus* as bipartite: "I wanted to write that my work consists of two parts: of the one which is here, and of everything which I have not written. And precisely this second part is the important one." *Wittgenstein: Sources and Perspectives*, ed. C. G. Luckhardt (Ithaca, NY: Cornell University Press, 1993), 94–95.

[20] Tom Stoppard, *Jumpers* (New York: Grove, 1974), 72.

part a dramatization of the language-game of the builders from the beginning of *Philosophical Investigations*.

Published in the 1980s, Thomas Bernhard's *Wittgenstein's Nephew* (1982) and David Markson's *Wittgenstein's Mistress* (1988) both recall earlier postmodern interest in Wittgenstein. Markson's final novel can be read as an extended meditation on the early Wittgenstein's propositional form or, as David Foster Wallace put it, as a prolonged answer to the question "What if somebody really had to *live* in a *Tractatus*ized world?"[21] The book begins with a simple conceit, although it is not one that Markson immediately makes plain to the reader. The protagonist, Kate, believes herself to be the last remaining person in the world. And, indeed, there are no other people in the book (thus giving *Wittgenstein's Mistress* one more person than Wittgenstein's *Tractatus*). What there are instead are Kate's rambling thoughts about relatively arcane matters ranging from art history to Greek mythology to classical music to existential philosophy. It would seem a rather strange way to spend one's time as the last person on earth, if one could imagine time as something to be spent in such circumstances. The narrative tone is minimalist and reminiscent of Beckett, who himself assembled "a substantial collection of books by and about Wittgenstein."[22] In addition to her thoughts and memories, Kate's world is populated by a small number of discrete objects: her home, her clothing, a few boxes of books. Markson does not involve himself in the nitty-gritty of, say, how she secures food, what she eats, and so on. Kate's world is all that is the case.

A handful of the novel's digressive and overlapping ideas mention Wittgenstein in particular:

Although come to think about it I once read somewhere that Ludwig Wittgenstein himself had never read one word of Aristotle.
In fact I have more than once taken comfort in knowing this, there being so many people one has never read one word of one's self.
Such as Ludwig Wittgenstein.
Even if one was always told that Wittgenstein was too hard to read in any case.
And to tell the truth I did read one sentence by him after all, which I did not find difficult in the least.
In fact I became very fond of what it said.

---

[21] David Foster Wallace, "The Empty Plenum: David Markson's *Wittgenstein's Mistress*," *Review of Contemporary Fiction* 10 (2): 219 (Summer 1990).
[22] Andre Furlani, *Beckett after Wittgenstein* (Evanston, IL: Northwestern University Press, 2015), 3.

You do not need a lot of money to buy a nice present, but you do need a lot of time, was the sentence.

On my honor, Wittgenstein once said that. (100)

This is the most extended meditation on Wittgenstein in the novel. There are three or four other such segments – one on how Brahms carried candy in his pocket for children and thus likely gave some to the young Wittgenstein, one on how Wittgenstein regularly fed the same seagull during his time in Galway, and another on how Wittgenstein carried sugar cubes in his pocket to give to horses when he went on walks near Cambridge. And, of course, there is no evidence that Wittgenstein did say what, on her honor, Kate says he said. But were it only for these remarks, Wittgenstein would have no greater claim to giving his name to the title than Shakespeare or Shostakovich or any of a dozen other artistic and cultural figures that preoccupy Kate's thoughts. Beyond content, however, the novel's "stylistic conceit – propositions, and comments on propositions," as Joseph Tabbi remarks, "derives from a fanciful reading of Wittgenstein's *Tractatus*."[23]

Kate is thus Wittgenstein's mistress – or her book is – in the sense that she or it represents some intimate but illicit relationship with Wittgenstein's thought. Markson alludes to the book's title when Kate remarks that "Wittgenstein was never married, by the way. Well, or never had a mistress either, having been a homosexual" (220). In an interview with Tabbi, Markson recounts the origins of the book's memorable title.

JT: Tell me about the title.
DM: Originally I was calling it *Wittgenstein's Niece*. Never knowing, of course, that Thomas Bernhard would eventually publish something called *Wittgenstein's Nephew*. ... *Wittgenstein's Mistress* had been on the same scratch sheet with *Niece*, and I decided I liked it better by then.
JT: And meaning basically that your heroine is mistress to Wittgenstein's thought?
DM: Well, along with several other people's, yes. But as I started to say a few minutes ago, the Wittgenstein is frequently most obvious in the very way she questions so many of her own "propositions," as it were.[24]

We thus almost had *Wittgenstein's Nephew* and *Wittgenstein's Niece* within a few years of each other.

---

[23] Joseph Tabbi, "David Markson: An Introduction," *Review of Contemporary Fiction* 10 (2): 101 (Summer 1990).
[24] Joseph Tabbi, "An Interview with David Markson," *Review of Contemporary Fiction* 10 (2): 113 (Summer 1990).

Bernhard's novel features two characters, one a writer named Thomas Bernhard and the other Paul Wittgenstein, nephew of the famous philosopher. Set in Vienna, the novel centers around themes of music and mental illness that resonate with Ludwig Wittgenstein's biography, but the novel remains somewhat coy about the philosopher:

> I never talked to Paul about Ludwig, let alone about his philosophy. Only occasionally, and somewhat to my surprise, Paul would say, *Of course you know my uncle Ludwig.* That was all. We never once talked about the *Tractatus*. On one occasion, however, Paul said that his uncle Ludwig was *the maddest member of the family. After all, to be a multimillionaire and a village schoolteacher is a bit perverse, don't you think?*[25]

Like Markson's novel, one can say of Bernhard's that it is not so much the literal or thematic content that is Wittgensteinian so much as the form. But Bernhard's form goes in the opposite direction of Markson's short propositions. *Wittgenstein's Nephew* is all one paragraph – precisely 100 pages long in my edition of the English translation – one long paragraph that circles back on itself repeatedly as it sketches a particular cultural landscape. Bernhard's work also recalls the philosopher's Austrian roots, for although Wittgenstein is often discussed in the context of Anglo-American philosophy, his cultural values and points of reference were always very much those of late Hapsburg, fin-de-siècle Vienna, as Allan Janik and Stephen Toulmin so convincingly demonstrated nearly half a century ago in *Wittgenstein's Vienna*.[26]

II. Late Wittgenstein in Contemporary Literature

More contemporary writing after Wittgenstein is less uniform in its references to the man and his work, but it finds more diverse ways to make use of Wittgenstein's concepts, arguments, or writings, particularly from the later philosophy. For example, when asked in an interview which writers have influenced her – the interviewer suggests Milton or Shakespeare – Leslie Marmon Silko responds rather differently: "Well, lately, the one person that's meant a lot to me is Wittgenstein. I think his

---

[25] Thomas Bernhard, *Wittgenstein's Nephew* (1982; New York: Vintage International, 1988), 63. It is unclear if Bernhard intends that this Paul Wittgenstein is the son of the philosopher's older brother Paul, the pianist who lost his right arm during World War I and for whom Ravel wrote "Piano Concerto for the Left Hand."

[26] Allan Janik and Stephen Toulmin, *Wittgenstein's Vienna* (New York: Simon & Schuster, 1973).

remarks on color turn into some of the most beautiful poetry I've ever read. People call Wittgenstein a philosopher and I call him a poet."[27] The poet Maggie Nelson also refers to Wittgenstein's writings about color:

> Or of Wittgenstein, who wrote his *Remarks on Colour* during the last eighteen months of his life, while dying of stomach cancer. He knew he was dying; he could have chosen to work on any philosophical problem under the sun. He chose to write about color. About color and pain. Much of this writing is urgent, opaque, and uncharacteristically boring. "That which I am writing about so tediously, may be obvious to someone whose mind is less decrepit," he wrote.[28]

Later in the same work, Nelson refers explicitly to the *Tractatus*, admiring its profundity despite its brevity.[29] And on the first page of *The Argonauts* (2015), Nelson refers immediately to Wittgenstein in a way that recalls DeLillo's interest: "Before we met, I had spent a lifetime devoted to Wittgenstein's idea that the inexpressible is contained – inexpressibly! – in the expressed. This idea gets less air time than his more reverential *Whereof one cannot speak thereof one must be silent*, but it is, I think, the deeper idea. Its paradox is, quite literally, *why I write*, or how I feel able to keep writing." In this passage, Nelson comes close to the second sense of "writing after" Wittgenstein – the sense of writing as searching, as an investigation – as she also does when she writes: "I insisted that words do more than nominate. I read aloud to you the opening of *Philosophical Investigations*. *Slab*, I shouted, *slab!*"[30] Nelson's interest in Wittgenstein represents a generational shift from the postmodern treatment, at times bordering on caricature, of the philosopher as mad scientist or silent mystic; moving beyond this binary, in a way that is less reverential but perhaps deeper, Nelson signals an interest in Wittgenstein's life and work that is more supple and personal even as it is also more political.

As the example of Nelson's work clearly evinces, and as Marjorie Perloff's study *Wittgenstein's Ladder* influentially established, Wittgenstein's philosophy factors as a recurrent influence on and figure in contemporary poetry.[31] "Part III of the *Black Plague*," poet and critic David Antin relates, "is pretty much an arrangement of words taken from a translation of Wittgenstein's *Philosophical Investigations*. About the

---

[27] Kim Barnes, "'A Leslie Marmon Silko Interview' (1986)," *Conversations with Leslie Marmon Silko* (Jackson, MS: University of Mississippi Press, 2000), 81.
[28] Maggie Nelson, *Bluets* (Seattle, WA: Wave Books, 2009), 10.
[29] Nelson, *Bluets*, 91.
[30] Maggie Nelson, *The Argonauts* (Minneapolis, MN: Graywolf, 2015), 3, 4.
[31] Marjorie Perloff, *Wittgenstein's Ladder: Poetic Language and the Strangeness of the Ordinary* (Chicago, IL: University of Chicago Press, 1996).

words, nobody owns them – not Wittgenstein, or the translator, or me – and anyone who wants them is welcome to use them again."[32] Georgina Colby reports that after the posthumous publication of *On Certainty* in 1969, Wittgenstein's work "was the subject of much spirited debate in Antin's circle."[33] Michael Palmer's *The Circular Gates* (1974) contains an epigraph from *The Brown Book*: "But do we interpret the words before obeying the order."[34] And a line in Palmer's "Notes for Echo Lake 4" (1981), "Did the lion finally talk," refers to Wittgenstein's famous remark in the *Philosophical Investigations*: "If a lion could speak, we would not understand him" (PI 235).[35] Describing a technique similar to Antin's, Rosmarie Waldrop relates "I had used – and misused – Wittgenstein phrases all through *The Reproduction of Profiles*."[36] When asked about his favorite philosopher in an interview, poet Robert Creeley replied "Wittgenstein is the one that's most provocative to me."[37] The world of contemporary poetry, one might say with another nod to Cavell, is replete with Wittgensteinian provocations.

In the early 1970s, Antin and Kathy Acker together read through Wittgenstein's writings.[38] In "Against Ordinary Language: The Language of the Body," Acker draws on a Wittgensteinian vocabulary in examining "the antagonism between bodybuilding and verbal language." Describing the minimalist language of the gym, Acker suggests that "This spoken language is kin to the 'language games' Wittgenstein proposes in his *The Brown Book*."[39] Later in the essay, after citing the *Tractatus* ("The sense of the world must lie outside the world. In the world everything is as it is [TLP 71, 6.41]"), Acker returns to the notion of a language-game: "If ordinary language or meanings lie outside essence, what is the position of that language game which I have named *the language of the body*? For bodybuilding (a language of the body) rejects ordinary language and yet itself constitutes a language, a method for

---

[32] David Antin, *Selected Poems: 1963–1973* (Los Angeles, CA: Sun & Moon Press, 1991), 93.
[33] Georgina Colby, *Kathy Acker: Writing the Impossible* (Edinburgh: Edinburgh University Press, 2016), 10.
[34] Michael Palmer, *The Lion Bridge: Selected Poems, 1972-1995* (New York: New Directions, 1998), 15.
[35] Palmer, *The Lion Bridge*, 77.
[36] Rosmarie Waldrop, *Curves to the Apple* (New York: New Directions, 2006), xi.
[37] Robert Creeley, "An Interview by Emily Keller," *The American Poetry Review* 12 (3): 28 (May/June 1983).
[38] Georgina Colby, *Kathy Acker: Writing the Impossible* (Edinburgh: Edinburgh University Press, 2016), 10.
[39] Kathy Acker, "Against Ordinary Language: The Language of the Body," *The Last Sex: Feminism and Outlaw Bodies*, ed. Arthur Kroker and Marilouise Kroker (New York: St. Martin's, 1993), 21.

understanding and controlling the physical world in this case is also the self" (25). Acker's meditations on language and the body dovetail particularly well with Wittgenstein's attention to vocal utterances that are not quite verbal but still very much part of language-games: "Whereas the cry of the beggar means nothing other than what it is," Acker writes, "in the cry of the beggar, the impossible (as the Wittgenstein of the *Tractatus* and Heidegger see it) occurs in that meaning and breath become one" (25). Even more than the Wittgenstein of the *Tractatus*, however, Acker's essay, with its interest in the language-game of the gym – what with all its grunts, counts, clichés, and repetitions – recalls Wittgenstein's insistence in the *Investigations* on how moves in a language-game gain their significance from being embedded in a form of life.

Wittgenstein's method and style of writing most obviously inflects the writing that comes after him. "Wittgenstein's is a poetic practice based on the interrogation of the meaning of words in the context of life practices," Antin notes, "That was what he meant by grammar."[40] One might similarly describe the poetic practice of Lydia Davis's short stories, some of whose titles alone can appear distinctly philosophical ("The Senses") and at times downright Wittgensteinian ("Grammar Questions"). The one-sentence "Hand" reads as if it were taken right out of Wittgenstein's *On Certainty*, a text which opens with a rhetorical question about a hand and then repeatedly returns to the figure: "Now do I, in the course of my life, make sure I know that here is a hand – my own hand, that is?" (OC §3). "Beyond the hand holding this book that I'm reading," Davis writes, "I see another hand lying idle and slightly out of focus – my extra hand."[41] Davis's "story" also recalls Wittgenstein's question from the *Philosophical Investigations*: "Why can't my right hand give my left hand money?" (PI §268 In fact, Davis's collected short stories – some perhaps better considered remarks – exemplify Wittgenstein's reflection to Norman Malcolm that "a serious and good philosophical work could be written that would consist entirely of jokes."[42] When asked a series of rapid-fire questions by the *Times Literary Supplement* in 2016, Davis responded to the query "Jacques Derrida or Judith Butler?" with "Neither. Wittgenstein."[43]

---

[40] David Antin, "Wittgenstein Among the Poets," *Modernism/Modernity* 5 (1): 161 (January 1998).
[41] Lydia Davis, *The Collected Stories of Lydia Davis* (New York: FSG, 2009), 530.
[42] Norman Malcolm, *Ludwig Wittgenstein: A Memoir* (Oxford: Clarendon, 2001), 27–28.
[43] "Twenty Questions with Lydia Davis," *Times Literary Supplement*, 14 November 2016. https://www.the-tls.co.uk/articles/public/twenty-questions-lydia-davis.

A different concern of Wittgenstein's work – aspect-perception – governs the opening set piece Ben Lerner's *Leaving the Atocha Station* (2011). In keeping with his morning routine, the protagonist, an American poet named Adam Gordon who is living in Madrid on a Fulbright Fellowship, is standing in room 58 of the Prado Museum, looking at Roger Van der Weyden's *Descent from the Cross*. On this particular morning, however, another man stands in the same room looking at the same painting:

> I waited for him to move on, but he didn't. I wondered if he had observed me in front of the *Descent* and if he was now standing before it in the hope of seeing whatever it was I must have seen. ... I was about to abandon room 58 when the man broke suddenly into tears, convulsively catching his breath. Was he, I wondered, just facing the wall to hide his face as he dealt with whatever grief he'd brought into the museum? Or was he having a *profound experience of art*?[44]

The interests of the passage are particularly Wittgensteinian. How do facial expression and other bodily or embodied reactions pertain to internal feelings? How do artworks inspire such internal feelings? Are such sensations fundamentally private? And, if so, can a shared, social, public language ever adequately capture or express them?

This opening scene gives way to a series of meditations that speak directly to concerns Wittgenstein addresses in the private language argument and the discussion of "seeing as." Attempting to describe a taste or "sting" in his mouth that he experiences in conjunction with acute anxiety, the narrator remarks: "I had known this chemical sting since I was a child and had assumed everyone knew it, that it was at least as universal as the coppery taste of blood, and somehow related, although later I learned that nobody I knew was familiar with this taste, at least not as I described it, not as the particular aftertaste of panic" (18). That this particular sensation, which the narrator assumed was biological and therefore generalizable, does not extend to any of his interlocutors leads him to question whether his private sensations or inner experiences are shared with or accessible to other people. In an interview in which he describes his interest in images and in "the power of captioning," Lerner refers to "the Wittgenstein thing, the duck/rabbit, the multistable figure where you can see it as a duck or you can see it as a rabbit?": "For me, part of what a novel does is that it's very invested in

---

[44] Ben Lerner, *Leaving the Atocha Station* (Minneapolis, MN: Coffee House Press, 2011), 8. Hereinafter cited parenthetically.

seeing as. You put an image in the book and then you invite the reader to see it *as* this, or *as* that, and that emphasis on the way text can subject images to redescription is really fascinating."[45] Lerner encapsulates Wittgenstein's appeal to artists, writers, and composers: the problems he is drawn to in his investigations – language-games, aspect seeing, private language – are often fundamentally aesthetic in nature.

Given the apparent lack of "authentic experiences," aesthetic or otherwise, the narrator engages in a series of performative ones. *Leaving the Atocha Station* reads as an extended meditation on acting "as if" or "as though" something were the case. "As I covered my face in my hands and writhed as though in pain," the narrator says after having been punched in the face (13). Expressions of pain are, of course, one of the most central uses of language in Wittgenstein's philosophy. So, too, with art and aesthetic experience in Lerner's novel. "I forced myself to listen *as if* the poem were unpredictable and profound," the narrator relates, "as if that were given somehow, and any failure to be compelled would be exclusively my own" (37). The narrator then goes on to interpret the expressions, actions, and words of others "as if" such and such were the case, only seldomly pausing to consider, for example, that "she might not have had the experience I ascribed her" (45). In such a way, he fashions a profound experience of art out of the failure to experience art profoundly, for "only then could my fraudulence be a project and not merely a pathology" (164). Lerner's aesthetic fraudulence is peculiarly Wittgensteinian.

Nicholas Mosley's ambitious novel of ideas *Hopeful Monsters* (1990) – which includes a humorous set piece in which Wittgenstein appears as a guest at a garden party – is similarly interested in the problem of seeing as or seeing as if. Although the novel's protagonist hopes to ask the philosopher whether two people can "be together in those areas of silence: or do you have to be on your own," he ironically never gets a chance to speak to Wittgenstein.[46] Mosley fills the episode with failed attempts at communication: the sycophant who asks Wittgenstein a torturously long question is answered curtly with "I don't think that is correct" (157); the hosts' daughter who extends her hand as an offer to

---

[45] Emily Temple, "Ben Lerner on the Porous Boundaries of Literature, Truth, and Plagiarism," *Literary Hub* (May 4, 2017), https://lithub.com/ben-lerner-on-the-porous-boundaries-of-literature-truth-and-plagiarism.

[46] Nicholas Mosley, *Hopeful Monsters* (1990; Normal, IL: Dalkey Archive Press, 2000), 156. Hereinafter cited parenthetically.

take Wittgenstein's plate is offended when he snaps "What do you want?" (157); when one of the narrator's friends attempts to speak to Wittgenstein, the philosopher "was turning away as if annoyed" (161). Wittgenstein's relentless "pursuit of truth," the writer William Gass remarks, "was often an excuse to be rude."[47] Mosley characterizes Wittgenstein the philosopher so as to represent the problems that characterize his philosophy. Almost every description of Wittgenstein's awkward behavior at the party reads as if it were an exercise in what the *Philosophical Investigations* treats as seeing as:

Wittgenstein was seated in a small room inside the house: the room was crowded; there were people sitting on the floor and looking up at him as if he had been set in some niche. He was a thin, blue-eyed, curly-haired man; he seemed precisely delineated as if there was a light on the wall behind him. He wore a tweed jacket and an open-necked shirt. It seemed that although people were seeing him as if set up in a niche, he was not posing.

I thought – It is as if he were looking at the people watching him and saying: "Is it you? Is it you?" (156–157)

This quality of seeing Wittgenstein doing one thing as if it were something else, or as if there were something additional, appears almost every time the character does, as when "he looked down at his plate as if there might be entrails on it" (157). "I continued to have his image of Wittgenstein," the narrator confesses, "as someone whom it was necessary for me to meet: it was as if he were a figure that I had to learn something from at a corner of the maze" (155). Mosley never leads his character into that particular corner, or niche, and the figure of Wittgenstein remains out of reach.

While at times Wittgenstein appears as a character in a novel, at other times a character in a novel appears to be Wittgenstein. "In any case, I recollect that before approaching him," the narrator of W. G. Sebald's *Austerlitz* (2001) writes of the book's eponymous protagonist, "I had been thinking at some length about his personal similarity to Ludwig Wittgenstein, and the horror-stricken expressions on both their faces."[48] Although the narrator's association of Austerlitz with Wittgenstein begins with the fact that both of them always carry the same kind of rucksack, it extends to "a certain physical likeness between him and the

---

[47] William Gass, "At Death's Door: Wittgenstein," in *Finding a Form: Essays* (Ithaca, NY: Cornell University Press, 1997), 150.
[48] W. G. Sebald, *Austerlitz*, trans. Anthea Bell (2001; New York: Modern Library, 2011), 40. Hereinafter cited parenthetically.

philosopher who died of the disease of cancer in Cambridge in 1951" (40). The narrator remarks that "whenever I see a photograph of Wittgenstein somewhere or other, I feel more and more as if Austerlitz were gazing at me out of it" (41). Here Sebald winks to the reader, for in fact a photograph of Wittgenstein's face has literally appeared earlier in the novel. When the narrator recalls his visit to the Nocturama in the Antwerp Zoo, he notes that several of the animals had "strikingly large eyes, and the fixed, inquiring gaze found in certain painters and philosophers who seek to penetrate the darkness which surrounds us purely by means of looking and thinking" (4–5). In the middle of this description – which perhaps alludes to the *Philosophical Investigations* mention of "the darkness of this time" (4) as well as to its injunction, "don't think, but look!" (PI §§36, 66) – Sebald includes a cropped photograph featuring the eyes of the artist Jan Peter Tripp and one of the eyes of Wittgenstein. Beyond their physical likeness, the narrator continues, the similarities between Wittgenstein and Austerlitz can be seen "in stature, in the way they study one as if across an invisible barrier, in the makeshift organization of their lives, in a wish to manage with as few possessions as possible, and in the inability, typical of Austerlitz as it was of Wittgenstein, to linger over any kind of preliminaries" (41). "I observe a face," Wittgenstein writes in the *Investigations*, "and then suddenly notice its likeness to another. I *see* that it has not changed; and yet I see it differently. I call this experience 'noticing an aspect'" (PI §203, xi §113). In implicitly referring to this passage by noticing the likenesses between Austerlitz and Wittgenstein, Sebald explicitly invites the reader to consider his character an alter-ego, *doppelgänger*, or some other version of the philosopher.

When the character Austerlitz discusses his own writing, he also sounds particularly Wittgensteinian, echoing the thoughts and sentiments Wittgenstein expresses in the Preface to the *Philosophical Investigations*. In this first paragraph of that Preface, Wittgenstein writes:

I have written down all these thoughts as remarks, short paragraphs, sometimes in longer chains about the same subject, sometimes jumping, in a sudden change, from one area to another. – Originally it was my intention to bring all this together in a book whose form I thought of differently at different times. But it seemed to me essential that in the book the thoughts should proceed from one subject to another in a natural, smooth sequence. (PI, remark 3, page 3)

Now compare Austerlitz, discussing his own work: "Even in Paris, said Austerlitz, I had thought of collecting my fragmentary studies in a book, although I constantly postponed writing it. The various ideas I entertained at different times of this book I was to write ranged from the concept of a systematically descriptive work in several volumes to a series of essays" (120–121). Both Wittgenstein and Austerlitz fail to realize these ambitious plans. "After several unsuccessful attempts to weld my results together," Wittgenstein writes, "I realized that I should never succeed" (PI, remark 3, page 3). Instead, he realizes that the very nature of his investigations required a different kind of philosophical writing: "For it compels us to travel criss-cross in every direction over a wide field of thought. – The philosophical remarks in this book are, as it were, a number of sketches of landscapes which were made in the course of these long and meandering journeys" (PI, remark 3, page 3). Sebald draws explicitly on this language in Austerlitz's description of his own writings:

> However, even a first glance at the papers I had brought here from the Institute to Alderney Street showed that they consisted largely of sketches which now seemed misguided, distorted, and of little use. I began to assemble and recast anything that still passed muster in order to re-create before my own eyes, as if in the pages of an album, the picture of the landscape, now almost immersed in oblivion, through which my journey had taken me. But the more I labored on this project over several months the more pitiful did the results seem. (121)

Sketches, landscape, journey: Austerlitz and Wittgenstein use the same terms to describe their writing. Even Austerlitz's parenthetical remark, "as if in the pages of an album," repeats the *Investigations*, where Wittgenstein concludes: "So this book is really just an album" (PI, remark 3, page 3). Austerlitz's sense of pitiful resignation – "the more I labored ... the more pitiful did the results seem" – parallels Wittgenstein's concluding remark in the Preface: "I should have liked to produce a good book. It has not turned out that way, but the time is past in which I could improve it" (PI §4). Austerlitz shares with Wittgenstein despair over not being able to write a conventional book as well as an inability to recognize the innovation represented by that failure. Part of the richness of Sebald's novel is that most readers will not notice these connections at all – they are not necessary – and yet, once noticed, the work takes on additional layers of signification.[49]

---

[49] Sebald's interest in the work and particularly the life of Wittgenstein extends beyond *Austerlitz*. The second of the four narratives that comprise *The Emigrants* (1992), for example, features a protagonist, Paul Bereyter, who bears multiple similarities to Wittgenstein, particularly, as Sebald notes in an interview, during the philosopher's "period as a schoolteacher in Austria." Carole Angier, "Who is W. G. Sebald?," in *The*

Sebald is only one of a number of artists, writers, and filmmakers who have been as captivated by the life of Wittgenstein as they are by the work. "I had the intention of doing a film script on Wittgenstein at one point," Sebald told James Wood in 1997, "and did a rough draft for it, so it's something that may yet happen."[50] Derek Jarman did direct a rather bizarre film, *Wittgenstein* (1993), inspired by the philosopher's life. Bruce Duffy's novel *The World as I Found It* (1987) takes its title from a line from the *Tractatus* – "If I wrote a book called *The World as I Found it*" (TLP 57, 5.63) – and imagines itself as a sort of "fictional biography" of Wittgenstein, Bertrand Russell, and G. E. Moore. Some of the same territory is covered in the graphic novel *Logicomix: An Epic Search for Truth* (2008) by Apostolos Doxiadis, Christos Papadimitriou, Alecos Papadatos, and Anne Di Donne. Wittgenstein's association with Cambridge inspired Lars Iyer's campus novel *Wittgenstein, Jr.* (2014).

As with the recurring interest in aspect seeing in the works of Lerner, Mosley, and Sebald, Wittgenstein's "private language argument" in the *Philosophical Investigations* factors into the works of multiple poets and writers. In her work *Midwinter Day* (1982), Bernadette Mayer explicitly considers the possibility of creating a private language in a passage that typifies writers' consistent interest in both the work and life of Wittgenstein: "Wittgenstein says there is no such thing as a private language. I think it would be worth trying to make one. … Wittgenstein's house was furnished with old crates though he was not poor and when he came to eat at your house he would wash all the clean dishes over again himself before the meal because he was afraid they were not really clean."[51] Similarly, Bellow's characters frequently confront the possibility – one that presents as threatening or despairing – of a private language. In *Mr. Sammler's Planet*, Artur Sammler seeks out "the privacy of his own room" where "he had mentally inscribed certain propositions" along the cracks in the plaster walls.[52] And in *Seize the Day* (1956), Tommy Wilhelm despairs that "Every other man spoke a language entirely his own, which he had figured out by private thinking;

Emergence of Memory: Conversations with W. G. Sebald, ed. Lynne Sharon Schwartz (New York: Seven Stories, 2007), 73.

[50] James Wood, "An Interview with W. G. Sebald," *Brick: A Literary Journal* 59 (1998), https://brickmag.com/an-interview-with-w-g-sebald.

[51] Bernadette Meyer, *Midwinter Day* (New York: New Directions, 1982), 68.

[52] Bellow, *Mr. Sammler's Planet*, 134, 136. I discuss the similarities between Bellow's fiction and Wittgenstein's philosophy at greater length in "Bellow's Private Language," in *Wittgenstein and Modernism*, 231–253.

he had his own ideas and peculiar ways."[53] J. M. Coetzee's *Elizabeth Costello* (2003) presents the possibility of a private language as a threat to the originality of the artist. "But you must surely concede that at a certain level we speak, and therefore write, like everyone else," Elizabeth Costello's son insists to her, "Otherwise we would all be speaking and writing private languages." His mother, a writer, remains reluctant to concede the point, given "all the effort I put into not writing like anyone else."[54] Wittgenstein's private language argument, as Coetzee knows, reveals the fallacy that meaning, communication – and by extension aesthetic innovation – require private mental content inaccessible to anyone else.

The private language argument and its inverse, Wittgenstein's idea of meaning as use, also preoccupied a prominent philosophical novelist of the next generation. David Foster Wallace's interest in Wittgenstein was one aspect of his deep and sustained engagement with philosophy. Wallace's father was the philosopher James D. Wallace, who took his doctorate from Cornell, where his dissertation adviser was Norman Malcolm. As an undergraduate philosophy major at Amherst, David Foster Wallace took a seminar on Wittgenstein and was captivated in particular by the *Tractatus* and then "gradually came to find greater value in the antitheoretical and anti-systematic philosophy of the later Wittgenstein."[55] Wallace considered becoming an academic philosopher, was admitted to Harvard's graduate program, but withdrew before completing his first semester.[56] In his first novel, *The Broom of the System* (1987), the protagonist Lenore Stonecipher Beadsman attempts to solve a mystery regarding her grandmother, a former student of Wittgenstein's who has disappeared from her nursing home. The book's title gestures to a remark early in the *Philosophical Investigations* when Wittgenstein asks: "When I say 'My broom is in the corner,' is this really a statement about the broomstick and the brush?" (PI §33, 60). Lenore's brother recounts a

---

[53] Saul Bellow, *Seize the Day* (1956; New York: Penguin, 1996), 79.
[54] J. M. Coetzee, *Elizabeth Costello* (New York: Viking, 2003), 8.
[55] Randy Ramal, "Beyond Philosophy: David Foster Wallace on Literature, Wittgenstein, and the Dangers of Theorizing," in *Gesturing Toward Reality: David Foster Wallace and Philosophy*, ed. Robert K. Bolger and Scott Korb (New York: Bloomsbury, 2014), 179.
[56] For an overview of Wallace's lifelong interest in philosophy, see James Reyerson's introduction to the published version of Wallace's undergraduate philosophy honors thesis, "A Head that Throbbed Heartlike: The Philosophical Mind of David Foster Wallace," in David Foster Wallace, *Fate, Time, and Language: An Essay on Free Will*, ed. Steven M. Cahn and Maureen Eckert (New York: Columbia University Press, 2011), 1–33.

time when their grandmother asked him to say "which part of the broom was more elemental, more *fundamental* in my opinion, the bristles or the handle." When the boy suggests the bristles are what makes the broom a broom, his grandmother corrects him, insisting that it depends on how the broom is being used, whether one is attempting to sweep with it, for example, or to use it to break a window: "Meaning as fundamentalness. Fundamentalness as use. Meaning as use. Meaning as use."[57] The grandmother is repeating the lessons she learned from her teacher, who writes in the *Philosophical Investigations* that "the meaning of a word is its use in the language" (PI §§25, 43).

Wallace's familiarity with the private language argument shows up in a rather unlikely venue: a book review of a usage handbook. In fact, the concerns about privacy and skepticism raised by Wittgenstein's philosophy pertain directly to those attributes of language that are most public and conventional. In 2001, Wallace reviewed Bryan A. Garner's *A Dictionary of Modern American Usage*, a book he greatly admired. No mere book review, however, Wallace's "Authority and American Usage" spans some sixty pages and includes some eighty-one footnotes. Arguing against the ideal of a purely descriptive approach to language and lexicography, a position "that might aptly be called Unbelievably Naive Positivism" (87) – Wallace claims that when it comes to "language behavior," one cannot coherently entertain the very possibility of a purely descriptive realism, as one might hypothetically be able to do (but not in fact) with natural phenomena.[58] One cannot do so in the case of linguistic practices because "such behavior is both *human* and fundamentally *normative*" (87). At this point Wallace turns to Wittgenstein, first in the body of the text, and then in a long footnote. "To understand why this is important" – the fact that language is both human and normative – "you have only to accept the proposition that language is by its very nature public – i.e., that there is no such thing as a private language – and then to observe the way Descriptivists seem either ignorant of this fact or oblivious to its consequences" (87, 89). This claim in turn occasions a footnote that covers two full pages and even bears a title: "INTERPOLATIVE DEMONSTRATION OF THE FACT THAT THERE IS NO SUCH THING AS A PRIVATE LANGAUGE" (87). The ensuing exposition is as accurate as it is amusing. Beginning from a position familiar to

---

[57] David Foster Wallace, *The Broom of the System* (1987; New York: Penguin, 2016), 149–150.
[58] David Foster Wallace, "Authority and American Usage," in *Consider the Lobster and Other Essays* (New York: Little, Brown, 2006), 87. Hereinafter cited parenthetically.

readers of Wittgenstein, Wallace observes how it is tempting to think there is the possibility of a private language. One's experience of pain, for example, seems so vivid and yet so particular that it is difficult to imagine that specific experience of pain being anyone else's experience of pain. From there, it is but one or two steps to what Wallace describes as "the adolescent pot-smoker's terror that his own inner experience is both private an unverifiable, a syndrome that is technically known as Cannabic Solipsism" (87). With apologies for going on at length, Wallace then offers a relatively succinct yet thorough summary of Wittgenstein's private language argument, with an assist from the work of his father's dissertation advisor.

Wallace's essay then takes an unexpected turn from the private language argument to a discussion of Standard Written English versus Black English Vernacular that has provoked strong critical responses.[59] Wallace's recognition of the racial and cultural implications of Wittgenstein's arguments initially parallels certain aspects of Amiri Baraka's "Expressive Language" (1963). At first glance, Baraka's interest in Wittgenstein hearkens back to the mid-twentieth-century moment when writers were regularly reading the *Tractatus*. In *The Autobiography of Leroi Jones* (1984), Baraka writes that while he was living in the Village in the late 1950s, shortly after he heard about Allen Ginsberg and first read "Howl," "I began to read Heidegger and Wittgenstein and Husserl. Wittgenstein's *Tractatus* became an emotional reference for me."[60] And in "Expressive Language," Baraka takes up issues of a particularly Wittgensteinian flavor, questions of meaning, language-games, and forms of life: "Speech is the effective form of a culture," announces the essay's opening sentence.[61] But although "Expressive Language" draws

---

[59] See in particular Alexis Burgess, "How We Ought to Do Things with Words," in *Gesturing Toward Reality*; Samuel Cohen, "The Whiteness of David Foster Wallace," in *Postmodern Literature and Race*, ed. Len Platt and Sara Upstone (Cambridge: Cambridge University Press, 2015), 228–244; Lucas Thompson, "Wallace and Race," in *The Cambridge Companion to David Foster Wallace*, ed. Ralph Clare (Cambridge: Cambridge University Press, 2018), 204–219.

[60] Amiri Baraka, *The Autobiography of Leroi Jones* (1984; Chicago, IL: Lawrence Hill Books, 1997), 221. In his chapter on Baraka in *In the Break: The Aesthetics of the Black Radical Tradition* (Minneapolis, MN: University of Minnesota Press, 2003), Fred Moten juxtaposes Baraka's "improvisation through the very idea of logical structure" (99) with "the aphoristic and deeply improvisational form of Wittgenstein's work" (101).

[61] Amiri Baraka, "Expressive Language" (1966) in *Home: Social Essays* (New York: Akashic Books, 2009), 159. Hereinafter cited parenthetically. Baraka also approvingly refers to Wittgenstein in "The Revolutionary Theatre" (1965): "Wittgenstein said ethics and aesthetics are one. I believe this." *Home*, 200.

on a conceptual vocabulary reminiscent of the early Wittgenstein – "Can the concept of God exist in a perfectly logical language?" (172) – Baraka's primary argument bears a closer comparison to the later Wittgenstein. "Semantic philosophers," he writes, "are certainly correct in their emphasis on the final dictation of words over their users. But they often neglect to point out that, after all, it is the actual importance, *power* of the words that remains so finally crucial. Words have users, but as well, users have words" (160). And the power of words and their users reflects social, cultural, and economic influences on language. Baraka's concept of culture – "Culture is the form, the overall structure of organized thought" (162) – is analogous to Wittgenstein's notion of a form of life. Because different cultures develop specific linguistic practices, cultural difference inevitably leads to social hierarchy: "Being told to 'speak proper,' meaning that you become fluent with the jargon of power, is also a part of not 'speaking proper.' That is, the culture which desperately understands that it does not 'speak proper,' or is not fluent with the terms of social strength, also understands somewhere that its desire to gain such fluency is done at a terrifying risk" (163–164). Wallace's argument in "Authority and American Usage" betrays little understanding of that risk.

Writing after Wittgenstein has moved a long way from the stentorian, peremptory tone of the first sentence of Wittgenstein's first published work: "The world is all that is the case." Perhaps that movement represents a more capacious understanding of the world and all that comprises it. Contemporary writers have increasingly begun to write after Wittgenstein in the vein of Maggie Nelson, who, in ways that are similar to Baraka in emphasizing language users as well as uses of language, pursues a distinctly Wittgensteinian line of reasoning when discussing gender fluidity. "Words change depending on who speaks them," Nelson writes in *The Argonauts*, "there is no cure. The answer isn't just to introduce new words (*boi, cis-gendered, andro-fag*) and then set out to reify their meanings (though obviously there is power and pragmatism here). One must also become alert to the multitude of possible uses, possible contexts, the wings with which each word can fly."[62] "The meaning of a word is its use in the language." The sentence sounds about as dry, about as mundane, as one could imagine. But in Wittgenstein's philosophy and in the "writing after Wittgenstein" that follows it, "meaning as use" has

---

[62] Nelson, *The Argonauts*, 8.

come to be used in any number of meaningful ways. With the centennial anniversary of the publication of the *Tractatus* upon us, we have one hundred years of writing after Wittgenstein with which to reckon, a century's worth of acknowledgment of his work's continued importance to writers who continue to find myriad uses to which to put it.

2 A Wittgensteinian Phenomenology of Criticism

Toril Moi

Abstract: Can there be something like a "Wittgensteinian" literary criticism? If so, what could it possibly be, given that Wittgenstein sought to make us give up the craving for generality? Through an analysis of "The Avoidance of Love," Stanley Cavell's epochal 1969 essay on *King Lear*, Toril Moi shows that a reader inspired by Wittgenstein does not have to set out to apply a given theory, or to answer certain "Wittgensteinian" questions. Rather it entails a wish to acknowledge the concerns of the text, and respond to them. For Wittgensteinian critics, the text is not an object to be "approached" but action and expression. The critic sets out to answer questions that matter to her, and stakes herself in her own perceptions and judgments in the act of reading. "The problem of the critic, as of the artist," Cavell writes, "is not to discount his subjectivity, but to include it; not to overcome it in agreement, but to master it in exemplary ways." To do this requires training. This chapter sets out the implications of all these claims, argues against formalist views of literature and reading, and insists on the fundamental role of human judgment, and acknowledgment in the work of criticism.

Keywords: J. L. Austin, Stanley Cavell, Literary Criticism, Literary Theory, Acknowledgment, Expression, Formalism, Wittgenstein against Theory, Explanation, Phenomenology of Criticism.

Give Up Literary Criticism!

In this chapter, I'll ask whether there can be such a thing as a "Wittgensteinian" literary criticism.[1] But even before it can get off the ground that project runs straight into an obstacle, namely Wittgenstein's

---

[1] I am grateful to my two editors Robert Chodat and John Gibson, and to Claus Elholm Andersen, Sarah Beckwith, Rita Felski, Anders Öhman, David L. Paletz, and Kevin Spencer for generous feedback.

famous "Give up literary criticism!" As the distinguished British literary critic F. R. Leavis (1895–1978) tells the story, one day around 1930, Wittgenstein came up to him and said, without any kind of preamble: "Give up literary criticism!" Grievously offended, Leavis wanted to retort "Give up philosophy, Wittgenstein!" but held his tongue.[2] Did Wittgenstein mean to say that literary criticism is a worthless intellectual pursuit? Leavis certainly thought he did.[3] But Wittgenstein was equally hard on philosophy. He himself gave up philosophy in 1920, and only returned to it in 1929 when he realized that he had new, compelling questions to answer. He also regularly told his students to give up academic philosophy. One such student was Maurice O'Connor Drury, who writes that Wittgenstein "constantly urged his pupils not to take up an academic post and become teachers of philosophy." Taking this to heart, Drury trained as a psychiatrist. But, he insists: "Wittgenstein never advised anyone to give up philosophy, if by that is meant thinking about first principles and ultimate problems. When I said goodbye to him for the last time at Cambridge and we both knew he had not long to live, he said to me with great seriousness: 'Drury, whatever becomes of you, don't stop thinking.'"[4]

Wittgenstein's advice to give up philosophy embodies a strong critique of academia, and an equally strong sense of personal and existential seriousness. If you have no burning questions, you shouldn't be doing philosophy at all. Since Wittgenstein detested most academic philosophy, he would probably have detested most academic literary criticism too. The real question arising from his "Give up literary criticism!" is whether literary criticism can be existentially serious, expressive of genuine thinking, and also committed to Wittgenstein's hallmark philosophical "struggle against the bewitchment of our understanding by the resources of our language" (PI §109).

Can There Be a Wittgensteinian Literary Criticism?

It's by no means clear that there can be a "Wittgensteinian" criticism. Wittgenstein refused to provide theories, and thought of his philosophy

---

[2] F. R. Leavis, "Memories of Wittgenstein," in *Portraits of Wittgenstein*, eds. F. A. Flowers and Ian Ground (New York: Bloomsbury Academic, 2016), 543.
[3] See Leavis, "Memories," 548.
[4] Maurice O'Connor Drury, "Contribution to Ludwig Wittgenstein: A Symposium: Assessments of the Man and the Philosopher," in Flowers and Ground, eds., 1045.

as therapeutic – not intended to lay down requirements for what we must do, but to clear up confusions and help us find the way out of metaphysical mazes and back to the ordinary. In the light of such commitments, the very idea of creating a concept called "Wittgensteinian literary criticism" would seem to run counter to the spirit of his philosophy.

But it also seems wrong to say that there is no such thing. Literary critics who spend serious time with Wittgenstein's late philosophy often say they have been transformed by the experience. Questions we once took to be interesting now strike us as beside the point; ways of proceeding we once took for granted no longer seem compulsory. But when called upon to give an account of what has changed, of what it is we do now that we didn't do before, we often get somewhat lost for words. I often say things like: "I look and see," "I notice something and ask: 'Why this?'" "I try to let the work teach me how to read it." Or I talk about a newfound sense of freedom to do what I find interesting, a sense that theory-inflicted shackles fall away, that I am now reading both literature and literary theory in a different "spirit." And here I reach for "spirit" or "attitude" to mark my distance from terms such as "method," "theory," or "approach."[5]

Literary critics looking for clear directions for how to do "Wittgensteinian literary criticism" will find such talk nebulous. Yet try as I might, I am simply incapable of coming up with anything remotely like the well-worn recipes for how to do New Critical, or deconstructionist, or Lacanian (and so on) readings. In literature departments, "theory" has regularly been taught as if the point was first to learn the theory (or approach), and then apply it to literary texts. But what do we do when there is no theory, and no desire to provide one? When the philosophy that inspires us to look at things differently makes both the theory-building impulse and the impulse to apply anything at all to a text seem fundamentally misguided?

All this makes me wonder whether doing criticism after Wittgenstein might be a fundamentally unteachable practice. If so, Wittgenstein's philosophy is likely to remain forever marginal to literary studies. Stanley Cavell notes that the success of New Criticism in academia was

---

[5] See Toril Moi, *Revolution of the Ordinary: Literary Studies after Wittgenstein, Austin, and Cavell* (Chicago, IL: Chicago University Press, 2017), 1–2. My "spirit" may be getting at some of the same things as Rita Felski's "mood" and "thought style" in *The Limits of Critique* (Chicago, IL: University of Chicago Press, 2015), 1–2.

a "function of the way it is *teachable*" (AL 269).[6] In the same way, one part of the success of deconstruction was surely the way it turned out to be an eminently teachable practice of reading.

These questions – about whether there can be such a thing as a "Wittgensteinian literary criticism," and if so, whether it is the sort of thing that can be taught – have puzzled me for years. This chapter is an attempt to reach a greater measure of clarity about them. But how to begin? Wittgenstein would advise me to give up the "craving for generality" and focus instead on examples.[7] An example is not in principle more ambiguous than a theory or a definition (cf. PI §71). An example doesn't have to represent anything, doesn't have to stand for a class of similar cases. It's just a particular case that invites reflection and analysis.

Thinking about examples clarifies the question of teachability. Often, the only way to teach someone how to go on, how to continue on their own, is by pointing to examples (see PI §71).[8] The study of examples, then, is itself a mode of teaching and learning, and one we all know well, for this is how we learn our first language. Wittgenstein calls this "training," as opposed to "explanation" (PI §5).

The point of working with an example is to invite dialogue. For if you can't see what I say I see in the text, the next step is to discuss the matter, to try to get clear on whether we imagine the case at hand differently, and what our respective views overlook and what they entail. "Disagreement is not disconfirming: it is as much a datum for philosophizing as agreement is," Cavell notes (AP 95).[9] His great teacher J. L. Austin also relishes disagreements: "A disagreement as to what we should say is not to be shied off, but to be pounced upon: for the explanation of it can hardly fail to be illuminating."[10] An analysis (description) of a particular case (example) can only ever be an invitation to look and

---

[6] Stanley Cavell, "The Avoidance of Love: A Reading of *King Lear*," in *Must We Mean What We Say?* (Cambridge: Cambridge University Press, 2002). Page references will be given in the text, marked AL.
[7] Ludwig Wittgenstein, *The Blue and Brown Books: Preliminary Studies for the "Philosophical Investigations,"* 2nd ed. (1960) (New York: Harper Torchbooks, 1965), 17.
[8] I discuss the difference between a philosophy of examples and theory-building philosophies in chapters 3 and 4 of *Revolution of the Ordinary*.
[9] Cavell, "Aesthetic Problems of Modern Philosophy," *Must We Mean What We Say?*, 95. All page references to this essay will be given in the text marked AP.
[10] J. L. Austin, "A Plea for Excuses," in *Philosophical Papers* (Oxford: Oxford University Press, 1979), 184.

see, to consider whether, or how far, you can see what I see in that particular case. Just as I stake my subjectivity in my claims, you will stake yours. You test my claims against your own convictions, perceptions, and experiences. Sometimes you convince me, sometimes I convince you. But even when we can't find common ground, it doesn't follow that nothing has been achieved: the investigation itself will still have been illuminating. The best examples are the ones that inspire more thought, the ones that turn out to be "good to think with."

To get anywhere with examples, we need to begin the inquiry with an experience of difficulty, a sense of confusion, of being lost: "A philosophical problem has the form: 'I don't know my way about'" (PI §123). Wittgenstein's choice of words strikes me as deliberately poised between intellectual life and ordinary life, between philosophy and existence. My confusion might be intellectual and philosophical, but it might be existential too. We turn to the example, then, in search of a response to a problem. (In my experience, to discover what my problem actually is (as opposed to what I initially might think it is), is the hardest part of the work.) The ensuing investigation is not supposed to lead to an explanation, but to a description: "And this description gets its light – that is to say, its purpose – from the philosophical problems" (PI §109). If we have no problem, the investigation will be empty, for it will have no purpose.

But how do we know when to stop the inquiry? We are done when we have "established an order in our knowledge ... for a particular purpose" (PI §132). Or in other words: when we have managed to come up with a clear view in response to the specific problem we began with. In §133 of the *Philosophical Investigations*, Wittgenstein declares that the goal is not to "refine or complete the system of rules for the use of our words in unheard-of ways." The goal, rather, is "*complete* clarity," which means that "the philosophical problems should *completely* disappear" (PI §133). Then we can rest: "The real discovery is the one that enables me to break off philosophizing when I want to. – The one that gives philosophy peace...." In short: the original problem itself gives me the criteria for when to stop. When that problem disappears, the nagging stops, and I can relax. Of course, if I keep reading and thinking and living, new problems will surely arise. But right now I have earned my peace.

When it comes to the question of Wittgenstein and literary criticism, one example imposes itself, namely Cavell's pioneering essay "The Avoidance of Love: A Reading of *King Lear*," first published in 1969. I will use it as my example simply because it fills me with the sense that if this isn't a case of Wittgensteinian writing about literature, then nothing is.[11]

What Is Cavell Doing in "The Avoidance of Love"?

What makes Cavell's reading of *King Lear* Wittgensteinian? It's not any overt appeal to Wittgenstein's authority, for the essay rarely mentions Wittgenstein's name and contains only one explicit reference to a passage in *Philosophical Investigations*, namely §133, which turns up in a discussion of "where and why and how to bring an interpretation to a close" (AL 269).[12]

What kind of questions does Cavell ask? What are his problems? The subtitle of "The Avoidance of Love" is "A Reading of *King Lear*." Cavell uses the term "reading" to signal that he thinks of literary criticism as the attempt to get clear on problems arising in our encounter with the text. The investigation will take the form of a description (a recounting), which, if successful, will make the problem disappear.[13] This makes it sound as if Cavell can be categorized as a "close reader" in the mold of the New Critics. But although he – like any brilliant critic – certainly pays close attention to the text, he doesn't share the New Critics' view of what is to count as being "outside" or "inside" the text.[14] Nor does he share their preference for ambiguities and tensions, and the concomitant disdain for the obvious. And Cavell's magnificent essay is as meta-critical and theoretical as it is text-reading.

---

[11] I should specify that when I write "Wittgenstein" or "Wittgenstein's philosophy" (and so on) I mean Wittgenstein's philosophy as read by ordinary language philosophers. By "ordinary language philosophy" I mean the tradition after Wittgenstein and J. L. Austin, as established by Cavell, and to which Cora Diamond has made vital contributions. I should also say that in this chapter, I use the term "literary criticism" (or just "criticism") in the sense of "reading" or "interpretation," which I take to be a subcategory of the more wide-ranging term "literary studies."

[12] Around 1969, literary critics generally used "interpretation" about the activity we tend to call "reading." In the introduction to *Pursuits of Happiness*, Cavell discusses the differences between "reading," "interpretation," and "performance" in relation to film. See *Pursuits of Happiness: The Hollywood Comedy of Remarriage* (Cambridge, MA: Harvard University Press, 1981), particularly 35–38.

[13] In "What We Mean by Reading," *New Literary History* 51 (1): 93–114 (2020), https://doi.org/10.1353/nlh.2020.0004, Elaine Auyoung shows that literary critics always have a "reading goal." Like me, she stresses that a professional "reading" is always a piece of writing.

[14] Cavell shows why this opposition won't hold in "A Matter of Meaning It," *Must We Mean What We Say?*, 213–237.

In fact, Cavell begins not by going straight to *King Lear*, but by asking what, if anything, grounds the belief – widespread among literary theorists at the time – that there is a "conflict between character criticism and verbal analysis" (AL 269). Then he goes on to show, quite brilliantly, why he disagrees with the critical dogma that declares that we must never treat characters as if they were real people.[15] He then launches his reading of Shakespeare's play by listing nine classic problems that have long puzzled critics. These are all questions arising from the text, for example: "How are we to understand Lear's motivation in his opening scene? How Cordelia's? ... Is Gloucester's blinding dramatically justified? ... Why does Edgar delay before revealing himself to his father?" (AL 271).

The first part of Cavell's essay is a straightforward effort to provide answers to the nine textual questions. But already in the introduction he gives clear notice that his inquiry won't end there. For he also intends to raise a new, metacritical question, namely: "Why it is, if what I say is correct, that critics have failed to see it" (AL 272). The question of why it is so difficult to see the obvious, is the focus of the second part. Even Cavell's list of questions gets a metacritical justification: the very existence of such long-standing critical cruxes, he notes, makes *King Lear* "particularly useful as a source for investigating the question of critical data and for assessing some causes of critical disagreement" (AL 271). An intrinsic part of Cavell's project, then, is to figure out something about the status of claims in literary criticism, and about the nature of critical disagreements. In this chapter, I shall show that "The Avoidance of Love" fundamentally asks what grounds a critic's conviction in her own claims, and that Cavell's answer to that question provides us with nothing less than a *phenomenology of criticism*.[16]

If we take phenomenology to be a way of doing philosophy which brackets questions of essence and ontology, and instead tries to grasp phenomena as they appear to human consciousness through thick descriptions, ordinary language philosophers will find its procedures, if

---

[15] I chart the dogma's origins, theoretical frailties, and continued existence in "Rethinking Character," in Amanda Anderson, Rita Felski, and Toril Moi, *Character: Three Inquiries in Literary Studies* (Chicago, IL: Chicago University Press, 2019), 27–75.

[16] The critics of the Geneva School (active 1950–1970) also considered the act of criticism from a phenomenological point of view, yet strike me as quite different from Cavell. Georges Poulet's lively essay "Phenomenology of Reading," *New Literary History* 1 (1): 53–68 (1969) would be a good starting point for further discussion.

not its underlying metaphysical commitments, congenial. Wittgenstein constantly entreats us to "look and see!" (PI §66), to pay attention to particulars, to examine specific language-games, to imagine what we would say in a given case. Austin writes that because he recommends using "a sharpened awareness of words to sharpen our perception of, though not as the final arbiter of, the phenomena," he was tempted to call his way of doing philosophy "linguistic phenomenology."[17]

As I worked through "The Avoidance of Love," I began to realize that Cavell describes the act of criticism as at once personal, existential, and philosophical. For him, criticism is an effort to convey an experience built on the critic's perceptions and judgment, an activity which gives rise to a range of different existential moods and states of consciousness: elation, joy, anxiety, arrogance, vulnerability, and conviction, and its stakes are acknowledgment and responsibility.

But such claims, many literary theorists would say, raise the question of the subject. One can't, after all, do phenomenology without positing that human consciousness exists in the midst of a world of phenomena. Cavell certainly assumes that there is always someone doing the reading and the writing, someone who stakes herself – her own perceptions and judgments – in the act of reading, someone who will have to risk sharing her insights with others, and who fears that she might find herself speaking in a void, that nobody will see what she sees. In the same way, Wittgenstein assumes that there is always someone doing the philosophizing. Neither Wittgenstein nor Cavell follows this up with any kind of "theory of subjectivity" (or a "theory of agency," for that matter), for none is needed. No particular picture of what a "subject" is, or how "subjectivity" works is entailed. Whatever we might believe about subjectivity, we can presumably agree that particular human beings do the reading, and the writing.

To lay out Cavell's rich account of what we do when we do literary criticism, I'll begin by discussing the key term of "acknowledgment." Then I'll discuss the work of the reader. Key concepts in my account will be experience, judgment, perception, obviousness, vulnerability, arrogance, and conviction. Finally, I'll show that Cavell's phenomenology of criticism also provides some criteria for settling what might, or might not, count as "Wittgensteinian" literary criticism.

---

[17] Austin, "Plea," 182.

Acknowledgment and No Approach

The key concept in Cavell's *Lear* essay is *acknowledgment*.[18] For Cavell, *King Lear* is a play about the disastrous consequences of turning away from love because love requires acknowledgment, and acknowledgment requires self-revelation. The avoidance of love is also the avoidance of self-knowledge, which is why *shame* becomes such a crucial motivation for Lear and other key characters. Confronted with the unfolding of the tragedy, the task of the critic – and the theater audience – is to resist the temptation to turn away, to remain fully present to the plight of the characters, to "make them *other* and face them" (AL 338). This is the first step toward acknowledgment: to recognize that other people are separate from us, and that their expressions of pain require our response.

"Acknowledgment" is Cavell's, not Wittgenstein's term. The concept arises out of Cavell's efforts to work out the implications of Wittgenstein's philosophy for the so called "problem of the other." To get there, Cavell builds on Wittgenstein's remarks about the pain of others, about pain as something we attribute to a living body (see PI §§283–288) and also on his remarks about embodiment in "Philosophy of Psychology – A Fragment," previously known as "Part ii" of *Philosophical Investigations* (see PPF §§19–26). When Wittgenstein writes "The human body is the best picture of the human soul" (PPF §25), Cavell responds "The crucified human body is our best picture of the unacknowledged human soul."[19]

In "The Avoidance of Love," acknowledgment is something a subject does. Since our actions and expressions necessarily reveal us, who we are, how we see the plight of the other, acknowledgment is also self-revelation. Acknowledgment is response: the attempt to see "how it is with" the other, and to express what we see. It requires us to do something truly difficult, namely direct our undivided attention to the other, maybe by mobilizing Iris Murdoch's "just and loving gaze."[20] Acknowledgment differs from terms such as "sympathy" and "empathy" precisely because it's not just a mental or emotional operation, or a state of mind. Acknowledgment, then, requires us to make ourselves present

---

[18] Cavell first developed the concept in "Knowing and Acknowledging," *Must We Mean What We Say?*, 238–266. I discuss acknowledgment in relation to literature in chapter 9 of *Revolution of the Ordinary*.
[19] Stanley Cavell, *The Claim of Reason: Wittgenstein, Skepticism, Morality, and Tragedy* (New York: Oxford University Press, 1999), 430.
[20] Iris Murdoch, *The Sovereignty of Good* (London: Routledge, 2001), 33.

to the other (as opposed to remaining a mere distant onlooker): "In both [in a theater, and in actuality], people in pain are in our presence. ... [T]here is no acknowledgement unless we put ourselves in their presence, reveal ourselves to them" (AL 333).

Much of "The Avoidance of Love" examines self-revelation, and the myriad reasons why it is so hard for us to face who we are and what we do. Over and over again, Cavell insists on this aspect of acknowledgment. To acknowledge the other in pain, we must "[reveal] ourselves, [allow] ourselves to be seen," he writes. The alternative is to remain hidden: "When we do not [reveal ourselves], when we keep ourselves in the dark, the consequence is that we convert the other into a character and make the world a stage for him" (AL 333). When we withhold acknowledgment, we *theatricalize* the other, turn her into a mere player on our stage. This is true in life as in literature.

Writing in 1967 and 1968, at the time of escalating war in Vietnam and the intensifying struggle for civil rights in the United States, Cavell ends his essay by explicitly drawing out the implications of his work for a citizen of the United States at the time. Tragedy was always political, he notes (see AL 347). If, when faced with the misery of others, we choose "silence, hiddenness, and paralysis," we are as responsible for new tragedies, as Lear is when he chooses to avoid Cordelia's love (AL 349). To acknowledge the other is to make the effort to see his "true need," Cavell writes (AL 346). The phrase echoes Wittgenstein's call for a revolution – a turning around – on the "pivot of our real need" (PI §108). But to get to that point – the point of seeing the true need of the other – Cavell notes, "will take a change of consciousness. So phenomenology becomes politics" (AL 346).

If acknowledgment is attention and response, as a reader I have to try to understand the work's claim on me. But since acknowledgment is personal, particular, and specific, I now have a double task: to understand the work, to acknowledge its concepts and concerns; and to figure out where I stand in relation to it, to get clear on what my own stake in the text might be.

There is no set way of doing this. Each act of acknowledgment is different, dependent on the particular relationship of the parties involved. The way of acknowledgment won't yield one "approach" or one "method."[21] Even the word "approach" appears wrong in this

---

[21] Timothy Gould, in his fine book *Hearing Things: Voice and Method in the Writing of Stanley Cavell* (Chicago, IL: The University of Chicago Press, 1998), argues that Cavell sets out a

context. To approach you isn't to acknowledge you. The problem of analyzing a text isn't the same as the problem of analyzing an object. When I read, the text is not outside me in the same way as a tree is outside me. On the contrary: the act of reading implicates me in the text from the start. If language is public and shared, as Wittgenstein thought, then there is no way for me to get outside the text's language, for it's also the medium of my own existence. Because we are already in its world, we never see the text as a totality from afar. Rather than considering the work as an inert object, criticism understood as acknowledgment treats it as action and expression, as a claim to which the critic responds.[22]

In this situation, there is no recipe for how to begin, or for where to go. All we can do is to find a "blur or block from which to start," as Cavell puts it in *The Claim of Reason*.[23] That "blur or block" may be a passage or a theme that haunts us, to which we always return, something that grabs our attention and refuses to let it go. Something we need to understand. Something that makes us ask, "Why this?" On this view, the most important part of the intellectual (philosophical, critical) work is to figure out what you want to know. This is why there can't be one, unified "Wittgensteinian" mode or method of reading. How you go about answering your question (which is all "method" can mean in this context), will depend on what you want to know, the state of your own knowledge, who you are writing for and what work you want your investigation to do.[24]

Educating Experience

To build a critical response, the critic needs to notice something. To notice something is to single out a feature – a metaphor, a genre, a mood, a turn of phrase (and so on) – and pay attention to it. In his crucial paper "Aesthetic Problems of Modern Philosophy," written five years before the *Lear* essay, Cavell insists on the point: "It is essential to making

---

"new model of philosophical method," which Gould calls "the model of reading" (131). I see my own arguments as consonant with Gould's. But the question of what counts as a method in philosophy is rather different from what counts as a method in literary criticism, and the topic would require a chapter of its own.

[22] I write more about the picture of texts as objects with surfaces masking hidden depths in chapter 8 of *Revolution of the Ordinary*.

[23] Cavell, *The Claim of Reason*, 6.

[24] I am paraphrasing Cavell in "Must We Mean What We Say?," in the collection of the same title, 20.

an aesthetic judgment that at some point we be prepared to say in its support: don't you see, don't you hear, don't you dig? The best critic will know the best points. Because if you do not see *something*, without explanation, then there is nothing further to discuss" (AP 93). But this feels daunting, particularly for beginners. For how do I know what is worth noticing?

I remember vividly the first time I visited the great art museums in Paris. I was seventeen. A country girl from the west of Norway, I had never set foot in an art museum until I stood there in the Louvre. My French friends appeared undaunted. They even had things to say about the nonfigurative paintings in the Jeu de Paume. But I grew mute. How was I supposed to be able to *say* something about works that came to me as UFOs from outside my solar system? Although I looked as carefully as I could, I felt as if I was incapable of actually *seeing* anything in these paintings: I could find no words. I felt stupid and agonized over my colossal lack of culture.[25] Back at the University of Bergen I had exactly the same experience with modernist poetry, which more often than not made me feel I was drowning in a kind of word soup. As with the paintings, I simply didn't know where to begin. But it turned out that I could learn. So let's not forget that to get to the point where one *can* notice *something* of critical interest in a text is in itself an achievement.

The good news is that the capacity to notice something can be taught. This is why future critics go to graduate school: to train their eye and ear, to become learned in their field, to understand the wider intellectual debates of their day. When done in the right way, the study of theory and philosophy trains the critical imagination by offering new ideas that refine and extend our range of perceptions. Done in the wrong way, it can give the student the impression that once she has learned the theory, it will tell her what to look for. Then, she might believe, she won't have to risk herself, her own judgment and insights, in the work of criticism. When theory is used as a security blanket in this way, it allows the critic to remain hidden, to avoid the work of acknowledgment, the self-exposure, and the responsibility that comes with it.

If reading is an adventure, as Simone de Beauvoir and Cora Diamond both claim, then a work of criticism is a kind of travelogue: a report on

---

[25] Maybe this experience explains why I read Pierre Bourdieu's *Distinction: A Social Critique of the Judgment of Taste*, trans. Richard Nice (London: Routledge & Kegan Paul, 1980) with such a sense of recognition.

an experience.[26] The best travel writers have an unusual capacity for observation, a strong sense of why their journey matters, and they know how to convey this. After all, a literary critic is also a writer; our readings are our writings. There is a challenge here: Are we capable of finding the right words? Of writing in ways that accurately convey the exact nuances of our thinking? Writing so as to convey why we care? Matters of style are also matters of philosophy.[27]

Some critics appear to yearn for the objectivity of the natural sciences. They advise their students to avoid the word "I." They fear leaving traces of their own intellectual excitement, dejection, frustration, elation in their writing. But why? Only a critic who believes that traces of her subjectivity will somehow vitiate her insights will have a problem with personal modes of writing. They forget that in most of the humanities, subjectivity, experience, and perceptions are not impediments to knowledge, but rather the conditions of possibility for having any knowledge at all.[28] A critic who tries to eradicate her subjectivity is just trying to pretend that she is not in fact the person doing the reading. But we can't escape our own humanity in this way. We read as the fallible human beings we are: "The problem of the critic, as of the artist," Cavell writes, "is not to discount his subjectivity, but to include it; not to overcome it in agreement, but to master it in exemplary ways" (AP 94). None of this implies that critics should never use an impersonal style. It's just a reminder that an impersonal style is also a style: a mode of expression chosen by a human subject.

If criticism requires the critic to stake her own critical subjectivity in her readings, the critic must train her judgment, develop her powers of perception and reflection – in short, she must educate her aesthetic experience to the point that she can trust it. Of course, experience is far from infallible. If on occasion it leads us astray, we need to go back, check our experience, train it some more.[29] This is true for ordinary

---

[26] For an analysis of Cavell's ideas about reading alongside Beauvoir's literary theory, and Diamond's suggestion that reading is an adventure, see Toril Moi, "The Adventure of Reading: Literature and Philosophy, Cavell and Beauvoir," *Literature and Theology* 25 (2): 125–140 (2011).

[27] Cavell writes on Wittgenstein's style as an expression of his philosophy in "The Availability of Wittgenstein's Later Philosophy," in *Must We Mean What We Say?* particularly 70–72.

[28] Ralph Berry makes a similar point in "Wittgenstein's Use," *New Literary History* 44 (4): 617–638 (2013).

[29] For more, see Cavell, *Pursuits of Happiness*, 12–13.

experience as well. The work in feminist consciousness-raising groups in the 1970s was essentially a crash course in the reeducation of experience. In those groups we learned that if we educated our experience for long enough, by discussing our perceptions and by gathering new information so as to be able to rethink our original understanding, then, eventually, our consciousness of ourselves and the world would shift. That's one way that "phenomenology becomes politics" (AL 346).[30] In the same way, we can train our aesthetic judgment and experience. All this training and learning and education gets us to the point where we can see something. So much of the hard work of literary criticism happens long before we can begin the investigation.

Arrogance, Conviction, and Vulnerability

Given the fundamental role of the critic's subjectivity in the act of criticism, how can we tell whether a critic is right? To find an answer, Cavell sets up a series of concepts rarely discussed in relation to the work of criticism: *melodrama, immodesty, arrogance, conviction*. "Criticism is inherently immodest and melodramatic," he declares (AL 311). The pleasure we take in our discoveries express joy in the new. Every critical essay is a shout of excitement: "Look! I have seen what nobody else has seen in *King Lear* before!" Cavell writes about the "peculiar exhilaration [of] a critical discovery," of the "joy in a major critical insight," but also about the "peculiar chagrin" arising from the "recognition of a critical lapse" (AL 312). Call this the melodrama of the literary critic.

Arrogance comes with the territory. "Arrogance is inherent in criticism," Cavell writes (AL 312). But it's inherent in philosophy, too, and in most kinds of work in the humanities. For what gives the critic or philosopher the right to say that she sees what we don't? That *she*, of all people, can bring the world, or the work to (self-)consciousness, as Cavell puts it (see AL 313)? This sounds presumptuous. But what would criticism be if it only told us what we already know? In any case, the best critics do see something we haven't seen. They can change our experience of a work forever. I am incapable of watching a performance of *King Lear* without measuring it against Cavell's understanding of the opening scene as demonstrating Lear's avoidance of love, his unspeakable fear of self-knowledge. Nor can I watch the end without seeing it, with Cavell, as

---

[30] I use this example in "The Adventure of Reading."

Lear's second betrayal of Cordelia. Until Cavell showed me how to look at these scenes, I missed their significance. His essay has enriched me, given me the capacity to see more, and more deeply, than I did before. That's what great criticism does.

Conviction makes us both arrogant and vulnerable. Arrogant because I can't just let go of my conviction, for it expresses my faith in the rightness of my reading. Vulnerable, first because my conviction makes me helpless: I simply can't help seeing what I see. But vulnerable also because conviction requires me to speak up, to see if others can come to share my view, which is far from a foregone conclusion, for a critical conviction is not grounded in philosophical reason, or scientific measurement, but in experience, perception, and judgment. By sharing what I see, I expose myself to the judgment of others. No wonder that so many literary critics feel overwhelmed by anxiety when they first set out on their path, and that, even after writing for years, so many of us continue to feel that tension in the gut as we struggle to express our convictions.

In a later essay, Cavell speaks of the philosopher's necessary "arrogation of voice." His discussion rests on the idea that since nothing authorizes us to speak up (for who has the authority to allow (or deny) us the right to speak?), every critical or philosophical speech act is an arrogation of voice: in speaking out, I arrogate to myself the right to appeal to the judgment of others.[31] In criticism, as in Cavell's kind of philosophy, we put ourselves on the line. This can feel terrifying. Yet if we don't speak out, we will never discover whether there is an audience for what we have to say. The task of a teacher in the humanities is to help her students find their own voice.

Obviousness: Staking Oneself

"A critical position," Cavell writes, "will finally rest upon calling a claim obvious," and "a critical discovery will present itself as the whole truth of a work" (AL 311). He is well aware that both claims come across as ludicrously easy to dismiss: "How can a claim be obvious if not everyone finds it obvious? ... And how can a claim to total meaning be correct when so much is left out?" (AL 311). Such dismissals overlook the complexities of the concepts involved, for "they take a claim to

---

[31] See "Philosophy and the Arrogation of Voice," in Cavell, *A Pitch of Philosophy: Autobiographical Exercises* (Cambridge, MA: Harvard University Press, 1994), 3–51.

obviousness as a claim to certainty, and they take the claim to totality as a claim to exhaustiveness" (AL 312).

In a bravura analysis, Cavell shows what's wrong with such responses. The real question, he argues, is why critics habitually do make such "*vulnerable* claims" (AL 311–312). In the first case, the claim that something is "obvious" is seen as a claim to certainty. But this is to epistemologize the claim of obviousness, to impose on the claims of criticism standards of knowledge derived from the sciences, or from a fantasy that only perfect God-like knowledge truly counts as knowledge. Such standards and fantasies will inevitably disappoint: absolute certainty is simply not a feature of the kind of knowledge that criticism – or work in the humanities in general – can provide. And once epistemological disappointment sets in, skepticism might appear to be the only alternative.[32]

In the second case, the idea of "totality" is taken to be synonymous with "exhaustiveness." Clearly, no reading ever exhausts all the possibilities of a (great) work of literature. By using the word "totality," Cavell asks us to reconsider what it means to feel that a reading has come to an end. (This is where he invokes §133.) The critic's claim to "totality" or "completion," he argues, doesn't convey her sense that she has said everything one can possibly say about the work, but rather that her reading has made one particular problem disappear completely.

In literary studies, "obviousness" has simply not been a valued concept. In particular, it's strikingly absent from discussions of close reading.[33] So why is the concept so important to Cavell? Why does he insist that the difficulty of criticism is "the difficulty of seeing the obvious" (AL 310)? And doesn't he come close to contradicting himself when he claims, first, that he takes himself to have seen something in *King Lear* that other critics haven't, and second, that he considers that something to be *obvious*? How is it possible that other critics have failed to see what he has seen?

Like other intellectual works, a reading is built on evidence and arguments. Cavell's point is that the whole edifice nevertheless rests on *some* perception, *some* claim that the critic can't reason her way to, *something* she just takes in "without explanation," as Cavell puts it (AP 93). At some point, the critic simply has to say: "this is what I see." She just sees the

---

[32] See Cavell, *The Claim of Reason*, particularly part IV about skepticism and acknowledgment.

[33] It's missing, for example, in Jonathan Culler's fine discussion in "The Closeness of Close Reading," *ADE Bulletin* 149 (2010), https://doi.org/10.1632/ade.149.20.

work that way. Something strikes her as so obvious that she grounds her reading on it. This is what it means to "stake one's subjectivity" – to risk one's judgments, perceptions, learning – in one's reading. Elsewhere, as we have seen, Cavell writes that "at some point, the critic will have to say: This is what I see" (AP 93). He then refers to a famous passage in *Philosophical Investigations*: "Once I have exhausted the justifications, I have reached bedrock, and my spade is turned" (PI §217). The bedrock of our readings, the place where we can dig no further, the place where all our reasons and explanations run out, the place where we have to take a stand, is the perception we simply can't *unsee*.

Cavell's commitment to criticism as the difficult task of seeing the obvious is perhaps the most Wittgensteinian aspect of his essay on *King Lear*. He notes that the whole of "Wittgenstein's later philosophy can be thought of as investigations of obviousness" (AL 312). But the obvious can be hard to find. There is a difference between "what *seems* obvious" and what actually *is* obvious (AL 310). Intellectual fashions are often the culprits: they make us take dubious claims as unquestioned starting points, make us buy into a theoretical picture of how things *must* be (for example, what a play is, how to treat or not to treat characters, or what we need a theory of subjectivity for), with the result that we simply miss what is before our eyes (cf. PI §129), for "our perception of it is blanked" (AL 311). To see the obvious, to reach clarity, we need to free ourselves from the pictures that hold us captive (cf. PI §115). We do this not by conjuring up unheard-of ideas, but by *reminding* ourselves of what we already know: "The work of the philosopher consists in marshalling recollections for a particular purpose" (PI §127). "Marshalling recollections" used to be translated as "assembling reminders." In German, Wittgenstein uses the phrase: *ein Zusammentragen von Erinnerungen* – a gathering of memories. If critical confusion is a kind of forgetting, critical insight is a kind of remembering.

A Phenomenology of Criticism

Cavell's understanding of the act of criticism (reading), should now be clear. The critic is driven to her investigation by a nagging problem. To figure out exactly what the problem is, and how to express it is a crucial part of the work. Like ordinary language philosophy, criticism works on examples, rejects the craving for generality, and considers its own findings to be invitations to conversation and response. The critic is as responsible for her readings as for any other acts. Criticism (reading) is carried out by a subject who, in search of answers to questions that simply won't let her go, brings her experience, her powers of perception and judgment, and her scholarship (learning) to bear on a text. The critic's work makes her vulnerable, but also produces elation and joy, chagrin, and despondence. The critic stakes herself in her own readings. Criticism is intrinsically arrogant, in that the critic necessarily takes herself to have seen something other critics haven't. In the end, her conviction rests on her painstakingly earned sense that *something* in the work just is obvious. The critic's goal is acknowledgment, yet every act of criticism risks falling into the trap of avoidance, risks turning away from the difficult task of seeing the obvious.

This phenomenological account of criticism explains why some kinds of criticism strike me as "un-Wittgensteinian." To me, any kind of reading that sets out to make us forget that reading is a human experience with stakes and responsibilities comes across as a willful denial of the existential and phenomenological truth of the matter. The relatively fashionable rejection of the human in contemporary theory would be one example.[34] Such theorists blind themselves to what they actually do when they read, and write, and theorize. Or maybe they just forget to reflect on the fact that a theorist, too, is just a specific human being doing her thinking and writing in a particular place, at a particular time. As Cavell often reminds us, nothing is more human than the denial of the human (see, for example, AP 96).[35]

A number of formalist literary theories explicitly oppose discussions of characters' intentions, motivations, and reasons, an attitude which rules out any attempt at acknowledgment of characters or authors.[36] For formalists, talk of acknowledgment means anthropomorphizing or humanizing the literary text, which to them is just a set of shapes, figures, or structures. More generally, many literary critics assume that the task of literary criticism is to focus on the literary, or literariness, which to them simply means form. They take "literary" reading to be attention to *how* a thing is said, more than to *what* is said, as if the latter went without saying. A Wittgensteinian reader can't accept this picture,

---

[34] In *Revolution of the Ordinary*, I discuss some "posthuman" readings of Ferdinand de Saussure's linguistics (see 120–128).

[35] This is one of the three ideas that Cavell considers "characteristic of his manner" (see "Preface," *Must We Mean?*, xxv).

[36] For examples, see Moi, "Rethinking Character."

which takes for granted that there is a fundamental split between form and meaning, for this is a classic case of the "Augustinian vision of language," which Wittgenstein sets out to overcome in *Philosophical Investigations*.[37]

Modes of reading that treat the text as an object to be "approached," rather than as action and expression, will also run counter to the Wittgensteinian spirit, for they won't see the text as placing claims on us. One variation of this picture presents the text an object with a (suspect) surface hiding deeper truths. Such "approaches" easily end up on the skeptical seesaw, which Wittgenstein's philosophy helps us to get off. Instead of asking "Can you see what I see?" and instead of seeing that question as an invitation to further philosophical conversation, such critics will either worry about whether their reading is 100 percent right or true (the yearning for absolute certainty), or embrace skepticism by denying that the text means anything except what the reader puts into it ("this is just my reading"). More crucially: when a theory is turned into an "approach," understood as a set of steps the critic must take, it enables the critic to hide herself, to avoid staking her own subjectivity in her readings. All this conflicts with Cavell's phenomenological understanding of criticism as acknowledgment and just response.

In contrast, this account of criticism doesn't stand in opposition to various theories that literary critics like to draw on, for they don't address the same issues. In particular, there is nothing here that prevents the critic from writing as a politically committed human being. On the contrary, in so far as the critic must stake her own subjectivity in the act of reading, I would expect her to read as the feminist, Marxist, antiracist, postcolonial critic she is. Or as a psychoanalytic, historicist critic (and so on), if that's what she is. In my experience, thinkers from Hegel through Marx, Beauvoir, Foucault, and Lacan can be used in ways that do no violence to the Wittgensteinian spirit. Theories or philosophies that already lean heavily on the use of examples, specific cases such as psychoanalysis (Freud, Lacan) and phenomenology (Sartre, Beauvoir) can easily inspire work congenial to Cavell's account of criticism. There is considerable compatibility between Wittgenstein's vision of language and Mikhail Bakhtin's understanding of discourse as a fundamentally dialogic social phenomenon.[38]

---

[37] See PI §1 and Moi, *Revolution of the Ordinary*, chapter 1.
[38] See my brief discussion of Bakhtin in *Revolution of the Ordinary*, 198–199.

Nothing creates that unmistakable Wittgensteinian "spirit" in a piece of literary criticism better than the critic's understanding of Wittgenstein's later philosophy. But mere knowledge of that philosophy is no guarantee: Wittgenstein, too, can be used in ways that turn his thought into another "theory," another "approach."

Literary criticism inspired by Wittgenstein can be about anything: "Ordinary language philosophy is about whatever ordinary language is about," Cavell writes (AP 95).[39] Wittgenstein-inspired work can be deeply historicist, or it can focus on the phenomenology of aesthetic forms. It can ask about values and meaning, about ethics and politics. The critic's knowledge of Wittgenstein often reveals itself not through invocations of his authority, but in the critic's interest in words, concepts, language-games, self–other relations, in her worries about skepticism and responsibility, or in her willingness to acknowledge that she is, in fact, using herself as an example, as a touchstone for her readings.

In "The Avoidance of Love," Cavell explicitly aligns the work of criticism with the work of ordinary language philosophy. Both practices require the same sort of commitment and interests. In both cases, the problem is to discover what data, and what kinds of appeal, one does, in fact, find convincing in claims about meaning. In both cases, "the issue is one of placing the words and experiences with which philosophers have always begun in alignment with human beings in particular circumstances who can be imagined to be having those experiences and saying and meaning those words. This is all that 'ordinary' in the phrase 'ordinary language philosophy' means, or ought to mean" (AL 270). By insisting on the similarity, Cavell draws attention to the *work of thinking* in literary criticism. I think this is why Cavell uses the term "philosophical criticism" to describe what he is doing in the *Lear* essay (see AL 313).[40]

I find that the most "Wittgensteinian" readings are those that are compatible with the phenomenology of criticism I have outlined in this chapter, and that investigate literary questions in ways that also have philosophical and existential implications. This is precisely what Cavell

---

[39] This is the second of the three formulations Cavell considers "characteristic of his manner" ("Preface," *Must We Mean?*, xxv).

[40] The phrase "philosophical criticism" also appears in a footnote, which singles out Michael Fried's writing, not just his "intensely theoretical or speculative" essays like "Art and Objecthood" but also his short pieces on the British sculptor Anthony Caro, which "consists of uninterrupted descriptions" as exemplifying the mode (see AL 333 n. 16).

does in "The Avoidance of Love." Concluding that *King Lear* is a play about the failure of acknowledgment, the fear of revealing oneself, and the avoidance of the claims of the other, Cavell does not hesitate to say that these are also existential and political problems. But there is more: his insights in what criticism is arise from his reading of the play. If previous critics have failed to see what he sees in *King Lear*, he reasons, it because the same questions also arise for literary critics. What blinds us to the claims of the text? Why do we hide ourselves? Why is it so hard to pay unflinching attention to the particular other in front of us? The phenomenology of criticism is the phenomenology of acknowledgment.

3 Appreciating Material
Criticism, Science, and the Very Idea of Method
Robert Chodat

Abstract: This chapter explores the impulse to understand reading and criticism in the terms provided by the natural and social sciences, asking both what generates such an impulse and whether it can deliver on what it promises. Such an impulse dates back to the early days of literary studies as an academic discipline, if not longer, but it has returned with a vengeance in the early twenty-first century. The chapter explores two recent instantiations of the impulse: the effort to use Big Data to understand the history of the modern novel, and the hope to understand aesthetic experience in the terms developed by neuroscience. Each of these models presents itself as a radical departure from traditional aesthetic criticism, and promises to break down boundaries between disciplines in ways that would revolutionize how we understand the practice of criticism. Wittgenstein's writing on language, the mind, and aesthetics, the chapter argues, helps us understand the misplaced assumptions and conceptual weaknesses that pervade these efforts. Instead of giving us the generalizing causal accounts that define the most coherent and rigorous scientific disciplines, criticism and aesthetic understanding arise from a kind of immersive experience, a prolonged encounter with a singular artifact, and one in which empirical studies have no clear explanatory role.

Keywords: The Modern Novel, Aesthetic Experience, Aesthetic Criticism, Aesthetic Understanding, Scientific Explanation, Naturalistic Accounts of Reading and Criticism, Big Data, Neuroscience, Singular Artifacts, Readings and Immersive Experience.

I may find scientific questions interesting, but they never really grip me. Only conceptual and aesthetic questions do that.
—Wittgenstein, 1949 (CV 79)

I

In the first of his "Lectures on Aesthetics," Wittgenstein suggests that the traditional vocabulary of aesthetics – grand but contentious words such as "beautiful" – rarely plays any role in real-life talk about artworks. And as he often does, Wittgenstein supports his thought by drawing an analogy to another everyday sphere. "What does a person who knows a good suit say when trying on a suit at the tailor's? 'That's the right length,' 'That's too short,' 'That's too narrow.'" Good tailors sometimes say nothing at all, "but just make a chalk mark and later alter it," and knowledgeable customers might simply look pleased with a garment and wear it often. Such responses grow partly from learning rules – being "drilled" to know what's "correct." But they also involve a "feeling for the rules," a sense of how to "interpret" them in a given case. When all this happens, when someone knows how to choose an appropriate cloth, how to handle it, how to communicate with tailors, how to innovate in new cloth-related situations – then we have, says Wittgenstein, "what we call an appreciator of material" (LC 3–8).

"Appreciator of material" is a surprisingly apt phrase in the context of a volume about literature and its study. "Material" has well-established uses in literary contexts, meaning "topic" or "original idea," as when Henry James speaks of novel-writing as "the transformation of the material under aesthetic heat."[1] But "material" can also refer, as with Wittgenstein's tailor, to physical substances, to objects whose dimensions, weight, or mass can be calculated. Warehouses store materials, machines are assembled from them. These two uses of "material" – "theme for art" and "physical object" – are quite dissimilar, but Wittgenstein's remark is suggestive because the second has been almost as common in modern literary studies as the first. To be sure, few literary scholars have tried to weigh *Hamlet* as they might a piece of magnesium. But literary phenomena have often been pictured as entities extended in time and space, material products of a causal sequence that responsible readers aim to identify, much as one could with a piece of lumber or brass. Wittgenstein speaks of a tailor's material in order to bring our aesthetic language back to the rough ground. Material-talk in literary studies has, by contrast, shaped a much larger picture of the field's object of study.

---

[1] Henry James, "The Lesson of Balzac," in *The Question of Our Speech; The Lesson of Balzac: Two Lectures* (Boston, MA: Houghton Mifflin, 1905), 92–93.

This is a high-altitude claim, and in what follows, I'll clarify it with two examples that raise the question of how criticism will be practiced in the twenty-first century. But the basic motivation for such materialism isn't hard to discern. Describing literary phenomena as objects with properties means describing them in terminologies developed by the modern sciences, and thus aligning the study of literature with the fields that serve as our culture's standard of genuine knowledge. Winning some of this authority was clearly the idea of the scholar who insisted in the first issue of *PMLA* (*Publications of the Modern Language Association*) that, as long as "teachers of modern languages ... do not realize that their department is a science," as long as they fail to see that "a scientific basis dignifies our profession," the public will believe "that *anybody* can teach French or German or ... English."[2] But it has also been the motivation of subtler thinkers who have expressed more nuanced views of the sciences. Think here of the New Critics, who worried about the waning of Christianity but who also insisted that, as one spokesman said, "criticism must become more scientific, or precise and systematic," carried out by "the collective and sustained effort of learned persons" in universities.[3] Or think, a few decades later, of structuralism and poststructuralism, which produced a steady stream of expert vocabularies and "rigorous" (one of Derrida's favorite words) analyses, even as they were being assaulted for antiscientific "relativism."[4]

---

[2] H. C. G. Brandt, quoted in Gerald Graff's *Professing Literature: An Institutional History* (1987; Chicago, IL: University of Chicago Press, 2007), 67–68.

[3] John Crowe Ransom, "Criticism, Inc.," *Virginia Quarterly Review* 13 (4): 586–602 (Autumn 1937); quotation at 587. On the New Criticism's complex attitude toward science, see Gerald Graff, "What Was New Criticism? Literary Interpretation and Scientific Objectivity," *Salmagundi* 27: 72–93 (Summer–Fall 1974).

[4] As Toril Moi says, Derrida's aim is above all to provide a "general system" that will account for all past and future cases, and this project generates his own dazzling array of technical terms: *différance*, mark, supplement, iterability, trace, etc. (see her *Revolution of the Ordinary: Literary Studies after Wittgenstein, Austin, and Cavell* (Chicago, IL: University of Chicago Press, 2017), 65–69.) One could argue, of course, that the main goal for Derrida and much of "high theory" was more a systematic or taxonomic description of literary, linguistic, and cultural phenomena than a full-blooded explanatory and predictive account of the sort that is typical of the modern empirical sciences. Still, as Vincent Descombes has suggested in a discussion of Lacan and Lévi-Strauss, these theoretical schools were seldom shy about discussing "causality," "effects," "mechanisms," and "materiality," and they were prone to disparaging previous scholars for being insufficiently "scientific" and "rigorous" (see Descombes, *The Mind's Provisions: A Critique of Cognitivism*, trans. Stephen Adam Schwart [Princeton, NJ: Princeton University Press, 2001], chapter 5).

Wittgenstein is illuminating here because he provides a way of recognizing both the variable forms that materialism can take as well as the sorts of "therapies" they might require. Trained as an engineer, he was hardly unaware of how the causally bound universe shapes our thought and talk. Indeed, few philosophers have attended more meticulously to our condition as material bodies existing in a material world, and nowhere does he encourage us to think that poems and novels transpire in an otherworldly ether. Thinking, says *The Blue Book*, is an "activity" that's "performed by the hand" when we write, "by the mouth and larynx" when we speak (BB 6); and later, reflecting on the mistaken ambitions of formal logic, Wittgenstein insists that he is writing "about the spatial and temporal phenomenon of language, not about some non-spatial, non-temporal phantasm" (PI §108). But few thinkers have also more sharply scrutinized the muddles that can emerge when a scientific model "elbows all the others aside," as he says, making them look "paltry by comparison, preliminary stages at best" (CV 60). Nowhere, that is, does his persistent emphasis on our embodied condition come at the expense of the *meaningfulness* of our speech and action – including those elaborate, densely layered actions that go into the creation, display, and understanding of artworks.

What interests me, in short, is not the specific artists, themes, features, or styles that Wittgenstein himself appreciated. I want instead to ask what constitutes "appreciation" as such, and what would make it – rather than some other activity – essential in artistic and critical contexts. Seen in this light, Wittgenstein partakes of a long-standing tradition that contrasts the different intellectual projects that have marked modern culture and its educational institutions.[5] As I'll suggest, in the twenty-first century, when such differences are being increasingly planed away, these deliberations are worth considering as much as ever.

---

[5] For other accounts of Wittgenstein's relation to debates over the *Natur-* and *Geisteswissenschaften* – including his relationship to Comte, Dilthey, Weber, Gadamer, Barthes, and others – see Richard Allen and Malcolm Turvey, "Wittgenstein's Later Philosophy: A Prophylaxis Against Theory," in *Wittgenstein, Theory and the Arts*, eds. Richard Allen and Malcolm Turvey (London: Routledge, 2001), 1–35; Ulrich Arnswald, "On the Certainty of Uncertainty: Language Games and Forms of Life in Gadamer and Wittgenstein," in *Gadamer's Century: Essays in Honor of Hans-Georg Gadamer*, eds. Jeff Malpas, Ulrich Arnswald, and Jens Kertscher (Cambridge, MA: MIT Press, 2002), 25–44; P. M. S. Hacker, "Wittgenstein and the Autonomy of Humanistic Understanding," in *Wittgenstein, Literature, and the Arts*, 39–74; Georg Henrik von Wright, "Humanism and the Humanities," in *The Tree of Knowledge and Other Essays* (Leiden: Brill, 1993), 155–171.

II

Since the turn of our century, the long-standing hope for scientific respectability among literary scholars has been intensified by a new empirical turn, one that recalls some of the naked positivism of the profession's earliest years. From this perspective, "high theory" might have made us more cosmopolitan over the last half-century, licensing theorists to keep up with the latest news from Paris and Frankfurt, but critics have remained provincial all the same. For they've ignored the work of the bona fide scientists working across the quad, in labs that are developing the procedures and technologies that will define the future.

Consider, first, Franco Moretti's small book about Big Data, *Graphs, Maps, Trees* (2005), an influential attempt to expose the "secularized theology" of conventional literary scholars, their reverence for "rare and curious works, that do not repeat themselves, exceptional – and which close reading makes even more exceptional, by emphasizing the uniqueness of exactly *this* word and *this* sentence here."[6] Following "the natural and the social sciences," Moretti wants instead to use digital technology to make "the reality of the text" undergo "a process of deliberate reduction and abstraction," one that yields "fewer elements, hence a sharper sense of their overall interconnection. Shapes, relations, structures. Forms. Models." Such "distant reading" will, suggests Moretti, provide a *"specific form of knowledge"* that would be unavailable to someone without his own "great respect for the scientific spirit" (GMT 1–2). A traditional scholar of the nineteenth century might know two hundred novels, but the databases prove that this number "is less than one percent of the novels that were actually published: twenty thousand, thirty, more, no one really knows." Such a corpus, he says, represents not "a sum of individual cases," but a "collective system that should be grasped as a whole" (GMT 4).

With a series of graphs depicting the results of his research, Moretti shows, for instance, the strikingly similar pattern that marks the

---

[6] Franco Moretti, *Graphs, Maps, Trees: Abstract Models for Literary History* (London: Verso, 2005), 3; henceforth cited parenthetically as GMT. "Secularized theology" appears in Moretti's *Distant Reading* (London: Verso, 2013), 67; henceforth cited parenthetically as DR. I'm focusing here on Moretti because he has probably done more than anyone to make Big Data seem relevant to literary studies. For a blistering analysis of other scholars who have (apparently) used Big Data in more sophisticated ways, including the work of many scholars who have worked closely with Moretti, see Nan Z. Da's "The Computational Case against Computational Literary Studies," *Critical Inquiry* 45: 601–639 (2019).

development of the novel in different countries – Britain, Japan, Italy, Spain, Nigeria – across different centuries. In every case, we see a leap, in a span of twenty years or so, from five to ten new novels being published per *year* to one new novel per *week* (GMT 5). And in every case, the leap portends a fall: in all these countries, a few decades after the initial spike, the publication of novels collapses (GMT 9–12). Moreover, Moretti finds that, from around 1740 to 1900, Britain witnessed the rise of forty-four distinct genres, ranging from the "Courtship novel" and "Oriental novel" at the start to the period to the "New Woman novel" near the end, many of them appearing and disappearing simultaneously, in "clusters" (GMT 17–19).

Moretti's earlier work comprised a far-reaching account of the history of the European novel, but the methods of *Graphs, Maps, Trees* are a new tack.[7] As he says elsewhere, the concern for "the relationship between form and ideology" that marked his early criticism (DR 89) grew later into "the study of morphological evolution," which then developed "into the analysis of quantitative data" (DR 179). For reasons of space, says Moretti, *Graphs, Maps, Trees* focuses on data about "book history," and Moretti acknowledges that he is "building on" the work of fifteen other scholars, experts in British, Spanish, Indian, Japanese, French, Danish, and other national literatures. He cites the names of these various experts in order to underline that "quantitative work is truly *cooperation*" (GMT 4–5). A single person, after all, can never read twenty thousand books, so one needs teamwork, even "labs." But this complication is actually a "fantastic opportunity" (DR 89), for the "data" one seeks in such an enterprise "are ideally independent from any individual researcher" (GMT 5). Data-analysis fosters collaboration, which in turn fosters objectivity, which in turn yields a "more rational literary history" – which is ultimately, says Moretti, "the idea" (GMT 4).

My second example of the empirical turn adapts what is perhaps the only scientific field to have garnered as much attention (and funding) as Big Data over the last few decades: neuroscience. It's hard nowadays to glance at a newspaper and *not* hear a gleeful hint – from early-childhood researchers and criminal justice experts to marketers and office managers – that, as Paul Churchland once put it, our ordinary folk psychology will someday seem as useful as alchemy. A brain might be more complicated than a liver, but it no more operates according to special

---

[7] See, e.g., Franco Moretti, *The Way of the World: The Bildungsroman in European Culture* (London: Verso, 1987).

physical laws than do such unglamorous organs, and knowing its details will yield finer-grained explanations of human behavior.[8]

Including behavior surrounding the arts. Thus William P. Seeley demonstrates, as he says, "the utility of neuroscientific research to philosophy of literature" by noting:

> Imaging studies and surface electromyography research measuring muscle responses have been profitably used to investigate, model, and explain how these cognitive processes contribute to narrative understanding, and in consequence narrative appreciation, at a neurophysiological level.[9]

Similarly, G. Gabrielle Starr explains the "materiality of aesthetic pleasures," not just "narrative understanding" but "aesthetic experience" generally:

> [I]n general anatomical terms, neural activation moves from sensory cortex forward toward the basal ganglia (reward processes) and toward the hippocampus and amygdalae (memory and emotion ...). Activation in the orbitofrontal cortex follows, but there are interactive loops that reach between these frontal areas and the basal ganglia so that higher-order, complex processes of cognition, and emotional and reward processes, may continually feed one another.[10]

As these comments suggest, the "materials" that matter to neuroaesthetics are not artifacts in a public culture (e.g., books) but the networks of neurons and axons in an individual head. More than Moretti, that is, neuroaesthetics focuses on a work's reception; hence the fMRI studies.[11] Discussions of aesthetic experience, says Starr, are typically discussions of objects: urns, landscapes, melodies. But we really should talk about *events*: walking around an urn, imagining dwelling in a landscape, savoring the movements of a piper's melody. Doing so foregrounds the "dynamism and temporality" of aesthetic experience, "even at a minute level" (18), a dynamic interaction that is "instantiated neurally through brain systems for emotion and reward, as well as through the default mode network" (21). These biological systems buzz whenever we feel pleasure, but "there is a tipping point," says Starr, "at which

---

[8] Paul Churchland, "Eliminative Materialism and the Propositional Attitudes," *Journal of Philosophy* 78: 67–90 (1981).

[9] William P. Seeley, "Neuroscience and Literature," in *The Routledge Companion to Philosophy of Literature*, eds. Noël Carroll and John Gibson (New York: Routledge, 2016), 269–278.

[10] G. Gabrielle Starr, *Feeling Beauty: The Neuroscience of Aesthetic Experience* (MIT Press, 2016), 15, 24. Henceforth cited parenthetically by page number.

[11] But Moretti has – tellingly – expressed sympathy for a neuroscientific research into reading; see *Distant Reading*, 160.

appreciating or liking turns into a response that is both distinctly powerful and distinctly aesthetic" (24). Art has a particularly high "computational value," for it offers an array of perceptions and images that would be mostly unavailable elsewhere – "*novel kinds of rewards*" that reorganize our existing neural representations of what's obtainable and desirable. There's no a priori reason that hammers struck on twisted metal cords should be enjoyable. But if brains have been shaped in certain ways, and if the cords are struck in certain patterns, a piano can "continually expand the context that maps emotions onto the world around us into previously uncharted territory." Thus music gains a "durable value" in our lives (25–26).

III

The development of the research university, wrote Thorstein Veblen in 1918, shifted "the power of aspiration" from "the cults of faith, fashion, sentiment, exploit, and honor" to "the concerted adulation of matter-of-fact."[12] A revival of such adulation in literary studies was predictable in our own day, given recent trends: the calls, for instance, for "consilience" among fields of knowledge, the growing "metric fixation" among administrators, the perception that the humanities are hampered by "a miasma of endlessly contingent discourses and representations of representations" – all developments that mesh nicely with a corporate ethos of abolishing "silos" and unleashing "innovation."[13] The question, however, is not whether the motives for the empirical turn in literary studies are understandable, but whether these projects actually do what they

---

[12] Thorstein Veblen, *The Higher Learning in America* (1918; London: Transaction, 1993), 7.
[13] "Consilience" is the term made famous by the biologist E. O. Wilson, *Consilience: The Unity of Knowledge* (New York: Vintage, 1998). "Metric fixation" is discussed by Jerry Z. Muller, *The Tyranny of Metrics* (Princeton, NJ: Princeton University Press, 2018). The "miasma" of the humanities is diagnosed in Edward Slingerland, *What Science Offers the Humanities: Integrating Body and Culture* (Cambridge: Cambridge University Press, 2008), 9. On silos, see Steven Pinker in "Science Is Not Your Enemy," *New Republic* (August 6, 2013): "If anything is naïve and simplistic, it is the conviction that the legacy silos of academia should be fortified and that we should be forever content with current ways of making sense of the world. Surely our conceptions of politics, culture, and morality have much to learn from our best understanding of the physical universe and of our makeup as a species." For an intelligent review of these and other calls for interdisciplinarity, see Jonathan Kramnick, "The Interdisciplinary Fallacy," *Representations* 140: 67–83 (Fall 2017).

want – namely, provide knowledge that is as coherent as what one typically finds in the sciences, and with the same capacity to achieve widely accepted results and hence authority. Wittgenstein, I'll claim, clarifies not just why these projects can't do what they want, but also how they deflect us from what *does* happen when we talk about literature and the arts. Mimicking the sciences exemplifies the attitude against which Wittgenstein warned more than any other: what in the *Blue Book* he calls "our craving for generality," particularly our wish to account for phenomena, like the scientist, with the smallest number of elements and laws (BB 18). "Crystalline purity" is not a discovery of this sort of enterprise, but one of its requirements (PI §107). Such explanations are certainly attractive: "It is charming to destroy prejudice," as Wittgenstein remarks. (Recall Moretti snickering over "rare and curious works.") But these explanations "are not borne out by experience, as an explanation in physics is," no matter how enticing they seem. The specific content of such pseudoscientific explanations is thus less significant than "the *attitude*" they express (LC 24–26). And what they mostly express is a "contemptuous attitude towards the particular case" (BB 18), an unwillingness to "*look and see*" what is before us (PI §66).

Recall, for instance, Moretti's basic method in *Graphs, Maps, Trees*: using data on book history to quantify the history of the novel. The method shirks what should be an obvious question: are "book" and "novel" so uncomplicatedly interchangeable? I usually know how to identify stacks of rectangular pages gathered into portable objects that can lie flat, and I can distinguish them from scrolls and clay tablets. It takes me a lot longer, however – and requires considering an indefinite range of features and exceptions – to distinguish novels from *their* relevant neighbors: epics, romances, dramas, dialogues, etc. By the same token, I can easily find out how books have been "produced" over time, either by hand or by machine, but well-trained experts will give conflicting answers to the question of when a "novel" has been "produced," depending on which fibers of the concept – books like *The Golden Ass*? like *Religio Medici*? like *Jacques le fataliste*? like *Middlemarch*? like *The Tower Treasure*? like *Neuromancer*? – they use. As Moretti notes, quantification is possible only when a series is "composed of homogenous objects" (GMT 25). But he does little to say why "novel" is one such "object," and the long, quarrelsome history of theorizing about the genre suggests why doing so would be fruitless. And it's the "blurred edges" (PI §71) of "novel" that make it hard to understand, in turn, Moretti's charitable appeals to his fellow novel-researchers. Ornithologists can in good conscience use data gathered by other ornithologists about the digestive system of hummingbirds because they agree about what counts as both a hummingbird and a digestive system – agreement that can be easily explained even to middle-school students. But it's not at all obvious, at least without extensively analyzing their work, whether Moretti's fifteen scholars are using "novel" in exactly the same way. Research programs function only where there is widespread agreement in judgments; and we have no idea if such agreement has been reached here.[14]

If Moretti conflates aesthetic genres with material objects, neuroscience conflates aesthetic understanding with material processes, and a similar move makes the "conjuring trick" (PI §308) work. Recall, first, Wittgenstein's dictum: "an 'inner' process stands in need of outward criteria" (PI §580) – which here reminds us that fMRI images of somatosensory cortexes won't be images of a mental state if we haven't already learned the publicly available criteria for that state. Unless family and teachers have already taught us what counts as angry *behavior*, pictures of angry brains will be indiscernible from pictures of sad, bored, or merry brains. More than that – and this more radical point distances Wittgenstein from his behaviorist contemporaries – the range of behaviors associated with any mental state is massively underdetermined.

---

[14] One answer to this criticism might be that, for Moretti's claims to make sense, readers must agree over what counts as what only in *most* cases, and understanding that there was a massive growth in novels in the nineteenth century is all we need to make interpretive claims about the development and character of the genre – which, as we know from his penetrating other books, is Moretti's real aim. But this thought drains Moretti's project of everything that was supposed to be new and urgent. No doubt readers *do* agree much of the time about what counts as what; that's how genres and subgenres get formed and accepted. But such rough and ready agreement is quite different from the "collective system" that Moretti suggests exists over and above the "sum of individual cases" of texts. There is a long-standing question about whether family-resemblance concepts could ever be the objects of study in a scientific program (is there a science of "games"?), and without first doing at least some of the work required to answer *that* question, Moretti won't be able to explain how his book is providing the "specific form of knowledge" he promised. Without the claim to science, all we have is the idea that a tradition of novels developed in the nineteenth century – but we already knew that. Other critics sympathetic to the use of Big Data have been somewhat more attuned to its limits. See, e.g., Johanna Drucker, writing in a special forum on Moretti's work: "Designing a text-analysis is necessarily an interpretive act, not a mechanical one, even if running the program becomes mechanistic. ... The [automated] methods are based on epistemological assumptions that get translated into metrics and always operate only within the limits of current technical capacities" (see Johanna Drucker, "Why Distant Reading Isn't," *PMLA* 132:631 [2017]).

"Anger" seems obvious: "He's angry at his father," we effortlessly say as the toddler screams on the floor. But consider:

> [of a young painter who moves to Paris] "He's angry at his father."
> "I'm angry at myself for getting bad grades last semester."
> "I'm at this protest today because I'm angry about where our country is now."
> "The White House was angry about the leaks."

Trained specialists can reliably identify tumors and blood clots, but no more than "reading" (PI §§156–171), "being guided" (PI §§170–178), "understanding" (PI §§318–348), and "expectation" (PI §§442–465) will *all* these shades of "anger" share any *one* physical property.[15]

Likewise, for all the explananda of neuroaesthetics: mental "rewards and emotions," "experiencing art," "understanding narrative." Doubtless the micro-level processes that Starr and Seeley describe – activation of the sensory cortex, reward processes in the basal ganglia – do sometimes occur when we get absorbed by a Bach concerto. But to identify only *that* as "aesthetic experience" is to ignore the span of activities in which we weight, with varying degrees of intensity, whether something is fitting, pleasant, ugly, beautiful, cliché, stunning, unsatisfying, or sublime: judging if a door is too low (LC 13), turning on a lamp to create a mood, parting a child's hair, admiring a friend's turn of phrase, marveling at an elegant solution to a math problem, applauding a deft double-play, leglessly dancing at 4 a.m. in a Berlin club, wordlessly marking a pair of pants with chalk. What counts as a "reward" or "understanding" in each of these activities is vividly different, and refusing to identify them as "aesthetic experiences" – to say, with Starr, that there's a "tipping point" in the brain when mere "liking" becomes a "response that is ... distinctly aesthetic" – is to draw a boundary without clarifying its specific purpose (PI §§68–69). For Wittgenstein, there is no such *thing* as "anger," "understanding," "being guided" – or, so I'm claiming, "experiencing art." A "primitive interpretation of our concepts" begets "psychophysical parallelism," a "prejudice" that posits direct casual links between physiological processes and psychological terms (Z §611). Like Augustine watching his elders (PI §1), we think of words in terms of locations rather than applications; and off our theories race.

---

[15] See also PI §571. For a good discussion of such psychological terms, see Warren Goldfarb, "Wittgenstein on Understanding," *Midwest Studies in Philosophy* 17: 109–122 (1992).

IV

Poems, novels, and other texts obviously couldn't exist without the fleshly mechanisms that make sound waves in the air or marks on a page. But to recall Wittgenstein's terms to his students, what matters about such texts, what distinguishes them from rocks and stones and trees, is not merely their "material" but our manners of "appreciation," our ways of engaging with them. As I've indicated, our manners take an indefinite range of forms, and this heterogeneity has been, I think, the single biggest motivation for casting literary studies as a scientific enterprise. Talking about literature means using categories without clear extensions (including "literature"). It means discussing works that test and even defy our standing linguistic and storytelling practices, and that dramatize psychological, moral, political, and cultural conflicts that we don't (any longer?) know how to settle. And it means reflecting on an open-ended range of perceptual, affective, and cognitive experiences. When Moretti remarks that he wants a more "rational" literary history, his adjective betrays an anxiety that marks both the discipline and the educational institutions that house it. Put bluntly: discussions of poems and stories just seem too anarchic, too riddled with ad hoc impressionistic avowals, too *irrational*, to constitute anything we would recognize as legitimate knowledge.

With his criss-crossing "sketches of landscapes," his thoughts never "force[d]" along "a single track" (PI preface), Wittgenstein seems to provide little relief here. But a lack of comprehensive system isn't the same as irrationality. Indeed, Wittgenstein's later work can be said to explore the sorts of rationality and sense-making that mark our lives and language beyond the relatively narrow canons provided by logic, mathematics, and the empirical sciences. His goal is to understand the patterns of significance that are neither necessary nor arbitrary, yet which durably braid our experience; that "did not emerge from some kind of ratiocination" but which I display "day in, day out by my actions and also in what I say" (OC §§475, 431).[16] Asking how we learned color-words (PI

---

[16] Indeed, it's striking how little the terms "rationality" and "irrationality" appear in the later Wittgenstein. Few philosophers have more inventively reflected upon unfamiliar or alien ways of communicating, interacting, and living (think of all the far-off tribes, expressive animals, and sci-fi thought experiments), but few philosophers are also less prone to declaring a coherent, intelligible practice "irrational." Several passages of *On Certainty* imagine someone who is "unbalanced" – crazy, insane, etc. – but those are exceptions more than rules.

§29), imagining a group of builders (PI §§2–8) or a learner "adding 2" (PI §§185–188), "marshalling recollections" (PI §127), "finding and inventing *intermediate cases*" that clarify our language (PI §122) – none of these strategies would have a point if they didn't illuminate the depths of order woven into our language-games. Even if that order is something we are prone to underappreciate, or wish to escape.[17]

To understand the sense-making I mean, let me return to Wittgenstein's phrase and ask: What is "appreciation"? The term can seem dusty and antiquated, dubiously untheoretical, but as I'll briefly suggest now, it can in fact steer us in the right direction to the same degree that "material" tends to steer us in a wrong one.

For starters, a reminder of something everyone knows: textbooks routinely summarize the theory of special relativity without reprinting Einstein's paper. The 1905 article, that is, is in some important sense disposable, and its claims can be clarified, updated, and extended without unduly damaging the theory itself. But nobody doubts that summaries of "To Autumn" or *To the Lighthouse* omit a good deal – perhaps even all – of what's most important about them. Paraphrase might not constitute heresy, but it's manifestly different than the text itself.

All this suggests that conceptual priority, in literary contexts, lies in specific texts, in words that audiences must encounter firsthand – what Kant would call the "singular presentation of the object."[18] As I come to learn about literature, I never actually read literature as such. I instead read particular works, particular sets of words organized into particular patterns by particular authors writing at particular moments. And gradually – through examples and by practice (PI §220) – I build up a general idea of how to classify a given work (is it *literature*, and if so, what sort?), which features and patterns matter, what role it played for its author, how it fit into the moral and political culture of its day, how it stands in our own time, and so forth. The very idea of a "collective system" (in Moretti's term) of "literature" could be imaginable only by someone who has *already* devoted a gigantic amount of time reading singular instances of it and who has *already* learned to make these immensely complicated judgments. Likewise, talking of "aesthetic experience" – "aesthetic" as opposed to something else, and understood in neural or other terms –

---

[17] Cf. Stanley Cavell: "Discovering the depth of the systematic in language was not Wittgenstein's intellectual goal, but his instrument." See *The Claim of Reason: Wittgenstein, Skepticism, Morality, and Tragedy* (New York: Oxford University Press, 1979), 30.

[18] See Kant, *Critique of Judgment*, trans. Werner S. Pluhar (Indianapolis, IN: Hackett, 1987).

makes no sense unless one specifies the particular object that has allegedly generated it. We talk, notes Wittgenstein, about "'the effect of a work of art' – feeling, images, etc." But unusual effects can be caused by anything, and as much by nonart (drugs, sleeplessness, etc.) as by art. "Doesn't the minuet itself matter? – hearing *this*: would another have done as well?" (LC 29). What I most want to understand about the minuet is the minuet, not the chain of inner events that might occur in its presence.[19]

If "appreciation" starts with a concrete thing, of what does it consist? Less of *interpretation*, I want to say, than of *immersion*: a form of attention, participation, and care that precedes any genuine account of a thing's "meaning." "The sort of explanation one is looking for when one is puzzled by an aesthetic impression," remarks Wittgenstein, "is not a causal explanation, not one corroborated by experience or by statistics as to how people react" (LC 21). Two things stand out here. First, note that what prompts aesthetic discussion is our being "puzzled." Something *grabs* or *draws* us, and *matters* to us; we don't just walk away indifferent; we want to grasp and make sense of what's before us, but can't find our way around. Second, the puzzlement isn't dissipated by viewing the work as an effect of prior causes. "The puzzlement I am talking about," Wittgenstein suggests, "can be cured only by peculiar kinds of comparison," analogies that sharpen our sense of what a *particular* work displays. We contrast, say, the way a certain story ends with the way another story (one existing, imagined, in draft, etc.) ends. Doing so helps clarify the events recounted earlier in the narrative, or something about the protagonist's future, or the text's attitude toward a certain sociopolitical value. Or we offer a metaphor to describe an author's work, an image that will evocatively synopsize a characteristic style, mood, or subject-matter. "Why," we ask, "does the poem use this word here?" Our answers to this question – "Because it recalls that moment in an earlier stanza, and marks a change of mood ..." – don't identify a causal chain, but make the poem intelligible: *reasonable*, in some modest sense of that word. We might very well judge that a technique has different purposes

---

[19] Elsewhere Wittgenstein remarks: "You must ask how we learnt the expression 'Isn't that glorious!' at all. – No one explained it to us by referring to sensations, images or thoughts that accompany hearing!" (Z §170). And in 1947, prompted by Tolstoy's "bad theorizing": "You might say: the work of art does not aim to convey *something else*, just itself. Just as when I pay someone a visit, I don't just want to make him have feelings of such and such a sort; what I mainly want is to visit him, though of course I should like to be well received too" (CV 58).

in different eras, and different readers will inevitably offer different comparisons and analogies: they point to different texts, different authors, different genres, all depending on their own interests and purposes. Here as much as anywhere, we notice that "language is a labyrinth of paths," approachable from various sides (PI §203). But we are nevertheless trying to articulate something that is *there*, in the work, something that other people might also recognize. "Our discomfort takes the form of a criticism," and not a report on my state of mind (e.g., "My mind is not at rest") (LC 15). We aren't just reporting on our own stream of impressions, and in this sense the process isn't just easy subjectivism.

All this resembles Wittgenstein's descriptions of his own philosophical activity, which aims to provide "an order for a particular purpose" – "one out of many possible orders, not *the* order" (PI §132). How this practice differs from the sciences can be clarified by considering how such puzzlement *ends*. What, asks Wittgenstein, "would be the criterion that you had pointed out the right thing" when making comparisons between texts? The right thing is what makes you "satisfied"; some description suddenly seems "fitting" (LC 19–20). If my comparison of the ending of two stories doesn't click for you, I can try to describe what I see; but if this description doesn't persuade you, then I haven't given you an explanation, and nothing requires that you accept it. If you and I are to share an understanding of a work – and as Cavell says, our response to a work, "unshared, is a burden," a form of mutual estrangement – then I have to try another comparison.[20] Likewise, if I find a poem mawkish, I won't be proven wrong by a survey showing that ninety-nine percent of readers find it profound. By contrast, if I don't grasp a scientist's explanation of photosynthesis, it doesn't mean that the explanation is mistaken. Perhaps I'm not educated enough to understand it; perhaps the scientist was inarticulate. Either way, the legitimacy of the explanation stands, as it were, outside of my own response to it. Scientists get puzzled in their work, and disagree with one another all the time about the best explanations. But unlike literary critics, they also have widely accepted procedures for bringing the puzzlement and disagreement to

---

[20] Cavell, *Must We Mean What We Say?*, 192. Cf. Wittgenstein in 1948: "I give someone an explanation [of a musical phrase] and tell him 'It's as though . . .'; then he says, 'Yes, now I understand it' or 'Yes, now I see how it's to be played.' It's most important that he didn't have to *accept* the explanation; it's not as though I had, as it were, given him conclusive reasons for thinking that this passage should be compared with that and the other one" (CV 69).

a close – even if the process ends only after decades of debate, ongoing experiments, or the arrival of new technology.

None of this makes Wittgenstein a simple-minded formalist. His very definition of a language-game – "language *and the actions into which it is woven*" (PI §7, my emphasis) – suggests an aversion to treating texts as isolatable objects. If, as he says, "the intention *with which* one acts does not 'accompany' the action any more than a thought 'accompanies' speech" (PP, 280), then talking of works inevitably means talking about intentions – even if those intentions aren't easily legible or easily condensed into a kernel.[21] Moreover, the "actions" into which language is "woven" extends far beyond individual speakers. Wittgenstein insists as relentlessly as any literary historicist on understanding the circumstances of our utterances. From the 1930s onward, he was generalizing the Fregean context principle that his earliest work had endorsed: not only do specific words mean in the context of a proposition, but a proposition means only as part of a larger linguistic act, a linguistic act means only in the context of a particular practice, a practice only in the context of a sociohistorical moment, a sociohistorical moment only in

---

[21] The distance between Wittgenstein's concept of intention and those of the theories I've been describing is worth mentioning in passing. Neuroscience is as famously skeptical about intention as poststructuralism (the brain has no pontifical cells), and Moretti similarly marginalizes it: since "the human and social sciences" tell us that "conscious motives" are "ex post constructions," analysis can "disregard" our self-explanations "as mere rationalizations" (see Moretti, "A Response," *PMLA*, 123: 688 [2017]). Like "anger," "being guided," or "aesthetic experience," "intention" in a Wittgensteinian context doesn't refer to an inner process, a hidden spirit or life-force that the reader needs to uncover. The intentions of a work, like the intentions of an action, are all there on the surface; act and intention are mutually constitutive. As I note here, this hardly means that intentions are always fully intelligible. A friendly wave is sometimes indistinguishable from a nervous warning, and likewise we often don't know how to take a given line, passage, or work. Nor must "intention" in an artistic context be understood as something clear and distinct. "A work of art," as Stanley Cavell puts it, "does not express some particular intention (as statements do), nor achieve particular goals (the way technological skill and moral action do), but, one might say, celebrates the fact that men can intend their lives at all ... and that their actions are coherent and effective at all in the scene of indifferent nature and determined society" (see *Must We Mean What We Say?*, 198.) It makes sense, that is, to ask what a particular word in *King Lear* means, but it's much harder to know – as centuries of criticism suggest – what would count as "the" meaning of the play as a whole. The basic point, however, is that none of these scenarios require that what we are "really" talking about is isolatable objects any more than we are talking about material objects or material processes. Our attitudes toward a text and toward a random string of marks simply aren't the same, and what is expressed in the former is not gotten by measuring their letters (PI §§284–285).

the context of a wider *Lebensform*.[22] Even someone reading a poem or novel for the very first time will be using a great deal of "stage-setting" (PI §257) – a rough sense of "the whole hurly-burly of human actions, the background against which we see any action" (Z §567), including a sense of what's possible and necessary in our physical universe.[23] And more specialized contexts – traditions of art and its criticism – are also crucial, an indispensable source of comparisons and analogies: how other artists have handled a theme, reworked certain forms, expressed certain moods, responded to certain conditions. "What belongs to a language-game is a whole culture," remarks Wittgenstein, and when we overlook the "complicated role" that aesthetic judgments play in "what we call a culture of a period" (LC 7), we are liable to sound like the Europeans who clumsily talk about African art (LC 8–10) or the modern connoisseurs who discuss medieval coronation robes apart from the ceremonies in which they originally played a role (LC 9–10).

Seen in this light, empirical approaches to literature can be said to offer some useful reminders. Big Data underlines that what we deem "poems" or "fiction" (and "great poems" and "great fiction," too) arise within a much wider social, political, and economic field. Neuroscience reminds us that only creatures with a particular biological make-up can appropriately respond to – can have an "experience" of – poetry or fiction. The question is not only whether these broader contexts help us make sense of a work or experience, but also whether they actually constitute an *explanation* of it. Wittgenstein suggests that they don't. Not

---

[22] As Hans-Johan Glock puts it (citing PI §50 and other passages), the later Wittgenstein suggests that even an utterance such as "Shame!" is a proposition, in spite of the fact that it lacks subject and predicate and isn't expressed through a propositional clause – a view that is at odds with what we ordinarily call a "proposition" or "sentence" (see Glock, *A Wittgenstein Dictionary* (Oxford: Blackwell, 1996), 318–319. The contextualism of Wittgenstein's thought is one of the main things that have prompted commentators to draw comparisons to some of the major influences on literary theory. Affinities between Wittgenstein and Foucault, for instance, motivate much of the work of Ian Hacking; see his *Historical Ontology* (Cambridge, MA: Harvard University Press, 2004). Wittgenstein's relation to Marx and Marxism has likewise been recognized; see, e.g., *Marx and Wittgenstein: Knowledge, Morality and Politics* eds. Gavin Kitching and Nigel Pleasants (New York: Routledge, 2002).

[23] "Stage-setting" was Elizabeth Anscombe's invention in her original translation of Wittgenstein's sentence: "so vergisst man, dass schon viel in der Sprache vorbereitet sein muss." I'm using it here both because it's colorful and because it has become an immediately recognizable part of English-language Wittgenstein commentary. But I fully realize that Hacker and Schulte are more accurate when they translate the remark to read: "one forgets that much must be prepared in the language."

because these contexts are in fact negligible, or because generalizations about authors, texts, audiences, or literary history are impossible, but because these contexts and generalizations don't fully explain why one would be drawn toward, would be puzzled by or care for, a particular work in the first place. To turn our inquiries around our "real need" (PI §108), we first have to recognize that different kinds of descriptions have different weight in different contexts.

V

What are the *forms* of criticism, then? What attitudes might it express, what projects might it pursue? Aesthetic understanding is imagined in Wittgenstein as a fundamentally improvisational practice – a matter of testing out this or that stance toward an object, asking whether one is "satisfied," proposing comparisons. In the end, there is no obvious way that such testing and proposing constitute a "method" of the sort that could be easily taught or institutionalized. Nor is it clear whether they constitute *arguments* that could persuade others once and for all. "Lectures on Aesthetics" briefly imagines a person asking how to read blank verse, and the answer comes when someone else "says it ought to be read *this* way and reads it aloud to you. You say: 'Oh yes. Now it makes sense'" (LC 4). Similarly, Wittgenstein's writing on aspect-perception – a segment of his work that has had considerable influence on recent philosophical aesthetics – emphasizes not only the irrelevance of *causal* questions (PPF §§114, 170, 183), but also the makeshift quality of the entire practice.[24] I am "struck" by likenesses between a man and his son (PPF §239); I "suddenly" see the solution of a puzzle (PPF §131) or recognize an acquaintance in a crowd (PPF §143); an aspect "lights up" (PPF §140), forcing from us "a cry of recognition" (PPF §144). Elsewhere a musical training exemplifies this fluidity: "I have a theme played to me several times and each time in a slower tempo. Eventually I say '*Now* it's right,' or '*Now* at last it's a march' ..." (PPF §209). "Can one learn this

---

[24] Paul Guyer divides the reception of Wittgenstein in aesthetics into two "waves," the first of which (roughly in the 1950s and 1960s) focused on questions about the definition of art, and the second of which took up the reflections on aspect-perception. In this second wave, Guyer singles out the work of Cavell and Richard Wollheim for extended treatment (see Paul Guyer, *A History of Modern Aesthetics, Volume 3* [Cambridge: Cambridge University Press, 2014], chapters 11–13).

knowledge?" Wittgenstein asks at one point. "Yes; some can learn it. Not, however, by taking a course of study in it, but through *'experience'*."

Can someone else be a man's teacher in this? Certainly. From time to time he gives him the right *tip*. ... What one acquires here is not a technique; one learns correct judgments. There are also rules, but they do not form a system, and only experienced people can apply them rightly. Unlike calculating rules. (PPF §355)

As Toril Moi has observed, literary scholars bring certain "moods" and "mindsets" to a text, certain political commitments and moral concerns. But a mood is not a method – not a clearly defined series of steps that will allow us to reach a replicable result.[25]

To some readers, such remarks might recall debates in the 1970s and 1980s over whether criticism was itself a form of literature, and they might cite Wittgenstein's well-known remark that philosophy "ought really to be written only as *poetic composition*" (CV 24): a thought that, as in Schlegel or Nietzsche or Derrida, seems to obviate the line between "primary" and "secondary" texts.[26] A more persuasive idea – one that better fits with the tailor altering suits in "Lectures on Aesthetics" – is that criticism for Wittgenstein should be seen as a kind of *craft*: less a set of lyrical inventions than a practical effort to get us to slow down, to see what is before our eyes, to grasp a synoptic view of some particular problem. Here a less famous aphorism is apt: "A thinker is like a draughtsman whose aim it is to represent all the interrelations between things" (CV 12).[27] Reviewing criticism's persistent craving for scientific legitimacy, however, brings out something further about the practice of

---

[25] Moi, *Revolution of the Ordinary*, 192–193. "Moods" and "mindsets" are terms Moi adopts from Rita Felski.

[26] For some discussion of Wittgenstein's remark, see David Schalkwyk, "Wittgenstein's 'Imperfect Garden': The Ladders and Labyrinths of Philosophy as *Dichtung*," in *The Literary Wittgenstein*, eds. John Gibson and Wolfgang Huemer (London: Routledge, 2004), 55–74; Marjorie Perloff, "'But Isn't the Same at Least the Same?' Wittgenstein and the Question of Poetic Translatability," in *The Literary Wittgenstein*, eds. John Gibson and Wolfgang Huemer (London: Routledge, 2004), 34–54. On the question of whether criticism "really" is literature, see (among many others) Geoffrey H. Hartman, *Saving the Text: Literature/Derrida/Philosophy* (Baltimore, MD: Johns Hopkins University Press, 1981); Philippe Lacoue-Labarthe and Jean-Luc Nancy, *The Literary Absolute: The Theory of Literature in German Romanticism*, trans. Philip Barnard and Cheryl Lester (Albany, NY: SUNY Press, 1988).

[27] For a view of Wittgenstein as draughtsman, see Allan Janik, "Wittgenstein, Loos, and Critical Modernism: Style and Idea in Architecture and Philosophy," in *Wittgenstein and Modernism*, eds. Michael LeMahieu and Karen Zumhagen-Yekplé (Chicago, IL: University of Chicago Press, 2017), 71–88.

criticism, which we might call its *existential* dimension. No matter how many books we've read, how much we know about literary history, how many facts we have about the culture of a given period, how much data and research we accumulate, our judgments about a work are inescapably our own. Which other texts does this resemble? Which of its features matter, and how? Is it "literature"? Other people often clarify what I think; Wittgenstein's own writing dramatizes a continuous back-and-forth with other voices. But in the end, no expert is fully authorized to decide every one of these questions for me.[28] And that, too, separates literary studies from scientific fields. "People nowadays think that scientists exist to instruct them," writes Wittgenstein on the brink of World War II, and "poets, musicians, etc. to give them pleasure. The idea *that these have something to teach them* – that does not occur to them" (CV 36). Whatever else Wittgenstein means here by "teach," his own practice suggests what we learn above all, in the realm of art, is that nobody else can settle for me the matters that matter most.

---

[28] For a vivid version of this observation, see R. M. Berry, "Riposte to Brian Lennon and Loren Glass," *electronic book review* (February 6, 2010), https://electronicbookreview.com/essay/r-m-berrys-riposte-to-brian-lennon-and-loren-glass (accessed April 5, 2019).

4 A Vision of Language for Literary Historians
Forms of Life, Context, Use
Sarah Beckwith

Abstract: Wittgenstein did not address the question of history directly or extensively. But his vision of language is pervasively historical and has implications for the way we do literary history. This chapter examines the idea of use at the heart of Wittgenstein's vision of language, especially how it differs from the question of context, and how it is related to "forms of life." After exemplifying these concepts in Wittgenstein by revisiting some of the early remarks in the *Philosophical Investigations,* I explore the Oxford English Dictionary (OED) to show how the teaching of the differences in the use of words is at the heart of its practice. Finally, I highlight the work of an exemplary critic, William Empson, who regarded his work as an important corrective to the OED, and whose work is highly attuned to the history of use. The implications of Wittgenstein's vision of language with its fundamental revision of linguistic agency show that much contemporary historical criticism is not historical enough.

Keywords: History, Historicism, Linguistic Context and Use, Forms of Life, Linguistic Agency, Literary History, Dictionaries, Sandra Laugier, Stanley Cavell, William Empson.

"Always historize!" said Fredric Jameson.[1] The mood was imperative, total. In my neck of the woods – medieval and early modern studies – we are all historicists now. We work within literary periods, and our academic guilds, societies, journals, not to speak of our livelihoods, are defined from within the assumptions of literary history. But for the last thirty years or so, historicism has been gripped by a certain picture of language, and a set of related but distinct *doxas*: the death of the author, the intentional fallacy, and the idea of the "subject." Yet there are more

---

[1] Fredric Jameson, *The Political Unconscious: Narrative as Socially Symbolic Form* (Ithaca, NY: Cornell University Press, 1989), 9.

ways of doing literary history than are dreamed of in this philosophy. What got lost in this picture was linguistic agency. That is where Wittgenstein comes in.

Wittgenstein did not have much to say about the discipline of history. But his vision of language is historical through and through. He helps us see that there are myriad ways for literary criticism to do historical work, of being alert to history's presence. To see how and why that is the case, it is necessary to see how Wittgenstein's vision of language is historical.[2] I do this by examining that vision, taking up Wittgenstein's ideas of forms of life, context, and use.

I once had a funny misunderstanding with a member of staff. The conversation took place when I was Chair of an academic department with a Difficult Colleague who habitually stepped over the bounds of propriety in ways difficult to manage. On this occasion the member of staff began to tell me that she was tired because she had been up until two in the morning. She had to fetch Anna from a bar. I immediately began to feel quite concerned. What was she doing fetching Anna from a bar so late at night? I said I thought that this was an *astonishing*, inappropriate thing to ask of her. In my view she was not *in any way* obliged to fulfil such an outrageous, importunate request. She told me that she thought this simply came with the territory and we proceeded to have a polite disagreement. This went on for a bit. At a certain point in the conversation, I got the idea that this had been a frequent occurrence, that she seemed to have even a certain benign if weary placidity about the whole event, and was in any case not shocked by it in the way I was. These things happen was the gist of it; this is, surely, just the kind of thing you expect. For a moment I paused in my professional and personal anxiety about the demands on her time, on her life, my ideas about what sorts of responsibilities this imposed on me, my protective feelings, and the ones of outrage. It suddenly dawned on me that the daughter of my member of staff had exactly the same name as the Difficult Colleague. We had been talking entirely at cross-purposes.

It would be easy to describe this as a simple case of mistaken identity. Her Anna was her daughter. Mine was the tricky and demanding colleague. She was referring to her daughter; I to my colleague, only we had never grasped the plain fact of two Annas during the course of the

---

[2] "Vision of language" is Stanley Cavell's terminology. See chapter 7 of *The Claim of Reason: Wittgenstein, Skepticism, Morality, and Tragedy* (Oxford: Oxford University Press, 2nd ed., 1999); henceforth *CR*.

conversation. Once this was clear, we settled back into an amused appreciation of our past dialogue beyond the chasms of mutual incomprehension.

To whom did the name Anna refer? Much more was at stake in this conversation than reference. I understood my colleague to be complaining about Anna in the first instance. From her point of view this might have entailed an answering sympathy in me. What she got was a lecture on parenting from one in no position to give it. She complained; I demurred, mildly reproached her, advised her. It was becoming clear during the course of the conversation that I was upsetting and offending her. On my side, I was helping her set some boundaries in her job. Had this conversation gone on we might have found ourselves at more than cross-purposes. Our hitherto cordial and friendly relationship was feeling all of a sudden more than a bit shaky. Undoing the confusion about Anna changed our conversation: we both saw what each of us had been doing in so speaking. Each of us misconstrued not merely Anna, but each other and the situation we were in. This kind of miscommunication is a common hazard of conversation.

Had I not understood my dialogue partner (as at last I did) I would not have appreciated the context of the conversation. This time I understood the context only after I understood *her*, what she was doing in speaking, what her words therefore meant in the use of the moment.

When Wittgenstein said that for a large class of cases "the meaning of a word is its use in our language," he radicalized the idea of context, expanding it utterly beyond its confinement to reference and representation alone.[3] In "Ordinary Language as Lifeform," Sandra Laugier claims that it is "Ordinary Language Philosophy's primary methodological ambition ... to arrive at a conceptual analysis that allows us to recognize the importance of *context* in our uses of language, thought, and perception – that is in our various ways of *engaging* the real."[4] To appreciate the force of this claim we need to understand how Wittgenstein thought about language and the world. We will also have to reckon with Wittgenstein's conception of *speaking* as an activity, a (human) form of life, the conditions of possibility for significance and sense, and the

---

[3] "For a *large* class of the employment of the word 'meaning' – though not for *all* – this word can be explained in this way: the meaning of a word is its use in our language," *Philosophical Investigations* (PI §43).

[4] Sandra Laugier, "Wittgenstein, Ordinary Language as Lifeform," in *Language, Forms of Life, and Logic*, ed. Christian Martin (Berlin: De Gruyter, 2018), 285.

necessities bound up in speaking. If, as Wittgenstein claims, it is through use that both the word and the world come into view, we will also need to revise our idea of agency in speech, how conceiving speech as action, event, and expression transforms what a context is. Wittgenstein's intrinsically historical vision of language might show that most historicisms are not historical enough. Wittgenstein's work deepens our concepts of convention: he reveals that dominant pictures of language tend to miss (while also depending on) the bonds and necessities involved in acts of speech, in the normative reach of words. They make our agreements and accords too shallow and refuse what responsibility we have in our words by ascribing to language what we ourselves fail to mean or quite how and why we cannot be articulate on any particular occasion. (In this way of thinking, the fact of speaking becomes as important as what we might say.) Wittgenstein's vision of language is profoundly at the service of a recovery of the world, past and present.

I'll begin by examining Wittgenstein's seminal idea about speaking as a form of life, especially as it resonates with the work of J. L. Austin, and as it is taken up by Stanley Cavell who has most appreciated the humanistic, literary, historical, and radical potentialities of Wittgenstein's work. (For it is Wittgenstein's idea of forms of life that show us that word and world are already invoked together, there is no gap needing to be bridged or filled between one and the other, a picture Wittgenstein labels Augustinian). I'll then show the difference between context and use. After a brief discursus on examples of patterns of use in historical dictionaries, I explore the work of William Empson in his *The Structure of Complex Words* (*SCW*). Empson is my example of a critic for whom meaning is involved in use. Empson regarded this book as an important corrective to the work of the historical dictionary.[5] His work in *SCW* offers us provocative and path-breaking literary histories that make available "period style." *SCW* was published in 1951, and the *Philosophical Investigations* in 1953, only a few years before Austin gave his famous lectures at Harvard that became *How to Do Things With Words*.[6] The historicism that has established itself since the 1980s has obscured (dehistoricized, in fact) the intervention of these works in their

---

[5] *The Structure of Complex Words and Related Writings*, ed. Helen Thaventhiran and Stefan Collini (Oxford: Oxford University Press, 2020); henceforth *SCW*.
[6] J. L. Austin, *How to Do Things with Words*, eds. J. O. Urmson and Marina Sbisa (Cambridge, MA: Harvard University Press, 1962), based on lectures given in 1955; henceforth *HTD*. Cavell heard the lectures at Harvard and began his own seminal interpretations of Austin's (and Wittgenstein's) work also in the 1950s, offering his first paper on Austin in

own time. Understanding how radical this intervention was is an important step to grasping Wittgenstein's potential for historical work in literary studies and criticism.

Forms of Life: PI §§19, 23, 241–242; PPF §345

Why start with forms of life, a phrase Wittgenstein uses both in the singular and in the plural at four key points in the *Philosophical Investigations*.[7] I start with some glosses on the remarks in which this phrase appears because it is a key idea in combatting the "Augustinian" picture of language. When beginners learn to speak, they are not or not only learning the names of things, or being told the meaning of those words by the elders, as in Augustine's famous staging cited to open the *Philosophical Investigations*. Wittgenstein has various inventive, patient, and stunningly various ways of showing us that there is a difference between instruction and initiation. He asks us to reflect on how we learn to speak and presents us with a child not yet initiated into language. The idea of forms of life and the idea of initiation come together in the logic of the *Investigations* to combat the pervasive philosophical idea that a word has no meaning unless something corresponds to it.[8] To learn our language the child has to learn from us, follow us, share our reactions as she does the things we do. Wittgenstein's forms of life are invoked to call our attention to the patterns and regularities in the myriad ways we do things, including talk. "Instead of saying either that we *tell* beginners what words mean, or that we *teach* them what objects are," says Cavell, "I will say: We initiate them into the relevant

---

1957; see Stanley Cavell, *Must We Mean What We Say? A Book of Essays* (1969; Cambridge: Cambridge University Press, 2002), xviii.

[7] For a recent examination of the idea of "forms of life" in relation to other concepts in Wittgenstein, such as grammar and language-games, see Toril Moi, *Revolution of the Ordinary: Literary Studies After Austin, Wittgenstein, and Cavell* (Chicago, IL: University of Chicago Press, 2017), 54–61. I have also found two papers of Sandra Laugier's very helpful: "Voice as Form of Life and Life Form" in *Nordic Wittgenstein Review* 4 (2015) 63–82; and the paper cited in note 4. In addition, Juliet Floyd has written a meticulous and comprehensive analysis of Wittgenstein's changing terminology on forms of life; see her "Chains of Life: Turing, *Lebensform*, and the Emergence of Wittgenstein's Later Style," *Nordic Wittgenstein Review* 5 (2): 7–89 (2016). For an earlier treatment, see Naomi Scheman, "Forms of Life: Mapping the Rough Ground," in *The Cambridge Companion to Wittgenstein*, eds. Hans Sluga and David G. Stern (Cambridge: Cambridge University Press, 1996), 383–410.

[8] Craig Fox, "Wittgenstein on Meaning and Meaning Blindness," in *Wittgenstein: Key Concepts*, ed. Kevin Dean Jolley (Durham, UK: Acumen, 2010), 31.

forms of life held in language and gathered around the objects and persons of our world."[9] These routes of initiation are both strong and fragile: strong because we accept them trustingly and naturally in continuing responsiveness to each other, fragile because they turn on so very little – that, for example, the child laughs when you do, wants to clap his hands and tap his feet in rhythm with you, looks at what you look at, grasps your hand at your touch, finds the same things remarkable, the same things worth care and attention, repulsion, or longing. For initiation to take place the elders have to assume authority in their culture and responsibility for what they are saying, and the initiate has to be inclined to follow them.

As a form of life speaking is "as much a part of our natural history as walking, eating, drinking" (PI §25). In his *Lectures on Philosophical Psychology* Wittgenstein had remarked that, "if a child looked radiant when it was hurt and shrieked for no apparent reason, one could not teach him to use the word pain."[10] If, as he says in PI §142, there were no characteristic, patterned expressions of pain, fear, or joy, "if rule became exception, or exception rule; or if both became phenomena of roughly equal frequency – our normal language-games would thereby lose their point." The surreal morphing lump of cheese, growing and shrinking unpredictably mentioned in the same remark makes the procedure of weighing futile. It is another example of the weave and pattern of the natural histories that must be in place before such activities as measuring, or exclaiming in delight, crying in sympathy, quaking with fear, and the expressions associated with them, make sense. If we can decide to use napkins, rather than our sleeve, to wipe our mouths, or the common tablecloth as was once the case, if we opt to use knives and forks rather than fingers, it is still our mouths we wipe or feed. And if we mourn by secluding ourselves for several days, or by throwing ourselves on a funeral pyre like Dido, or by sprinkling earth into the fresh grave, we commonly cry about our losses.

---

[9] CR 178.

[10] *Wittgenstein's Lectures on Philosophical Psychology 1946–7*, notes by P. T. Geach, K. J. Shah, and A. C. Jackson, ed. P. T. Geach (Hemel Hempstead: Harvester Wheatsheaf: 1988), 37. See also PI §257: "What would it be like if human beings did not manifest their pains (did not groan, grimace, etc)? Then it would be impossible to teach a child the use of the word 'toothache'." Again, PPF Fragment I, §2: "'Grief' describes a pattern which recurs, with different variations, in the tapestry of life. If a man's bodily expressions of sorrow and joy alternated, say, with the ticking of a clock, here we would not have the characteristic course of the pattern of sorrow or of the pattern of joy."

When Wittgenstein controversially says in Fragment xi of the *Philosophy of Psychology*, §345: "What has to be accepted, the given, is – one might say – *forms of life*," he means these general facts of nature. They are not subject to our decision, yet to reject them (by imagining, say, a private language) is to refuse how public, how social is our mindedness and the very condition of our humanity.

When the beginners follow the elders in the scene of initiation, what they learn is more than the elders know, and more than they can say.[11] As Cavell famously points out, we learn words only in certain contexts, not in all the contexts in which they can and might be used, or will go on to be used.[12] So the idea of initiation into forms of life replaces the idea of rules, replaces the Augustinian picture and its ills. Why is this important, more than an academic matter? Because the Augustinian picture in Wittgenstein's patient, curative elucidation makes us hopelessly pursue a link *between* our minds and the world, crossing a *gap* between them (through universals, or through rules). Yet that picture of "between" is unnecessary: the between is a "picture" that exiles us from each other and the world, for we will thereby miss where meaning comes into view in use and practice. Wittgenstein wants to lead us out of our exile from ourselves and each other, from the quandaries and confusions in the philosophical tradition that imagine that our connection to reality is through naming, from the unhandsome grasp that tightens our grip on ourselves so needlessly.

Wittgenstein first introduces the term "form of life" in PI §19 in relation to language-game 2, which he asks us to consider as "a language for which the description given by Augustine is right" (PI §2). The builders (A and B, not Jones and Smith or Cunningham and Zopowski) have a language meant to "serve for communication." Wittgenstein first describes their activity: A is building with four different types of building materials (blocks, pillars, slabs, and beams). B has to give A the building materials in the right order so that A can make use of them. They make use of a "language" consisting solely of the words that correspond to the

---

[11] CR 178.

[12] Stanley Cavell, "The Availability of Wittgenstein's Later Philosophy" in *Must We Mean What We Say?*, 52: "We learn and teach words in certain contexts, and then we are expected, and expect others, to be able to project them into further contexts. Nothing insures that this projection will take place, (in particular, not the grasping of universals nor the grasping of books of rules), just as nothing insures that we will make or understand the same projections."

building blocks. Wittgenstein says that Builder B has learnt to bring the stone at Builder A's "call." "To imagine a language is to imagine a form of life," says Wittgenstein in PI §19, so what are the builders' lives like? If, as he says at §23, *"speaking"* (Wittgenstein's italics) is part of an activity, a form of life," what can we imagine the builders doing? Wittgenstein nowhere says they are speaking, talking, or conversing. He terms Builder A's words "calls" (*Ruf*), and their language "communication." Their form of life consists only of commands. It is not clear that we can even call them that for we can't as yet distinguish commands from reports, exclamations, insinuations, countermands, or descriptions. Can the builders josh or joke around? Blaspheme or curse? Can they bitch about the boss, countermand his orders, have a good chin-wag about the shoddy materials they are asked to heave and handle? Can they cast ironical aspersions on the whole enterprise they labor for, call for a rebellion against capitalist exploitation rather than another beam or slab? Can they do this together, or must one call out indefinitely, the other indefinitely carry the stones he calls for, like Sisyphus, or like Nelson Mandela on Robben Island? If Builder A suddenly shouts BRICK! will Builder B fetch one, call him a BLOCK head, sing Goodbye Yellow Brick Road, call for mortar? Will he rather stand utterly still, nonplussed at this unprecedented improvisation?

It is no wonder that we have trouble imagining the form of life of these builders, and therefore imagining their language as akin to the way we speak. For how could I ask Builder A or Builder B anything? One gives orders and the other reacts. How could we talk to each other in this way? How could they talk to each other? In his essay on Wittgenstein's builders, Rush Rhees says of one who learns to speak: "When he learns to speak, he learns to tell you something; and he tries to."[13]

Paul Standish recounts a lovely anecdote about his son telling him something for the first time. His little boy comes into his study very excited; he babbles away in determination and frustration, for he is finding it hard to make himself understood. Something about a toilet, his sister, and a pet dinosaur. The crisis is over. His wife has rescued the pet dinosaur from the toilet bowl into which his sister drastically cast it: but this is so important an event in his life that he wants to tell his father. Standish says this:

---

[13] Rush Rhees, "Wittgenstein's Builders," in *Discussions of Wittgenstein* (New York: Schocken Books, 1970), 79.

He has come to tell you what has happened. He is registering from your reaction the importance of what has happened, and in so doing finding out something about what the world is like. But he is also, in finding something to say, discovering the world as something we can speak about and discovering himself as having something to say. These are crucial steps in discovering what the world is.[14]

His son is not making sounds in imitation of others; he is *saying* something and so learning to both have a world and to know what the world is. This is what Wittgenstein means by routes of shared interest that we agree in, rather than about (§§241–242). That is why we might be tempted to think the builders are less or more than human: they will not, cannot grow in language as a child grows. They cannot therefore find, discover, take on the adventure of words.

Forms of life in Wittgenstein's understanding are intrinsically historical, public, and social. You cannot have a one-off form of life isolated in time; it depends on patterns of variation, and repetition, on certain regularities. Forms of life are inherited. They become parts of our past with which we must reckon, and in which we have to find and express ourselves. They are not determinative (as in some models of history) but they are the inevitable, indispensable background in which we make sense. They are initially taken on trust, and for granted, and because forms of life are described frequently in Wittgenstein's work as a "weave," a "tapestry," or a "complicated form of life," interconnected strand on strand, it is hard to see, as J. L. Austin said, where conventions begin and end.[15] Over and over again, Wittgenstein wants us to expand our impoverished diet of philosophical examples, and out of the sacred inner recesses of our minds, out of the striving for connection with an unattainable world we can't reach, to take us to the activities we share, the interconnections between speech and action, and the background in place for a stretch of speech to be possible, to the conditions for mutual intelligibility.[16] Wittgenstein asks us to consider the myriad things we

---

[14] Paul Standish, "Crying and Learning to Speak," in *Mind, Language and Action: Proceedings of the 36th International Wittgenstein Symposium*, ed. Daniele Moyal-Sharrock (Berlin: De Gruyter, 2015), 493.

[15] "[T]his complicated form of life" is from Fragment i.1; "tapestry" can be found, for example, at Fragment i.2. "Weave" is a characteristic idiom, e.g., Preface, p. 3, and elsewhere.

[16] PI §593: "A main cause of philosophical diseases – a one-sided diet; one nourishes one's thinking with only one kind of example."

do with words, and takes us beyond an exclusive focus on naming, stating, or referring.[17] Putting weight on our agency in speech, glossing our agreement *in* rather than about judgments (PI §241), Cavell recalls two aspects of judgment in predication and proclamation. Here counting something as something, determining what it is (what it is called) depends on our calling it, proclaiming it, counting it under a concept at all.[18] Cavell, suggests that talking, claiming, calling, counting, are the major modes in which we word the world.[19] In a bravura passage in *The Claim of Reason*, he invokes J. L. Austin's idea that the distinctions in our language show the differences we have found worth making, as well as Wittgenstein's "surveyable representation" (*übersichtliche Darstellung*) of our use of words (PI §122):

> If to the pairs telling and counting, and counting and claiming, and claiming and acclaiming or clamoring, hence proclaiming and announcing, and denouncing and renouncing, and counting and recounting, or recounting and accounting, we add the notions of calling to account or accusing, hence excusing and explaining, and add computing and hence reputing and imputing; what we seem to be headed for is an idea that what can comprehensively be said is what is found to be worth saying.[20]

The relation at stake in this idea of speech is not between two things, mind and world, but rather between the people of the world in the world they share. Wittgenstein's vision of language shows that our language and the world are aligned in a range of speech acts: we can now talk about truth not alone in terms of whether a statement or a proposition is true, but whether it fits the circumstances, is appropriate, is right. We are asked to look at the "total speech act in the total situation," to align our language with the world.[21] Our agency in speech becomes central: Sandra Laugier has gone so far as to say that Wittgenstein reinvented subjectivity as voice.[22] Wittgenstein's understanding of linguistic agency shows us how we can deepen our historical understanding outside of causal explanations in the realm of speech as action, event, expression.

---

[17] *CR* 17.   [18] Ibid. 35.   [19] Ibid. 94.
[20] J. L. Austin, "A Plea for Excuses," in *Philosophical Papers* (Oxford: Clarendon, 1961); henceforth *PP*. Cf. *PP*: "Our common stock of words embodies all the distinctions men have found worth drawing, in the lifetimes of many generations" (82); and Cavell, *CR* 94.
[21] *HTD* 148.
[22] Sandra Laugier, developed in a series of articles, but see "Voice as Form of Life and Life Form."

Wittgenstein's vision of this talking life attunes us to the idea of culture as "the work of our life with language."[23]

Context/Use

In his introduction published in 1989, to Empson's *The Structure of Complex Words*, Jonathan Culler praises Empson's work for the subtlety of his grasp of context. Culler suggested that the invocation "of the social character of language and the need for reference to context is invariably a simplifying move, based on the assumption that the contextual determination will in fact produce more determinate meaning and thus cut down on the play of meaning, which is thought to be a function of decontextualization." He praises Empson, on the contrary, for showing that one cannot "oppose text to context" as if context "were something other than text."[24] Yet even though Culler sees these two views of context – the simplifying reductions of historicism and his version of Empson's view – as philosophically wide apart, the Augustinian picture of language is, in fact, common to both. Whether a piece of the world is brought in to narrow and determine the meaning of a passage or work, or word, or whether "context" is simply more text, an endless play of meanings, the picture is of a world (of objects, behaviors, etc.) and language that is not dependent on how *we* use words – that is, on what we are doing in speaking, or how a particular use contributes to the work being done. Culler is right that Empson's grasp of context is subtle but not for the reasons he gives.

Our historicism is better served by an idea of meaning as use, rather than an idea of context wedded unwittingly or not to an Augustinian picture of language. What gets elided in that picture is not only the particularity of the point in time, but the agency of the speaker. Literary historicism, since roughly the 1980s, has found multiple ways

---

[23] Stanley Cavell, "Declining Decline: Wittgenstein as a Philosopher of Culture," in *This New Yet Unapproachable America: Lectures After Emerson After Wittgenstein* (Albuquerque, NM: Living Batch Press, 1989), 48. This essay, along with Cavell's chapter, "Natural and Conventional" in *CR*, is one of the most original and profound readings of "forms of life." Here Cavell expounds an idea of culture as "system of modifications of our lives as talkers." "Culture as a whole is the work of our life with language, it goes with language, it is language's manifestation or picture or externalization" (48).

[24] Culler, introduction to *SCW* x–xi (Cambridge: Harvard University Press, 1989). For more on the picture of context in literary studies, see Rita Felski's chapter "Context Stinks!," in *The Limits of Critique* (Chicago, IL: University of Chicago Press, 2015), 151–185.

of evacuating agency from the author, character, and reader and granting mysterious agency to "the text," or language, rather than those who use it.[25]

Wittgenstein rarely uses the term context although that is the word the translators have frequently chosen in place of a variety of the words he actually uses. "*Zusammenhang*" is his most common word for context, but also *Verbindung, Geschichte, Situation* – connection/link, story, background, situation. *Zusammenhang* appears for example in PI §§161, 525, 584, 644, 665, and PPF vi §§38 and 39. As its component parts suggest "*Zusammenhang,*" is something like – "how something hangs or fits together (*zu/sammen/hangen*). And this is why understanding what something means is aligning words and world, seeing what goes together. The word invites perhaps the earlier sense I invoked by J. L. Austin – "the total speech act in the total situation."[26] It invites us, in a more Wittgensteinian idiom, to think about how things go or fit together.

We cannot, on this model, specify uses in advance, for Wittgenstein's picture is not a generalizable theory into which future cases fit (or not). Wittgenstein's investigations are necessarily retrospective in this sense: we can specify, and explore past uses. This is where dictionaries come in.

Dictionaries: OED

Wittgenstein's vision of language is historical through and through. It reveals the distinctions we have cared to make over many centuries of recorded history, the differences that have mattered to our kind in the full variety of endeavors. These differences, if they are alive in use, reveal us and our world. Furthermore, ordinary language philosophy's principal method is re-minder, and re-call, bringing words back (again and again) to their everyday use. Austin and Wittgenstein in different ways see the act of philosophy as an art of memory. We recall "what we should say *when*" (my italics) – in Austin's parlance, that is, to particular circumstances in time and place; and we recall and bring our words back to

---

[25] Toril Moi has addressed the question of agency in character in *Character: Three Inquiries in Literary* Studies, coauthored with Rita Felski and Amanda Anderson (Chicago, IL: University of Chicago, 2019).
[26] HTD 148: "The total speech act in the total speech situation is the *only actual* phenomenon which, in the last resort, we are engaged in elucidating."

use – that is to particular agents.[27] Wittgenstein says: "The work of the philosopher consists in marshalling recollections for a particular purpose."[28]

Wittgenstein's own simile for language is an *ancient* city: "a maze of little streets and squares, of old and new houses, with additions from various periods," in which there are also "new boroughs with straight regular streets and uniform houses."[29] In his book, *Philosophy and Ordinary Language: The Bent and Genius of Our Tongue*, Oswald Hanfling juxtaposes Wittgenstein's city of words with that of Descartes:

> Ancient cities which have gradually grown from mere villages into large towns are usually ill-proportioned, compared with those orderly towns which planners lay out as they fancy on level ground ... You would say it is chance, rather than the will of men using reason, that placed them so.[30]

The differences are striking and they are vital for thinking of Wittgenstein's vision of language as an essentially historical phenomenon. Descartes juxtaposes the work of chance with the work of reason: he prefers the utopian dream of the urban planner. Wittgenstein's ancient city contains those "straight regular streets and uniform houses" (one imagines boulevards, subdivisions), but they are a part and not the whole of his city. A planned city, as a planned language, has not gone well and it is hard to decide which is worse: Stevenage or Esperanto.[31] The past of Wittgenstein's linguistic city is alive, still there, shaping the paths we can travel. One can imagine cul-de-sacs, sprawl, ghettos, one-way streets, and gentrification, above all an unplanned mixture of ancient, old, and new. No single architect could have designed it, and it is never finished: "ask yourself whether our own language is complete" (PI §18). We did not start our language from scratch: it was there before us with its inherited structures and patterns and with an open-ended, unspecifiable future. It exists diachronically as well as synchronously, to use an older terminology.

---

[27] "When we examine what we should say when, what words we should use in what situations, we are looking again not *merely* at words ... but also at the realities we use words to talk about" (Ibid.).
[28] PI §127.   [29] Ibid. §18.
[30] *Philosophical Writings of Descartes*, trans. J. Cottingham (Cambridge: Cambridge University Press, 1985), 1/16, cited in Oswald Hanfling, *Philosophy and Ordinary Language: The Bent and Genius of Our Tongue* (London: Routledge, 200), 150.
[31] Wittgenstein did not think much of Esperanto either; see CV 52e.

One way of mapping an ancient city of words is with a historical dictionary. We can think of a historical dictionary such as the OED as a kind of map of the ancient city of a native language. Dictionaries try to keep up with our creative and ever-changing lives with language because, as Chaucer said, "in forme of speche is chaunge."[32] Now that the OED is published online it is easier to see the monthly new additions, for example. At the time of writing "plant-based" and "LOL" have been added, showing not simply that veganism is now more mainstream, but that abbreviations are part of a texting culture, one, apparently, that has lots of love to give. The OED is also a record of words that have fallen out of circulation and become obsolete. Moi calls a dictionary a "snapshot of our speaking and writing practices at a given historical moment."[33] It is the historicity of the moment(s) that I wish to stress for the purpose of this chapter.

The OED, seventy years in the making, first published in its entirety in 1933 as the *New English Dictionary on Historical Principles* (NED)was the first diachronic dictionary. The citations of distinctive uses of words make up well over half of the dictionary's entire text.[34] Its two and a half million quotations are culled from a huge variety of materials written in English from the middle of the twelfth century onwards. The design of the NED was to "furnish a complete account of the present meaning and past history of every English word whatsoever now in use, or shown to have been in use."[35] That means that the dictionary would not contain malapropisms or nonce-words. For a malapropism was a creative *mis*use of a word: in a mournful conversation about all our friends and acquaintances who were suffering from cancer, my mother said: "yes, it is very popular these days, isn't it?", now, naturally, a family joke. "Noncewords" are James Murray's coinage for words made for one occasion only and incapable of extension to other uses.

Any earlier fantasies about the linking of the OED to an "English Academy" along the lines of the French Academy that would contain, correct, or police was dispelled from the beginning (though not without

---

[32] *Troilus and Criseyde*, Book 2, 1.22, *The Riverside Chaucer*, ed. Larry D. Benson (Boston, MA: Houghton Mifflin, 1987).
[33] Moi, *Revolution of the Ordinary*, 33.
[34] Donna Lee Berg, *A Guide to the Oxford English Dictionary* (Oxford: Oxford University Press, 1993), 3.
[35] Lynda Mugglestone, *Lost for Words: The Hidden History of the Oxford English Dictionary* (New Haven, CT: Yale University Press, 2005), 71.

argument.)[36] For the dictionary, as Samuel Johnson had sagely said in his own famous one, was "the work of man from whom permanence or stability cannot be delivered."[37]

Recall here that Wittgenstein had considered as an epigraph to the *Investigations* a quotation from King Lear: "I'll teach you differences."[38] The first editor of the OED, Herbert Coleridge, a young man of twenty-seven years old, made the first list of words to be included in the dictionary, and he established principles that would be followed by other editors. He would read through the citations on the famous "slips" that formed the basis of lexicographical work – so that he could compare different senses and distinguish which ones merely reduplicated each other, and which made significant distinctions – and if so, how profound or important.[39] The early editors established a protocol whereby they collected hundreds of thousands of "slips" compiled at first by members of the Philological Society, but later by people throughout the British Empire. The slips were written on half of a piece of writing paper with this systematized format: the headword was at the top left with the quotation written below, with a separate slip for each quotation.[40] Words no longer in use were pronounced obsolete ("obs.") but entered, and eventually each word was complexly cross-referenced so that the dictionary is precisely a weave or web of words with myriad interconnections. In the 1989 edition of the OED, there are altogether 290,500 quotations showing the distinct uses of words. The online edition adds hundreds of words and examples every month; for example, 400 new entries have been added in the month I am writing these words.[41] Thus the citations, the usages, play a constitutive role, providing not "meanings" but distinctions people have cared to make.

Dictionaries are not much good for beginners in a language precisely because so much has to be in place for them to help.[42] Empson tells a

---

[36] Mugglestone cites some fascinating fantasies along those lines; see *Lost for Words*, 143.
[37] Cited by Mugglestone, *Lost for Words*, 161.
[38] Ray Monk, *Ludwig Wittgenstein: The Duty of Genius* (New York: The Free Press, 1990), 536–537.
[39] Simon Winchester, *The Meaning of Everything: The Story of the Oxford English Dictionary* (Oxford: Oxford University Press, 2003), 54.
[40] Winchester, *Meaning of Everything*, 57.
[41] The third edition of the OED is now in process: https://public.oed.com/history/oed-editions/preface-to-the-third-edition.
[42] This is a significant point in Cavell's examination of "umiak" in *Must We Mean What We Say?* 19–20: "We were all prepared for that umiak." Investigating the world and the word come to the same thing because we learn word and world together. Whether we

lovely story about some student essays on *King Lear* he read when he was teaching in Japan.[43] He found it difficult to explain to Japanese students the complexity of the word "quite," and why certain formulations about the play did not sound right: "the death of Lear is quite tragic"; "the Fool was quite a nice friend for Lear."[44] Most native speakers come to the dictionary with specific inquiries in mind when all else is in place for them to find the word they want, lack, or can't recognize.

A historical dictionary renders meaning through examples of use. Empson himself assiduously added to the dictionary and regarded his own work as an important lexicographical intervention.

The Structure of Complex Words

If you happen to look up the word "possess" in the OED, you will find the following definition under the bolded word: **possess** v. trans. 5b: "to gain sexual possession of (a woman), to have sexual intercourse with."[45] The "of (a woman)" might now seem tin-eared or sexist. But Empson, who made many suggestions to the OED's editors, was delighted that it was included. Under 5b you will find Thomas Kyd, Shakespeare, James Joyce, and others in their company as instances of this use.

According to Stefan Collini, *SCW* is "one of the great unvisited monuments of literary criticism."[46] Collini and Helen Thaventhiran, the editors of the magnificent new critical edition, speculate that the fields it abuts and combines in its inimitable, creative way – linguistics and philosophy – were becoming increasingly professionalized. The increasing professionalism of those disciplines might have made the work seem idiosyncratic, unacademic, unavailable. And although *SCW* always had a small but appreciative following – Empson has even been claimed as a

---

look up the word "umiak" in the dictionary or come across a small Inuit boat in a Northern clime and are told what it is called, in both cases we are aligning word and world, and a great deal already needs to be in place for this naming to be so much as possible.

[43] Empson does not specify the occasion, but he taught in Tokyo in the early 1930s, taking up a position at the University of Literature and Sciences. See John Haffenden, *Among the Mandarins* (Oxford: Oxford University Press, 2005).
[44] *SCW* 23.
[45] Noted by Charlotte Brewer, *Treasure House of the Language: The Living OED* (New Haven, CT: Yale University Press, 2007), 75, 166.
[46] Stefan Collini, *The Nostalgic Imagination: History in English Criticism* (Oxford: Oxford University Press, 2019), 115. Collini's chapter was a major inspiration for my turn to Empson in this chapter.

deconstructionist *avant la lettre* – the new (post-Saussurean) paradigms that swept all in their wake did not help to make the book "available."[47] In a highly generalized assimilation of Empson to New Criticism, he was dismissed in company with Cleanth Brooks, Yvor Winters, and the whole Cambridge crowd who had learned from I. A. Richards and F. R. Leavis. He was a "words on the page man."[48] In the polarized climate of the time, (underwritten as it was by the Augustinian picture of language) this meant he *must* be asocial and ahistorical, interested in form only.

He did indeed work close up in and with language; he had an astonishingly subtle and well attuned ear and he trusted it too. Yet this very quality – so personal, if not downright quirky, added to his taste for the most precise and telling distinctions, the sheer range of his reading across demotic, everyday, and literary uses, his habit of happy paraphrase for getting at meanings, and all this delivered with a mischievous joy and relish in language and literature as a reader and writer – these features helped to obscure the profound and original historicism as well as the historical significance of his work. There is no earnest self-importance about Empson's work; no sense that you have to be dismal to be serious, or that you might not trust your reader and keep her in mind at every point. His provocative and bluff casualness, love of colloquialisms such as "blowing the gaff" (a favorite), his irrepressible sense of humor, nicely aimed, and possibly the alarming fact that *SCW* contained pages of algebra also obscured the book's ethical and historical implications. Collini's *The Nostalgic Imagination* has argued convincingly that Empson is in fact "an idiosyncratic but unusually interesting historian of English ethical life."[49] To read him is to attune your own ear, and to be invited to a share an inheritance. Like Wittgenstein he encouraged us

---

[47] See Culler's introduction to the 1989 edition of *SCW*. Christopher Norris's important book on Empson showed just how far he was from the New Critics for whom he was mistaken; see Christopher Norris, *William Empson and the Philosophy of Literary Criticism* (London: Athlone Press, 1978). The phrase "post-Saussurean" comes from Toril Moi, who uses it to characterize the picture of meaning underlying a great many contemporary critical theories deriving ultimately from Saussure; see chapter 5 of Moi, *Revolution of the Ordinary*. The Saussurean picture is a version of what Wittgenstein called the Augustinian picture.

[48] This is an inaccurate understanding of Empson's vision of language; see William Empson, *Arguifying: Essays on Literature and Culture* (Iowa City, IA: University of Iowa Press, 1988), 125.

[49] Collini, *Nostalgic Imagination*, 116.

to "look and see," to resist the craving for generality by bracing and meticulous examinations of particular words, particular cases.[50]

Empson owes no explicit or formal debts to Wittgenstein and appeared not to have met him, although Wittgenstein appeared in one of his poems. Their circles in Cambridge definitely overlapped, for Wittgenstein was a charismatic, even infamous figure there. In *SCW*, Empson, like Wittgenstein, regards language as something we live in: like Austin, he respects the language of talkers: "talkers are often casual and often silly but they are up to something."[51] This Empsonian colloquialism precisely captures the point that talkers are doing something, and gives a lovely allowance for whatever interesting mischief they might be up to.

SCW considers some overlooked and workmanlike words: all, fool, sense, wit, dog, and honest. Tracking the use of these words in a variety of texts from the Renaissance to the Restoration, Empson showed how the words, or rather their uses, carry a resonant, far-reaching ethical and philosophical charge. He called them "vague, rich, intimate words" and claimed that part of his project in *SCW* was to illuminate words that could give a "period style."[52] In a short chapter such as this, where I aim to show Empson is exemplary of a persistently overlooked, historical mode of criticism attuned to meaning as use, I can only give a flavor of Empson at work. I focus on his playful, rich yet far-reaching chapter on the English Dog.

Empson's English Dog

Collini likens the layout of *SCW* to an outer ring of barbed wire surrounding an inner ring of ditches and ha-has, surrounding a labyrinth.[53] The first two chapters and the last six are more theoretical and philosophical, and importantly, written after the chapter on individual words, drafted over a number of years. The chapter on the English Dog is somewhere in the labyrinth after "wit" and "fool."

---

[50] Wittgenstein, PI §66, *The Blue and Brown Notebooks: Preliminary Studies for the 'Philosophical Investigations'* (New York: Harper and Row, 1960), 17.
[51] *SCW* 37.
[52] "Vague, rich, intimate" is from *SCW* 149. "Clearing up the feeling of period style" was an aim of the book; see 73.
[53] Collini, *Nostalgic Imagination*, 116.

Empson examines – with perfect pitch – how a variety of writers use the word "dog" over a considerable period of time. It is clear to me that he must have known G. K. Chesterton's Father Brown quip: "I always like a dog, as long as it isn't spelt backwards" and enjoyed using it against Chesterton's Christian orthodoxy (more than a bugbear of Empson's). "Compare the sound God, which begins at the back of your throat, a profound sound, with which you are intimately connected ("ich"), and then stretches right across to a point above the teeth, from back to front, from low to high, with a maximum extension and exultation."[54] In dog, he suggests, you do this backwards. The "do" sound is all at the front, the vowel taking it backward, moving the tongue up and down as if it might eject what is in it. "Then, (with a sudden movement of affection, or a discovery of the truth, or a final anathema), the word reaches across to something deep, personal in you, and despised."[55] This is splendid, accurate, pleasurable, a gentle cocking a snook at Father Brown. Empson has slowed us down to remind us of the sensuous joy in speaking. But if we are in danger of thinking this approach linguistically myopic, mere technical swagger, Empson ranges over sixteenth-century rogue literature, Restoration theater, Nashe, Jonson, Shakespeare, Dryden, Fielding, Shakespeare, and the OED uses, as well as those in common parlance, to sound the range of the word. He argues that from the sixteenth to the eighteenth century "dog" is released from its associations with lowliness, cowering, scorn, filth, and sycophancy. From a creature who lives on scraps, associated with habits both fawning and vicious, and with the philosophic etymology of the cynic, hence pissing at the world, *canis familiaris* begins to accommodate affectionate, even admiring acceptance of the dog in us. The rogue shaking his ears like a dog in sixteenth-century rogue pamphlets, recently compiled by A. V. Judges and reviewed by Empson, is his cue.[56] And he finds other examples of the dog's sexually loose manners, his "dogged" truthfulness and loyalty, and those features, coupled with his cleverness and carelessness of his own dignity, become worthy of respect, and approval. Empson leads us through a series of textured instances, sounding out on our ear the range of doggish responses in his canine repertoire of humanity. From these detailed soundings he makes the following claim: "Dog, it is absurd but half-true to say, became to the eighteenth-century skeptic

---

[54] *SCW* 154 [55] Ibid. 154.
[56] A. V. Judges, *The Elizabethan Underworld* (London: Routledge, 1930). Empson's review is included in the new edition of *SCW* 393.

what God had been to his ancestors, the last security behind human values."[57]

Empson has traced these subtleties through what he calls the "shrubbery" of smaller ideas "which may be the most important part of their influence."[58] He is tracing, therefore, the growth of a kind of humanism, a quiet, unannounced rebellion against the culture's long and strong streak of Puritanism, and accompanying hypervigilance of human appetites. Here is where human relations happen – in the intimate, vague, and rich words of everyday life. Dog is thus in this period a "complex" word, that is, part of an established, yet overlooked use, moreover a use, that once grasped, gives us, precisely, the feel and flavor of what we call a "period."

Empson is attuned to minute registers that reveal a large historical landscape. You need to know, he said, "as well as all the serious opinions of a man in a society, how much weight he would allow, when making a practical decision, to some odd little class of joke phrases, such as excite, he would feel, sentiments obvious to any agreeable person, and yet carry such doctrines more really complex than the whole structure of his official view of the world."[59] Collini calls this a kind of "informal intellectual history."[60]

The first two chapters in Empson's book are "Feelings in Words" and "Statements in Words." Those designations – and his attack on behaviorism in his Appendices – show him to be concerned about a fundamental intellectual climate that gripped philosophy and adjacent "sciences" in the mid-twentieth century. The prevailing atmosphere of that philosophical culture is hard to recall. Cavell gives us a flavor of it in his memoir, *Little Did I Know*. He recalls a conversation between Hans Meyerhoff and a young teaching assistant in the logic course he was taking, in the exultant and exorbitant mood of the time. "We know now," said the teaching assistant, around whom a small crowd of students was gathering, "that every assertion is either true or false or else neither true nor false; in the former case the assertion is meaningful, in the latter case cognitively meaningless. If you go on saying to me that this line of Rilke's is cognitively meaningful, I smile at you."[61] In his memoir, *Little Did I Know,* Cavell declares that discovering an adequate mode of response

---

[57] *SCW* 157. [58] Ibid. 149. [59] Ibid. 163. [60] Collini, *Nostalgic Imagination,* 119.
[61] Stanley Cavell, *Little Did I Know: Excerpts from Memory* (Stanford, CA: Stanford University Press, 2010), 252–253.

to such assaults "became as if on the spot an essential part of my investment in what I would call philosophy."

Empson would prefer to avoid these "intellectual buzz-saws" but he understood clearly that such doctrines separate sense from emotion and render literary criticism "irrelevant," certainly frivolous, otiose as if when Keats said "Truth is Beauty," he "meant nothing at all except to excite emotion."[62] Empson says that we need a "more elaborate machinery" to disentangle the "Emotive from the Cognitive part of poetical language": "such at least is my own excuse for offering my own bits of machinery"[63] for "interpreting a word's action."[64] In so doing, as Alan Durant and Colin MacCabe have argued, Empson claims "serious investigative and epistemological rights for poetry."[65]

In one of the most devastatingly critical and profound chapters in *The Claim of Reason*, Cavell, who agrees with Empson on this score, shows that emotivism (in this case as represented by Stevenson's *Ethics and Language*) simply evacuated the moral terrain.[66] The chapter is called "An Absence of Morality." In Part 3 of *The Claim of Reason* he builds on the distinctions between "must" and "ought" so central to the path-breaking title essay of *Must We Mean What We Say?* Ought is prescriptive: must is normative. Ought implies there are other paths to take, though they might not be advisable according to you: if you say, "are you wearing that dress voluntarily?" you must mean there is something odd about it. That implication is necessary, a question of logic, not psychology.

Empson's quarrel with these destructive paradigms is similarly personal. When Empson explored "Implications," he dealt at once with the conditions and consequences of speech. His work then sees no distinction between doing historical and ethical work. For to understand what has to be in place for a stretch of speech to be possible, and to see (sometimes slowly, not at all, or in a flash) the implications of what we've said is to bring in our endless responsibility as language users. Empson, as I've said, never adopts a tone of high seriousness, yet the ethical import of his work is undisputable.

So his work is personal both in making a place for the personal in criticism, but also for trusting his own responses to what he reads. This

---

[62] SCW 13,14,18.   [63] Ibid. 18.   [64] Ibid. 20.
[65] Alan Durant and Colin MacCabe, "Compacted Doctrines: Empson and the Meaning of Words," in *William Empson: The Critical Achievement*, eds. Christopher Norris and Nigel Mapp (Cambridge: Cambridge University Press, 1993), 170–195.
[66] Emotivism posits moral judgments as expressions of feelings in contradistinction to propositions, assertions, or statements of fact.

does not mean he does not educate those intuitions, or follow what Cavell, in Emersonian mood, calls the tuition of his intuitions.[67] It means he starts there in an art and act of attention. We might find we are converted in our understanding of a piece at work because of what he has pointed out, or we might want to argue with him (he would have loved that too). Finding Empson inspirational (or Wittgenstein or Cavell) does not then mean that we need to reproduce their critical insights, tone, or approach. But we might be inspired to test out our own responses, which means being alert to them, and following them.

You might start with a dictionary in your investigation, as both Austin and Empson loved to do. Austin says a concise one will do. Richard Fleming started with one for his extraordinary book on evil; Stanley Cavell offered us his permanently useful "umiak"; Toril Moi meditates on Spanish bull-fighting – what we won't get from a dictionary, but only by grasping the very practice of the *corrida*.[68] I began my book on forgiveness with the telling differences between pardon, absolution, and forgiveness in the changing understandings of those speech acts in Shakespeare and the English Reformation.[69] The words can be "vague, rich, intimate" as long as we make them ours and see what they do in the mouths of others.

In times as troubling and divided as ours, such humane criticism might, through its great respect for the teaching of differences, show us forms of life we share.

---

[67] Stanley Cavell, *Disowning Knowledge in Seven Plays of Shakespeare* (Cambridge: Cambridge University Press, 1987), 5.
[68] Richard Fleming, *Evil and Silence* (Boulder, CO: Paradigm Publishers, 2010), 132.
[69] Sarah Beckwith, *Shakespeare and the Grammar of Forgiveness* (Ithaca, NY: Cornell University Press, 2011).

5 Wittgenstein and the Prospects for a Contemporary Literary Humanism

Espen Hammer

Abstract: According to Rita Felski, literary studies have for too long been restricted to what Paul Ricoeur famously called the "hermeneutics of suspicion." It should now return to the text itself as a locus not only of power, interest, and domination, but of literary value, inviting engagement intellectually, emotionally, and imaginatively. Via a reading of Wittgenstein's work on aesthetics, including his conception of aspect-perception, this chapter reflects on Felski's proposal, arguing that its opposition between suspicion and humanism might be too simple. While Wittgenstein offers a powerful defense of a humanist view according to which a literary text encourages responsiveness to expressive meaning, it is argued that his view can be extended to include meaning constituted in various historical contexts as well. As a result, the text, as Adorno and Said claim, can never escape its dual determination as both worldly and inherently meaningful.

Keywords: Rita Felski, Edward Said, Theodor Adorno, Hermeneutics of Suspicion, Literary Humanism, Aspect Perception, Expressive Meaning, Meaning & Interpretation, Modernism, Aesthetic Predicates, Aesthetic Autonomy.

In her 2015 *The Limits of Critique*, Rita Felski starts her influential discussion of the state and fate of literary studies by asking why literature matters. While to an outsider the question seems straightforward, a common response within the discipline, she notices, is to question the question. Values, it is being claimed, especially regarding such creations as literary texts, express particular points of view. Rather than admitting of "objectivity," "truth," or "adequacy," such points of view are constituted and sustained within more or less opaque contexts of power, interest, and domination, suggesting structures of meaning and sense-making over which the individual, purportedly responsible for the writing or reading of a text, has little or no control. Thus, rather than articulating value, which is thought to be naive and dogmatic, the theorist should demystify, destabilize, and denaturalize – in short, interrogate the text and the meaning it expresses by seeking to reveal its "constitutive other." Suspicion, Felski argues, has for at least half a century been both the mood and the method of literary studies: "Academics thrive in the rarefied air of meta-commentary, honing their ability to complicate and problematize, to turn statements about the world into statements about the forms of discourse in which they are made. We conduct such interrogations endlessly, and in our sleep. When asked to justify our attachments and defend our commitments, however, we often flounder and flail about."[1]

For a number of reasons – waning student numbers, diminishing career opportunities, insufficient funding, digitalization, commodification, and instrumentalization of research and higher education, but perhaps also its incessant skepticism about human expression and the concomitant desire to decenter and deconstruct its own discourses – practitioners of literary studies seem to find themselves in a deep legitimation crisis, struggling to justify their existence and demonstrate the value of their activities. Despite the general skepticism about value-statements just mentioned, the way they go about doing this ranges widely and includes both neoconservative ("canon-preserving") and neopositivist (or objectivist) proposals.[2]

Felski's own suggestion consists in calling for what she refers to as "postcritical reading," a form of engagement with literary texts that, unlike the still reigning "hermeneutics of suspicion" (Ricoeur), which always looked behind the text for hidden causes and motives, aims to return the text to the reader as a repository of meanings to be reflected upon, emotionally moved by, and imaginatively recreated.[3] Granting that interpreters will always be faced with a rich and sometimes unruly

---

[1] Rita Felski, *The Limits of Critique* (Chicago, IL and London: The University of Chicago Press, 2015), 15.
[2] Harold Bloom might be the most influential proponent of canon-preservation. Lisa Zunshine's cognitive literary studies and Franco Moretti's materialistic, empirical approach to the study of literature count in my view as examples of neopositivism.
[3] In *Freud and Philosophy: An Essay on Interpretation*, trans. Denis Savage (New Haven, CT: Yale University Press, 1970), 33, Paul Ricoeur refers to Marx, Nietzsche, and Freud as the three "masters of suspicion." For a book-length study of Ricoeur's account of the hermeneutics of suspicion, see Alison Scott-Baumann, *Ricoeur and the Hermeneutics of Suspicion* (New York: Continuum, 2009). For other discussions of Ricoeur's phrase, see Ruthellen Josselson, "The Hermeneutics of Faith and the Hermeneutics of Suspicion," *Narrative Inquiry* 14 (1):

surplus of meaning, Felski warns against viewing that surplus in light of some unified master trope of extratextual facts that explains the manifest meaning of the text. Rather, what should always be in the foreground is a commitment to the text as a phenomenon to be *engaged with*.

While I applaud this change of focus and epistemic interest, I agree with Felski that a straightforward replacement of the one with the other – of, say, antihumanism with humanism – can all too easily lapse into the dogmatic conservatism from which much of the field of literary studies has striven for so long to liberate itself. When she presents her positive view, however, Felski gestures more than she explicates and explains. She neither provides an account of the relation between critique and reading nor formulates a rigorous view of the nature of textual presence.

Taking Theodor W. Adorno's thesis about the twofold essence of art as my starting-point, I will claim that Ludwig Wittgenstein, while not explicitly a philosopher of literary experience, has a lot to offer when it comes to articulating the return to the literary text as an educative and self-forming exercise and project. Without lapsing into a discourse of origins and essences, Wittgenstein places the literary text firmly within the social world while rescuing its capacity to address, engage, and provoke. I plead for such a view of Wittgenstein by invoking and analyzing his late notion of the physiognomy of words. Although this concept does not receive any extended attention in his writings, it suggestively complements Wittgenstein's long-standing emphasis on the importance of capacities of discernment and reception in understanding. While the Wittgenstein I bring forward advocates a view of literary experience as relatively autonomous, I point out that, far from rejecting the activities associated with a hermeneutics of suspicion, his view of language-games allows for a number of equally legitimate approaches to a text. Some of these can involve what Felski (following Ricoeur) calls "suspicion." Drawing on some remarks by Edward Said, I end the chapter by calling for a renewed humanism based on Wittgensteinian premises.

Wittgenstein on Aesthetic Appreciation

Felski's approach to literary texts tends to base itself on an appeal to the excluded middle: either texts are, as orthodoxy holds, "heteronomous,"

1–28 (2004); and David Stewart, "The Hermeneutics of Suspicion," *Journal of Literature and Theology* 3 (3): 296–307 (1989).

calling for a type of analysis that places them firmly within socially structured contexts of power and ideology, *or*, as she wants to emphasize, they are relatively autonomous objects that allow for an engagement with strings of words as predominantly expressive, inviting readings and interpretations that pay attention to their unique ability to move and enlighten their audiences. But must we choose between the two? Might not the disjunction be inclusive, involving some degree of acceptance of both alternatives? Felski strikes me as deeply ambiguous on this point. On the one hand, she admits that suspicion and critique have been doing some good and should not be given up entirely. On the other hand, following the lead of Ricoeur's hermeneutics of trust, she proposes a reading that "restores" the text and that she thinks might help us "to articulate a positive vision for humanistic thought in the face of growing skepticism about its value."[4]

In the *Aesthetic Theory*, Theodor W. Adorno submits the following reflection, well worth quoting:

The double character of art – something that severs itself from empirical reality and thereby from society's functional context and yet is at the same time part of empirical reality and society's functional context – is directly apparent in the aesthetic phenomena, which are both aesthetic and *faits sociaux*. They require a double observation that is no more to be posited as an unalloyed whole than aesthetic autonomy and art can be conflated as something strictly social. This double character becomes physiognomically decipherable, whether intentionally so or not, when one views or listens to art from an external vantage point, and, certainly, art always stands in need of this external perspective for protection from the fetishization of its autonomy.[5]

Adorno offers a number of claims about the supposed double character of art. The two poles, he argues, tend to be mutually antagonistic, always resisting each other's appeals. While works of art can never escape their social determination, they can always resist it and struggle to secure their own autonomy. The two sides are endlessly at odds with one another. Yet, ultimately, each one of them is irreducible to the other.

The perhaps most difficult question in this passage is how the "double observation" of art can be achieved. How can two such opposed views be adopted simultaneously? Is Adorno making an epistemic point, claiming that the critic needs to employ two points of view – looking, as it were,

---

[4] Felski, *The Limits of Critique*, 186.
[5] Theodor W. Adorno, *Aesthetic Theory*, trans. Robert Hullot-Kentor (Minneapolis, MN: University of Minnesota Press, 1997), 252–253.

through two different lenses? Or is he rather making an ontological claim, suggesting that there are two incommensurable artistic or aesthetic realities? As I read him, bringing the double character of art into view requires the ability to entertain dual perspectives *and* attentiveness to how works of art in fact do display the relevant tension between heteronomy and autonomy. Indeed, many of his examples of such observational practices take the form of highlighting what he calls a protracted struggle buried within the works themselves. Enchanting and entertaining, drawing us to it as an object of consumption, the work seeks to be recognized as a commodity.[6] At the same time, however, certain works of art, by virtue of their internally imposed laws of form, resist their transformation into commodities, inviting their audiences to be receptive to their expressive qualities and, as Adorno adds, claims to possess truth-content (*Wahrheitsgehalt*).

Adorno makes a number of claims about how, especially in modern art, artistic form is able to countervail the alienating effects of reification. On his account, the tension between art's two poles reaches extreme levels in advanced modernist art such as Schoenberg's dodecaphonic music in which formal laws of self-organization – the strict rules associated with the twelve-tone row – are rigorously applied to the musical material. In such works, Adorno detects a privileged and unique mode of resistance to commodified society.

While Adorno highlights the dialectic and inner tension of aesthetic expression, his view of art and its potential for illumination and critique is deeply and perhaps exclusively beholden to the aesthetic commitments that were dominant in high culture during the historically specific period of high modernism. Wittgenstein, by contrast – at least so I will argue – while providing an account of aesthetic and literary expression that permits the critic to attend to the interplay between heteronomy and autonomy so crucial to Adorno, seems as interested in highlighting complex continuities between the two poles as he is to discuss discontinuities. In short, for Wittgenstein, art – and from now on I will primarily focus on literary works of art – brings culturally mediated meaning to expression in a *public* language, thereby offering spaces for a concentrated appreciation and discernment of both self and world.

---

[6] I aim to provide an account of this process in Espen Hammer, *Adorno's Modernism: Art, Experience, and Catastrophe* (Cambridge: Cambridge University Press, 2015), 95–100.

Apart from the occasional remark referring to aesthetic experience and works of art, Wittgenstein rarely addressed issues in aesthetics and literary studies. The one exception in which we find him paying extended attention to this set of topics is *Lectures on Aesthetics*, delivered to a private audience in Cambridge in the summer of 1938. Although the publication of these lectures is based on notes taken by his student Rush Rhees and cannot claim to be giving a verbatim report of what was said, they offer a unique and valuable insight into the philosopher's views of literary studies (or what he calls "poetical criticism"), connecting with and elaborating the thinking about language, language-games, and rule-following familiar from the *Philosophical Investigations* and much of the other late work.

Wittgenstein starts the lectures by polemicizing against the idea, familiar from the idealist philosophy of art from Plato and Aquinas to Kant, Hegel, Schopenhauer, and Croce, that aesthetics should be approached as a science aimed at clarifying certain generally occurring features of accomplished works of art such as the display of "beauty." To the extent that the subject of aesthetics is the nature of beauty – and hence of criteria for the rightful application of the term "beautiful" – it becomes, as he puts it, "entirely misunderstood" (LC 1). Attempting to support this view, Wittgenstein observes that adjectives like "beautiful" hardly play any role in competent aesthetic judging. Considered merely as an empirical observation, this claim might or might not be true. There are, of course, plenty of situations in which people will use them. Yet considered as moves within various language-games – which, after all, is where, for Wittgenstein, sense-making becomes possible – what kind of work do judgments such as "This is beautiful" actually do? (What is their relevant grammar?) The answer, Wittgenstein argues, is "very little." The predicate "beautiful" expresses approval. Yet observing someone characterizing a poem as beautiful does not tell us much about what it is that person actually finds in the poem to make it deserving of approbation. Indeed, calling a poem beautiful can be an expression of literary *incompetence*: it tends to be what someone will say who, while feeling that *something* needs to be said, finds nothing interesting or genuinely appropriate to say. Words like "beautiful" or "good" when considered merely as elements of sentences or judgments, and thus applicable "everywhere and nowhere in specific," are "entirely uncharacteristic" (LC 2) – semantically thin and with very limited capacity to bring a phenomenon into view and characterize it. The problem, one might say, hinges on the requirement, imposed by traditional aesthetics on its subject matter, of *abstraction*: that whatever qualifies as a suitable term on the basis of which to assess art must be applicable to some purportedly abstract and general feature of it, a feature that figures in all genuine instances and whose criteria of recognition are necessary and universal.[7] On such a view, to speak competently about art is to express sentences in which predicates of this kind are correctly employed. Although they must refer to particular objects, such expressions are "adequate" or "correct" only as carriers of semantic entities containing such abstract predicates.

In light of what has been said so far, one might think that the problem with traditional aesthetics has been its restrictive focus on certain highly general expressions. If it had picked fewer general ones, perhaps it would avoid the problem of abstraction. Yet Wittgenstein does not think that abstraction is only a function of generality. One might perfectly well come up with a revised list of aesthetic predicates and still find them empty when applied to actual works of art. For Wittgenstein, the real problem with traditional approaches to aesthetics consists rather in their tendency to consider language independently of its employment in actual language-games. It is there and there only that words make sense: "We don't start from certain words, but from certain occasions or activities" (LC 3).

On Wittgenstein's account, appreciation of art is akin to being initiated into, and mastering, the practices characteristic of a certain form of life or culture. There are rules entering into the understanding of what counts as a well-conducted performance of a Beethoven piece. There are things the teacher can state and make explicit. However, expert understanding can never be represented fully in those rules. Instead, one needs to be part of a whole culture surrounding the music:

> The words we call expressions of aesthetic judgement play a very complicated rôle, but a very definite rôle, in what we call a culture of a period. To describe their use or to describe what you mean by a cultured taste, you have to describe a culture. What we now call a cultured taste perhaps didn't exist in the Middle Ages. An entirely different game is played in different ages. (LC 8)

---

[7] In *Beyond Moral Judgment* (Cambridge, MA: Harvard University Press, 2007), 81, Alice Crary characterizes such an abstraction requirement as "a requirement to the effect that regularities constitutive of a sound discursive practice must transcend the practice in the sense of being discernible from a vantage point that abstracts from any sensitivities that we acquired in mastering it." She adds that "To say that Wittgenstein attacks such a requirement is to say that he attempts to subvert an understanding of the applications of words as fixed in a manner that is abstract in that it bypasses the need for reliance on acquired sensitivities."

Given the mastery that comes with this membership, genuine appreciation becomes possible. Someone who understands a piece of music will express this neither by using "interjections" ("Oh! How marvelous!") nor by putting forward aesthetic judgments of the formal kind just discussed ("This painting is beautiful"), but by being able to identify when it "works" and is "right" and to distinguish those cases from those that do not "work." The person of taste and appreciation displays competence by repeatedly being able to pass good judgments. In addition to knowing the language and a welter of facts and norms associated with the activity on display, such a person must have acquired, and be able to utilize and make evident, a particular kind of sensibility and "refined judgment." The connoisseur *reacts* aesthetically, expressing their reactions in a large range of different ways. Sometimes, such as when someone repeatedly returns to a painting or smiles during the performance of a particular passage in a sonata, it can be expressed tacitly. At other times, it can be expressed in various verbal responses, such as asking for a poem to be read differently or a painting to be hung higher on the wall. These are *criteria* of aesthetic competency; they tell us that someone knows what it is that really counts.

A proponent of what Alice Crary calls the "abstraction requirement" would at this point be likely to object to this line of reasoning by claiming that it proceeds by illicitly disregarding a necessary assumption. It is designed to bring us to say of someone who applies aesthetic predicates in a manner that we deem adequate that they are a competent critic. However, in order to deem the application of such predicates to be adequate, we must tacitly presuppose the possession of some general criterion or concept or rule that allows for the identification of specific cases as expressive of competence. In short, in order to tell that *this* is the competent thing to say, one must know what counts as being competent, and that has got to involve knowledge of some abstract, case-transcending rule. To explicitly say that there can be no such rule seems to be tantamount to saying that one can judge blindly, without rational grounding, and still count as competent.[8] In considering this objection from a Wittgensteinian point of view, the salient point to make is that

---

[8] Pierre Bourdieu would account for such a view in terms of his notion of habitus. See his *Outline of a Theory of Practice*, trans. Richard Nice (New York and Cambridge: Cambridge University Press, 1977), 78–86. According to Bourdieu, agents are socialized into a system of aesthetic appreciation structured by socioeconomic stratification and class.

the sensitivities acquired in mastering the practice in question are sufficient to ensure the proper continuity of the practice. A connoisseur can, of course, ponder general questions related to art and take an interest in theory. Yet the extent to which we would deem her competent as a critic would still depend on whether or not she masters the requirements associated with the practice of judging itself. As we have seen, these requirements cannot be represented in very general rules (although rules do, for Wittgenstein, have a place in aesthetic assessment), but are displayed in individual cases to individuals sharing the same sensibilities.

In the *Lectures on Aesthetics*, Wittgenstein makes a considerable effort to distinguish aesthetic explanations and aesthetic behavior from causal explanations made within the context of psychology. While granting that a psychologist might conduct experiments seeking to uncover causal mechanisms accounting for so-called "aesthetic behavior," he sees his own investigation as oriented toward the "concept" or "grammar" of the aesthetic relation. Aesthetic responsiveness cannot as such be made sense of as the effect of some preceding cause. Rather, it involves various stances that agents take toward the aesthetic object. If someone were to "explain" their aesthetic judgment by pointing to its supposed cause, they would no longer speak intelligibly. By being evaluative, aesthetic judgments are rational in the sense that they implicate the recipient as an agent capable of freely figuring out what the right response might be in light of the encounter with the aesthetic object. Aesthetic reactions can, as mentioned, display a considerable degree of spontaneity and involve very little thought. However, they are not wrung out of us in the way snoring is when air flows past relaxed tissue in one's throat. They do not conform to the repetitive patterns expressed by natural law. As we respond intelligibly to a work of art, we make moves within language-games. In order to do that – and display competence by making meaningful remarks – we need to have cultivated an ability to respond to the particular features at hand. We must, as Wittgenstein often points out, be able to "know our way about" the object and be able to continue projecting our words and behavior into ever new contexts while, in each case, recognizing both their flexibility and limitations. Someone who, in place of proper aesthetic responsiveness, only referred to what, given the underlying causal mechanism, is believed to be statistically correct, would have substituted the first-person or performative orientation – one's ongoing response – for a third-person or objective stance. As a result, we would no longer acknowledge that person as displaying aesthetic behavior: we would not know them as being responsibly implicated in the experience.

Commenting on Wittgenstein's ideas of how words are legitimately projected into new contexts, Stanley Cavell points to the importance of being able not only to find "new potencies in words" but "new ways in which objects are disclosed":

> An object or activity or event onto or into which a concept is projected, must *invite* or *allow* that projection; in the way in which, for an object to be (called) an art object, it must allow or invite the experience and behavior which are appropriate or necessary to our concepts of the appreciation or contemplation or absorption ... of an art object.[9]

We must, in short, be able to entertain the object or activity or event under a certain *aspect* – in art, specifically, see it in such a way as to make sense of it as the expressive entity it purports to be. A poem, for example, if read in a certain way, might seem lifeless and uninteresting. In the *Lectures on Aesthetics*, Wittgenstein reports having had such an experience with the eighteenth-century poet Klopstock. However, reading his poems with extreme emphasis on their meter, he suddenly found that what had been "moderately boring" became "*grand*":

> Take the question: "How should poetry be read? What is the correct way of reading it?" If you are talking about verse the right way of reading it might be stressing it correctly – you discuss how far you should stress the rhythm and how far you should hide it. A man says it ought to be read *this* way and reads it out to you. You say: "Oh yes. Now it makes sense." ... I had an experience with the 18th-century poet Klopstock. I found that the way to read him was to stress his meter abnormally. Klopstock put ‿—‿ (etc.) in front of his poems. When I read his poems in this new way, I said: "Ah-ha, now I know why he did this." What had happened? I had read this kind of stuff and had been moderately bored, but when I read it in this particular way, intensely, I smiled, said: "This is *grand*," etc. But I might not have said anything. The important fact was that I read it again and again. When I read these poems I made gestures and facial expressions which were what would be called gestures of approval. But the important thing was that I read the poems entirely differently, more intensely, and said to others: "Look! This is how they should be read." Aesthetic adjectives played hardly any rôle. (LC 4–5)

Like Kant, Wittgenstein does take aesthetic judgment to aspire to universality. It is not merely "subjective." The good tailor, the good

---

[9] Stanley Cavell, *The Claim of Reason: Wittgenstein, Skepticism, Morality, and Tragedy* (New York: Oxford University Press, 1979), 180, 183.

musician, or the good critic does not say "*this* is right" or "this is grand," etc. while adding "for me." He believes his interlocutor should agree, since not agreeing to "what is right" strikes him as irrational or somehow being in denial of the facts. However, his claim to rightness cannot be proven, if by proof one means the appeal to some sort of rule or criterion that, independently of one's response to the work, is supposed to decide for us. As for Kant, the universality at stake is based on the speaker's own response, for which he takes a certain degree of responsibility, but which at the same time will have to be based on acts of initiation and training.[10] Rather than pointing to a rule, he will have you see what he sees, respond the way he responds. Of course, both parties can find their own responses to be nonideal or inadequate. Faced with a Picasso painting or a Beethoven sonata, one might feel humble, limited in one's ability to truly appreciate it. The speaker might find he needs to know more. Or he might call on his interlocutor to become better educated. However, no authority can exist in these matters absent the willingness to insist on a particular way of seeing and experiencing the work as being *the right one*. When confronted with someone who most definitely is not willing or able to entertain a work of art the way you do, there is not much more to say. The discussants or critics will then perhaps have to conclude that they do not share the same sensibilities.

Unlike Kant, whose account of pure judgments of taste excludes all reason-giving, Wittgenstein believes that discourse should normally play a role in the formation of aesthetic judgments. Yet, rather than to prove anything, the aim of discourse is fundamentally to bring the critic's audience to *see* what the critic sees. Commenting on this implication of Wittgenstein's aesthetic reflections, Cavell writes the following:

> It is essential to making an aesthetic judgment that at some point we be prepared to say in its support: don't you see, don't you hear, don't you dig? The best critic will know the best points. Because if you do not see *something*, without explanation, then there is nothing further to discuss. Which does not mean that the critic has no recourse: he can start training and instructing you and preaching at you – a direction in which criticism invariably will start to veer. ... At some

---

[10] Kant expresses this thought in many different ways. In the context of Wittgenstein studies, a particularly revealing way of doing so is by way of the notion of *exemplarity*, of taking one's judgment to be exemplary of how all agents should react. See Immanuel Kant, *Critique of the Power of Judgment*, trans. Paul Guyer and Eric Matthews (New York: Cambridge University Press, 2000), 121.

point, the critic will have to say: This is what I see. Reasons – at definite points, for definite reasons, in different circumstances – come to an end.[11]

I mentioned aspects and aspect-perception, suggesting that the temporally extended capacity to see a work of art under a certain aspect is a crucial criterion of what counts as appreciating it.[12] The *Lectures on Aesthetics* were presented in 1938, and yet most of Wittgenstein's writing on aspect-perception, including the famous entries in what has traditionally been called *Philosophical Investigations*, Part II, as well as the late remarks on the philosophy of psychology collected in the *Remarks on the Philosophy of Psychology* and *Last Writings on the Philosophy of Psychology*, was being done after the war and as late as immediately before his death in 1951. However, judging from many of the remarks in the *Lectures on Aesthetics*, he is definitely anticipating, and making use of, many of the insights that appear more explicitly and with greater concentration some years later. This can certainly be said about the Klopstock example, where "seeing" the poem in the "right" way is crucial. However, the many remarks about seeing something in the right way, getting the object into view, and how important these capacities are for aesthetics and aesthetic behavior, point fairly unequivocally toward the general topic of aspect-perception. Indeed, in the *Lectures on Aesthetics* Wittgenstein employs several of the key concepts later used to elucidate the nature of seeing something under an aspect. One such concept is that of "attitude" (*Einstellung*). As we take up different attitudes to the seen, its valences, its modes of presentation, change. The attitude, Wittgenstein further argues, is expressed in the ongoing and culturally mediated ways in which a person goes on responding to the object. It reveals what something is being treated *as*. Moreover, what one sees in a work of art must be distinguished from the visual impression one might have of it. No change in what one sees in a painting (or "how it is seen") can be registered by replicating – perhaps by making a drawing – the visual impression. The experience is nevertheless immediate, leaving no room for distinguishing meaningfully between the object and how you see it.

---

[11] Stanley Cavell, *Must We Mean What We Say? A Book of Essays* (New York: Cambridge University Press, 1976), 93.
[12] For what is still the best book-length study of Wittgenstein's reflections on aspect-perception, see Stephen Mulhall, *On Being in the World: Wittgenstein and Heidegger on Seeing Aspects* (New York: Routledge, 1990). See also Avner Baz, "What's the Point of Seeing Aspects?," *Philosophical Investigations* 23 (2): 97–122 (2000).

When you "get it," the Klopstock ode you refer to does not count as an interpretation. You refer to the poem itself.

Wittgenstein's later account of "seeing-as" and aspect-perception revolves around precisely these concepts – attitude, expressive behavior, and responsiveness within culturally shaped environments, and the immediate beholding of something as something. In the *Philosophical Investigations*, Wittgenstein introduces the notion of "noticing an aspect" by reflecting on how a face can be seen differently when one notices its likeness to another:

> I observe a face, and then suddenly notice its likeness to another. I *see* that it has not changed; and yet I see it differently. I call this experience "noticing an aspect." (PPF xi §113)

As Wittgenstein acknowledges, the account seems paradoxical. The face *has not changed*, and yet to the person viewing it, it looks different. In the more well-known example of Jastrow's ambiguous figure of the duck-rabbit, a viewer can see it either as a duck or a rabbit; and there can either be a "continuous seeing" of one aspect to the exclusion of the other or a sudden "dawning" of an aspect. What accounts for the capacity to see one and the same image, an image that does not change, in two mutually excluding ways?

Accounts appealing to interpretation fail for the simple reason that they set up an untenable distinction between direct and indirect descriptions of the object. One sees something, an object, immediately – and yet one refuses to describe it as such. Instead, one claims to be referring to it indirectly, via the interpretation being offered. However, if there is, in fact, a visual experience of something, then it must be possible to describe it directly. The experience of the duck in the picture of the duck-rabbit can indeed be described directly: it is a duck that one sees. Behind this objection to the interpretation-view lies Wittgenstein's resistance to any views purporting to posit some sort of "neutral" world behind the one we in fact engage with.

Classical Gestalt theory adopted another approach. According to Wolfgang Köhler, whose work Wittgenstein studied, it is the organization of sensory content that changes when one experiences Gestalt switches.[13] In addition to shape and color, sensory content always appears to us as having a certain "organization" or "meaning."

---

[13] According to Joachim Schulte, *Experience and Expression: Wittgenstein's Philosophy of Psychology* (Oxford: Clarendon Press, 1993), 76, Köhler's work was "the most important

However, the purported change in the sensory content cannot be represented. If someone were to represent the change in their impression when the duck becomes a rabbit in the image of the duck-rabbit, they would simply keep drawing the same figure, namely the duck-rabbit. The aspect, in other words, under which we see something "as something," cannot be considered on a par with the object's shape and color. If it is, then the aspect becomes oblique and impossible to represent.

As already intimated from our reading of the *Lectures on Aesthetics*, when, according to Wittgenstein, someone sees something *as* something – for example a two-dimensional drawing as a three-dimensional figure – they treat it in certain ways (to the exclusion of others); thus what counts as an account of the phenomenon of seeing-as will be based neither on an appeal to interpretation nor to an attempt to identify some ineffable inner object, but will be oriented around an observation of the ongoing and fine-grained behavior of the viewer, how she *treats* the drawing: "What convinces us that someone is seeing the drawing three-dimensionally is a certain kind of 'knowing one's way about': certain gestures, for instance, which indicate the three-dimensional relations – fine shades of behaviour" (PPF xi §180). The attitude toward the drawing, Wittgenstein adds, becomes possible because the viewer has come to master a technique: they have been initiated into a certain practice, involving conceptual determination, imaginative projection of concepts, as well as abilities to both do things with the object and entertain nuances. The criteria of competence are revealed in the behavior, what one does with the object.

Among the examples Wittgenstein offers of aspect-perception is the experience of how images can present objects or persons that come *alive* to the viewer. Thus, in seeing them we attribute expression and, in exceptional cases, can find ourselves being *addressed* by the image:

I could say: a picture is not always *alive* for me while I am seeing it.
 "Her picture smiles down on me from the wall." It need not always do so, whenever my glance lights on it. (PPF xi §200)

Depending, in other words, on how it is viewed, an image of a face, for example, can be recognized as timid or sad, but also as presenting a *physiognomy*, a meaning or expression that the viewer can feel as being

---

single influence on Wittgenstein" during the years after the war when he worked on issues of perception.

addressed *to them*. The timidity or sadness is present in the image of the face, expressed *to* the viewer.

The concept of physiognomy – pointing to how images and signs can be experienced as having incorporated their own expressive meanings such as to establish a likeness to them – appears in conjunction with Wittgenstein's discussion of aspect-perception in *Philosophical Investigations* and remains one of his central occupations during the immediate postwar years. Applied to language, Wittgenstein (PPF xi §297) reports to feeling of certain words that they have a "field" (*Feld*) which typically becomes apparent and explicit when we concern ourselves with "subtle aesthetic difference." The word will have a "primary" or conventional meaning. However, it will also, at least insofar as it lends itself to aesthetic use and assessment, have "taken on" or embodied its own meaning. This latter type of meaning, which presupposes a sense of the primary meaning, Wittgenstein calls "secondary" (PPF xi §276). For Wittgenstein, the "field" and the "secondary meaning" indicate not only that understanding meaning in these cases cannot be an act of interpretation, but that meaning is experienced directly: we see it. He also claims that sentences can have a certain *ring* (*Klang*) (PPF xi §264). Thus, "aspect-blindness will be *akin* to the lack of a 'musical ear'" (PPF xi §260). Words like "Wednesday" and "Tuesday" can be fat or lean, depending on how one sees them. The name "Schubert," Wittgenstein reports, can by someone be viewed as fitting "Schubert's works and Schubert's face" (PPF xi §270). In several of the late writings on psychology, Wittgenstein refers to this as the word's "atmosphere":

> It's as if the word that I understand had a definite slight aroma that corresponds to my understanding of it. As if two familiar words were distinguished for me not merely by their sound or their appearance, but by an atmosphere as well, even when I don't *imagine* anything in connexion with them. – But remember how the names of famous poets and composers seem to have taken up a peculiar meaning into themselves. So that one can say: the names "Beethoven" and "Mozart" don't merely sound different; no, they are also accompanied by a different *character*. But if you had to describe this character more closely – would you point to their portraits, or to their music? (RPPI §243)

Wittgenstein's reflections on the surplus of meaning inherent in words, being available to discerning readers attentive to the "imponderable evidence" (PPF xi §360), suggests why translations of poetry can, even when they rigorously follow the conventional meaning of words and reproduce the formal structure, sometimes come across as being lifeless or without genuine poetic qualities: failing to respect the text's atmosphere, the secondary meaning, they give us something not worthy of our full attention. However, his conception of aesthetic appreciation and reading also brings a peculiar vision of "literariness" into view. On this view, engaging competently with a literary text involves precisely the struggle to bring into focus and appreciate the full meaning of a literary text that we have seen Wittgenstein at least implicitly providing an account of in the *Lectures on Aesthetics* and later, accompanying texts.

That meaning, it can now be claimed, is *autonomous*. It arises *within* the space opened up between reader and text. A reader unprepared for the specific demands placed on them by a text, and unwilling to seek them out, cannot hope to understand and appreciate what it has to offer. (The similarities with Kant are striking: If you don't expose yourself to a work in a way that brings your faculties – of the understanding and the imagination – into a state of harmonious interplay, then you cannot count as being receptive to it. Perhaps you bring moral or epistemic considerations to bear on it. In each of these instances you relate to something other than the aesthetic qualities.) Moreover, on Wittgenstein's view, literary studies and large swaths of the humanities, insofar as they aim to appreciate and evaluate human expression embodied in literary form, purport to be autonomous. While, of course, deeply situated in contexts of nonliterary life and pressures, they require for their proper practice their own modes of appreciation and judgment.

An Expanded Literary Humanism

The complex imagery at the end of James Joyce's short story "The Dead" calls for precisely this kind of appreciation. As Gabriel tries to fall asleep next to his wife who has just related to him the unnerving story of her dead lover, Michael Furey, it starts to snow, and this is how the text ends:

A few light taps upon the pane made him turn to the window. It had begun to snow again. He watched sleepily the flakes, silver and dark, falling obliquely against the lamplight. The time had come for him to set out on his journey westward. Yes, the newspapers were right: snow was general all over Ireland. It was falling on every part of the dark central plain, on the treeless hills, falling softly upon the Bog of Allen and, farther westward, softly falling into the dark of the mutinous Shannon waves. It was falling, too, upon every part of the lonely churchyard on the hill where Michael Furey lay buried. It lay thickly drifted on the crooked crosses and headstones, on the spears of the little gate, on the barren thorns. His soul swooned slowly as he heard the snow falling faintly through the universe and faintly falling, like the descent of their last end, upon all the living and the dead.[14]

This extraordinary passage, with its rich, meandering movements and flexible employment of free indirect speech, can of course be read in a number of different ways. Moreover, no search for a final answer in the author's biography can unpack its full significance. As Joyce's biographer Richard Ellmann wryly admits, "No one can know how Joyce conceived the joining of Gabriel's final experience with the snow."[15] However, in order to experience its power and, as Ellmann puts it, its "lyrical, melancholy acceptance of all that life and death offer,"[16] one must at the very least have a feel for the "softly falling snow." The snow falls both on the living and the dead, uniting them just as, for Gabriel, the story of Michael Furey who went to his grave so early, makes him feel close to his wife's dead lover. While alluding to a simile from the twelfth book of the Iliad, much of the imagery of the crosses invoke the Calvary – hence suffering, death, and (perhaps) a possible promise of transfiguration. To complicate all of this further, the snow is "general all over Ireland," uniting the living and the dead in some larger union to which Gabriel, expressed in the strange assertion that "the time had come for him to set out on his journey westward," feels mysteriously drawn. The west (of Ireland), more specifically Galway, is his wife Gretta's erstwhile zone of passion and real love: it is where she met Michael Furey. Yet Michael Furey, merging with the primitive and more impulsive country from which Gabriel has always felt alienated (and indeed has never entered, he now bitterly realizes), is dead: he sacrificed his life for the love he had of Gretta. In its imaginative absorption of stray material, the scene is one of quiet resignation, a sense of inevitable decline, and while the snow seems to share in that decline, it also throws a blanket over it, allowing the end of the story to suggest some degree of reconciliation with an otherwise indifferent universe. Thus, in a dream-like act of imagined synesthesia, Gabriel hears "the snow falling faintly through the universe."

None of this would be available to a reader unwilling or unable to read the text as the literary achievement that it undoubtedly is. A competent reader must have a feel for how the rich expressive quality of this

---

[14] James Joyce, *Dubliners* (Oxford and New York: Oxford University Press, 2008), 176.
[15] Richard Ellmann, *James Joyce: New and Revised Edition* (Oxford and New York: Oxford University Press, 1983), 250.
[16] Ibid., 252.

passage depends on the poetic atmosphere created by the specific use of words and their complex relations. Moving in and out of Gabriel's mind, as it were, the narrator invites the reader to experience all the ambiguities of his emotions as he jealously ponders his wife's continued passionate attachment to the memory of a relationship of which he himself has never been – and could never be – a part. The reader must see and accept how reference to "the dark of the mutinous Shannon waves" might be able to provide an exact image not only of the "Furey quality of the west," but also of how snow silently dissolves as it meets the surface of the dark, unruly, and mighty ocean, suggestive perhaps of passion and desire.

While, on Wittgenstein's account, the relationship between reader and text is autonomous, a proponent of the "hermeneutics of suspicion" (to use Felski's and Ricoeur's phrase again) might well be disposed to display a very different attitude to the text. A biographically and perhaps politically inclined reader might emphasize Joyce's sometimes negative feelings toward Ireland, his view that Ireland indeed is a land of the dead. A Marxist reading might see the relationship between Gabriel and Gretta, on the one hand, and Michael Furey, on the other, in terms of class, leaving Furey to represent the ambiguous feelings of the educated, progressive bourgeoisie toward members of the working class. A psychoanalytic reading, moreover, might draw attention to how Gabriel's dream-thoughts seem to set up a contrast between a miserable existence in the east (dominated by the ego and its demands) and yearnings for a different yet more dangerous existence in the dark west (dominated by the unconscious and its ambiguities of life and death).

As is well-known, the later Wittgenstein was interested in Freud and saw him as one of the few authors really worth reading. However, in the 1942 "Conversations on Freud," he distinguishes rather sharply between two ways of approaching psychoanalysis. The one, which he rejects, looks at symbol-formation and dreams in terms of their purportedly essential features. Appealing to causal mechanisms, dreams are believed to result causally (and necessarily, in a law-like fashion) from preceding, though unconscious, wishes. The other, which he recommends, "fits the dream into a context in which it ceases to be puzzling" (LC 45):

What is done in interpreting dreams is not all of one sort. There is a work of interpretation which, so to speak, still belongs to the dream itself. In considering what a dream is, it is important to consider what happens to it, the way its aspect changes when it is brought into relation with other things remembered, for instance. (LC 46)

Again, the concept of aspect-perception seems to play a crucial role. To decipher a dream, the interpreter must be able to relate it meaningfully to other experiences, and also to place it within the kind of context – perhaps sexual desire, but other contexts can equally be important – in which it might start to make sense. By pondering these relations, the bits and pieces might eventually fall into place, leaving the interpreter to say "'Ah, now I see why it is like that, how it all comes to be arranged in that way, and what these various bits are . . .' and so on" (LC 46).

Wittgenstein, in other words, was not averse to the hermeneutics of suspicion. His reflections on psychoanalysis demonstrate that as long it avoids the fallacies of appealing to essence and causal closure – *and* does not confuse the status of its own statements, which are in the service of elucidating an otherwise incomprehensible or hidden meaning, with the status of statements making up a literary expression – the employment of sophisticated accounts of preconscious meaning, whether to uncover the workings of ideology, power, or the Freudian unconscious, would in a field such as literary studies be perfectly legitimate.

This brings us back to Felski. On her recommendation, literary studies should largely recede from its long-standing commitment to the hermeneutics of suspicion and reconnect with the text as an autonomous source of human enjoyment and insight. A Wittgensteinian approach to literary studies would agree with Felski that literary texts indeed provide such autonomous forms of engagement. However, it would be closer to Adorno's account of the "double-nature of art" than to Felski's more decisive humanism. While Wittgenstein advocates a view of literary texts that invites the reader to be surprised, stirred, or called to account by the words they contain, he strongly denounces both essentialism and methodological unity. For Wittgenstein, an advanced reader of literary texts would be likely to place them in various contexts, inviting a number of different language-games and attitudes to inform her reading. His view avoids some of the difficulties pertaining to Adorno's theory, for which the "double-nature of art" entails a value-distinction between high and low, works of aesthetic negation and works of mere social effect. In comparison to that of Adorno, whose aim is deeply critical, Wittgenstein's pluralism comes across as relaxed and generous, calling for nothing more than respect for the integrity and individuality of particular language-games.

In one of his last essays, Edward W. Said called such a mode of thought "para-doxical."[17] As opposed to the older humanism of critics such as Eliot, Leavis, and Harold Bloom, which sought to preserve the prestige associated with a canon of purportedly great literary works by insulating them from all social and historical contextualization, Said's humanism encourages the critic to accept and indeed analyze the antinomian relation between "the space of words and their various origins and deployments in physical and social place."[18] Said not only argues for the equal legitimacy of intratextual and extratextual study, but also believes that the two *complement* each other. Although texts do address their readers directly and call for the kind of attention that I have highlighted in conjunction with my reading of Wittgenstein, one cannot fully appreciate the full range of their nuances without some knowledge of their history and origin. Moreover, the context of origin tends to reveal more than just unacknowledged constraints on textual transparency and determinacy. As Said sees it, rather than just weighing on the text as causally relevant yet exterritorial and hence textually destroying garbage – the politics, the desire, the power, and the suffering of real agents in real historical situations – the world from which the text emerges is never a tabula rasa. Rather, it comes inscribed with all kinds of discourses, information, and interpretation, pointing beyond themselves and potentially informing the text one is studying. At the same time, however, the true humanist realizes that the text under scrutiny can provide a privileged access to these layers of meaning. Epistemically, this involves a decentering and expansion of textual meaning. However, it does not obligate us to be "suspicious" of the text and reduce it to its context of origin. Instead, politically, it brings textual meaning in contact with socially and politically constituted meaning, allowing for semantically rich and sometimes progressively relevant interchanges between different discourses. Said calls this "worldliness" – that "all texts and all representations were *in* the world and subject to its numerous heterogeneous realities," assuring "contamination and involvement."[19]

---

[17] Edward W. Said, *Humanism and Democratic Criticism* (New York: Columbia University Press, 2004), 83.
[18] Ibid.
[19] Ibid., 48–49. In *The Limits of Critique*, Felski in fact seems to acknowledge the significance of such "worldly" readings: "Edward Said's reading of *Mansfield Park* as an allegory of imperialism, for example, made the work of Jane Austen newly intriguing and worthy of

Felski seems to be glimpsing the structure of this para-doxical thought. However, because her understanding of critique is so determined by the suspicious search for restraining, extratextual causes – Victorian society, imperialism, discourse/power, Western metaphysics – she ends up recommending a Manichean rather than a Saidean, expanded humanistic position: all outside influence *disturbs* or *disrupts* textual engagement. On Said's view, we might have to recant the purity and immediacy that Wittgenstein sometimes seems to associate with the genuine aesthetic attitude. However, what Wittgenstein has to say about attitude and appreciation strikes me as fully compatible with Said's expanded, worldly and "para-doxical" thought. It might require of us an ongoing willingness to bring discourses and language-games in contact with one another. However, at its most accomplished, as in Said's case, it can enrich our understanding of the text while at the same time permitting the exploration of transcendence and integrity characterizing the texts we value the most.

Concluding Remarks

The field of literary studies has for quite some time been struggling to articulate a viable sense of purpose and legitimacy. As Felski correctly argues, after decades of decentering the experience of texts, providing explanations of textual meaning in light of purportedly external and causally effective frameworks (power, desire, etc.), what seems needed is a new understanding and appreciation of how literary texts engage us as human subjects. How can that be provided without regressing back into the stale conservatism of canons and perennial value to which the hermeneutics of suspicion objected? I have argued that Wittgenstein can offer a way forward. When thought of in conjunction with his thinking about language-games, practices, and aspect-perception, Wittgenstein gives us a deeply compelling account of textual appreciation. However, while believing that bringing the text correctly into view is an autonomous activity (an activity relative to the language-games and techniques associated with this capacity but not transferable to other contexts), Wittgenstein acknowledges a plurality of mutually supporting and informing language-games such as to expand the operation of the critic to include "worldly" (Said) meanings when appreciating the work.

attention to a community of postcolonial critics who might otherwise have paid her writing scant heed" (115).

On this view, a competent critic attends to meanings that ultimately are mediated by the work's origin in a world beyond itself. Unlike Adorno, who sees the dual nature of art in terms of an ongoing battle between heteronomy and autonomy, the Wittgensteinian critic expands the work, and expands her conception of autonomy, discovering that both enable as well as constrain dimensions of literary sense-making.

6 Storied Thoughts
Wittgenstein and the Reaches of Fiction
Magdalena Ostas

Abstract: This chapter puts forward the thesis that fictional forms, and the imaginative reach they bring to thinking, serve as a kind of philosophical method for Wittgenstein in *Philosophical Investigations*. It explores how the original use Wittgenstein makes of fiction and stories revitalizes conversations in the space between literature and philosophy. For Wittgenstein's commitment to fiction as method, distinctively, allows him to sound out actualities and realities in the world. It is a uniquely truth-capable use of fiction that also highlights what novels, stories, films, performances, and other fictional forms are intrinsically capable of. The chapter begins by developing a contrast between Wittgenstein and Plato on the use of story. It continues into readings of central characters, figures, circumstances, and events in the opening sections of *Philosophical Investigations*. The discussion concludes with reflections on two novelists, Jane Austen and Virginia Woolf, whose interest in giving everyday life narrative form illuminates the stakes of Wittgenstein's commitment to story. The chapter more broadly asks central questions about how fictional forms put us in contact with consequential parts, pieces, and aspects of the world and how Wittgenstein's philosophy paves a new path into this connection between fiction and life.

Keywords: Fiction, Imagination, Narratives versus Stories, Fiction and Reality, Literary Form, Truth, Relationship between Literature and Philosophy, The Everyday, Plato, Jane Austen, Virginia Woolf.

Nothing is more important for teaching us to understand the concepts we have than constructing fictitious ones.
—Ludwig Wittgenstein, *Culture and Value*

I.

Philosophers have always told stories. The most famous story Plato told, for example, involved shackled men in a cave surrounded by plays of light – fire, shadows, sun – and his central storyline followed the conversations of a character named Socrates. Plato's avowed claim in the later books of *The Republic*, as literary critics well know, is that there is no use for poetic and literary representation in the ideal state, and he bans the poets from his republic. Yet the tools of Plato's argument – that is, how he assembles these philosophical claims about poetry and engages us in them – remain, especially for literary critics, essentially poetic. In this sense, Plato's use of story, allegory, and dialogue might appear to undermine his intent of pitting poetry against philosophy in a stalemate quarrel. Plato wants nothing to do with the poets and poetry, but as many readers remind us, his arguments are barren and blank without its force.[1]

The apparent conflict between Plato's dedication to truth in philosophy and his use of stories and other fictional forms can be the occasion for drawing a specific lesson, one that has oversaturated conversations in the space between literature and philosophy. The lesson teaches that Plato helps us to see philosophy's dependence on literary forms like figures, tropes, and allegories and that literature (or "literariness") is already at play in, and is even the condition of the possibility of, rational forms of thinking. Metaphors, stories, analogies, examples, and anecdotes – seemingly these have merely slipped into philosophy's rhetorical world, but they are then discovered in this line of interpretation to be essential to philosophical reflection and argument, the unwitting essences of thought.

This chapter explores the thoroughly original use Wittgenstein in his later philosophy makes of stories and other fictional forms, and it shows how Wittgenstein's distinct way of putting fiction to work for philosophy revitalizes and reshapes the conversations in the space between literature and philosophy. For within the company of philosophers normally invoked at the crossroads of literary and philosophical thinking, Wittgenstein is original in what I will call his commitment to fiction as method – that is, to using fictional accounts and fictional descriptions to

---

[1] See, for example, Christopher Janaway, *Images of Excellence: Plato's Critique of the Arts* (Oxford: Clarendon Press, 1995) and the essays by Julia Annas, Alexander Nehamas, and Martha Nussbaum in *Plato on Beauty, Wisdom, and the Arts*, eds. Julius Moravcsik and Philip Temko (Totowa, NJ: Rowman and Littlefield, 1982).

uncover new forms of philosophical understanding. Wittgenstein is singular in how he uses fiction, unexpectedly, to sound out and describe the contours of the world. The shackled men in Plato's cave never were, and although Plato conjures them to help teach us something about knowledge or appearance or art, they are not figures entangled in circumstances about which we would be inclined to say, "Yes, I recognize the world Plato has imagined as my world or as invoking my world. This is the world I live in too." Plato's prisoners, in fact, are there to help us comprehend something that in spirit opposes a response of recognition. The prisoners are actually figures who help us grasp Plato's contention that we cannot trust or believe the images that fall into our range of experience, the ones that we see and hear with our ordinary senses. Their role in Plato's story is not to confirm but potentially to upend our sense of security and certainty in our everyday encounters with things and with others in the world.

In a similar way, even the philosopher most radically enthusiastic about the power of story to teach and uncover, Nietzsche, conjured up characters like noblemen and beasts of prey and resentful slaves to help us – again – register something abstract or deep about our world and our history. Nietzsche's story about these characters yields a powerful insight about modern experience, to be sure, but it is essentially abstract and speculative because, like Plato's allegory, it pivots on our discovery that the world is not as we had thought. Nietzsche's story entreats us to imagine our experience differently than we have all along, to abandon the everyday naïve view.

One might say that Wittgenstein in his later philosophy, in contrast, aspires to help us return or reattend to our everyday experience. Thus, the power of fiction that Wittgenstein's later writings continually wield is not insight-seeking but actuality-seeking at its core. It is a belief *in fiction* to help us get clear on concrete, specific, and actual horizons of value that comprise our experience in the world exactly as we stand. When we hear Plato's description of the prisoners in the cave or Nietzsche's account of the slave revolt, we have to reach beyond each story, so to speak, and take on the intense or penetrating view in order to understand the insight it seeks to hold out to us. In Wittgenstein's later philosophy, stories work in exactly the opposing direction. They ask us to recognize ourselves (or to say that we don't recognize ourselves) in a world given to us for consideration *as one we might precisely recognize* – but a world that is, nonetheless, explicitly fictional. Wittgenstein writes the following in an early fragment: "For the place I really have to get to is a place I must already be at now. Anything that I might reach by climbing a ladder does not interest me" (CV 7e). In the routes thinking can take over the course of philosophical reflection, Plato's cave dwellers and Nietzsche's slaves are indeed like ladders, figures who force us to leave the ground in order to access what is meaningful and resonant.

In the contrast that I will develop, Wittgenstein's later philosophy, like fiction of all kinds, summons concrete scenarios, events, circumstances, happenings, and characters that are at once fictitious yet actual, what we might think of as not truthful but truth-capable[2], imaginative but also imaginable. This is at least how some of the most exciting work in literary studies and philosophical aesthetics today (from critics – to cite only a brief list – like Charles Altieri, Robert Chodat, Richard Eldridge, John Gibson, Bernard Harrison, Toril Moi, and Yi-Ping Ong) frames the central issue of fiction's relation to life. The guiding common insight is that, like Wittgenstein's sketches and stories, literary fictions do not come to hook onto the world in some manner (either a mysterious or a logical one) but are instead already a part of the world, born inside it, living within it, illuminating it, and casting it under suspicion. Thus there is no need for any additional explanation for the activity – already in operation – that gets called hooking, referring, mirroring, or representing.[3] Wittgenstein's philosophy casts new light on the question of

---

[2] I take the helpful phrase "truth-capable" from Kenneth Dauber and Walter Jost, "Introduction: The Varieties of Ordinary Language Criticism," in *Ordinary Language Criticism: Literary Thinking after Cavell after Wittgenstein*, eds. Dauber and Jost (Evanston, IL: Northwestern University Press, 2003), x.

[3] See Charles Altieri, "Presence and Reference in a Literary Text: The Example of Williams' 'This Is Just to Say,'" *Critical Inquiry* 5 (3): 489–510 (Spring 1979), doi:10.1086/448003, and *Reckoning with the Imagination: Wittgenstein and the Aesthetics of Literary Experience* (Ithaca, NY: Cornell University Press, 2015); Robert Chodat, *Worldly Acts and Sentient Things: The Persistence of Agency from Stein to DeLillo* (Ithaca, NY: Cornell University Press, 2008) and "Empiricism, Exhaustion, and Meaning What We Say: Cavell and Contemporary Fiction," in *Stanley Cavell and Literary Studies: Consequences of Skepticism*, eds. Richard Eldridge and Bernard Rhie (London: Continuum Books, 2011), 208–223; Richard Eldridge, *Leading a Human Life: Wittgenstein, Intentionality, and Romanticism* (Chicago, IL: University of Chicago Press, 1997) and *Literature, Life, and Modernity* (New York: Columbia University Press, 2008); John Gibson, *Fiction and the Weave of Life* (Oxford: Oxford University Press, 2007) and "Narrative and the Literary Imagination," in *Narrative, Philosophy, and Life*, ed. Allen Speight (Dordrecht: Springer, 2014), 135–150; Bernard Harrison, *Inconvenient Fictions: Literature and the Limits of Theory* (New Haven, CT: Yale University Press, 1991) and *What Is Fiction For? Literary Humanism Restored* (Bloomington, IN and Indianapolis, IN: Indiana University Press, 2014); Toril Moi, "The Adventure of Reading: Literature and Philosophy, Cavell and Beauvoir," *Literature and Theology* 25 (2): 125–140 (June 2011), doi:10.1093/litthe/frr014, and *Revolution of the Ordinary: Literary Studies after Wittgenstein, Austin, and*

how fictional works put us in direct contact with the world's most significant and even precious aspects and do not "reference" or refer to extant realities. As Bernard Harrison has phrased the matter, "If literary texts possess the power to administer shocks to the systems of categories and assumptions which we inhabit, they must put us in contact with something harder and more authoritative than other texts: with reality, in fact."[4] And as John Gibson puts it, the fact that "a frame of fiction can function to open up a view of the real" means that literary works do not make truth claims about reality but actually "use it."[5] It turns out that fictions, paradoxically and wonderfully, are capable of truths – of showing the world we live in to us. In the context of the everyday realities that so often seem to elude our full grasp or attention – the realities we live that are after all continuously right there – fiction for Wittgenstein is actually necessary to noticing, seeing, and understanding. It can be a tool of revelation.

Wittgenstein's stories – like novels, plays, performances, films, and other fictional forms – in this way seek out and test the parameters of what we are willing to confirm our world actually looks and feels like. The sketches that populate *Philosophical Investigations* give the imagination a terrain for exploring its own sense of what is real and important, and each one is an invitation to imagine something and observe the impact of that imagined happening on the ideas and convictions we hold: say you go shopping for apples (PI §1), what if you're building a house (PI §§2–21), what if you suddenly feel pain and try to speak or write (PI §§258–272). Circumstances such as these described in *Philosophical Investigations* are unextraordinary, and thus as in a novel or film they are transformed solely by virtue of being included in the field of attentiveness that unfolds before us. Look more closely, each section and sequence in *Philosophical Investigations* seems to say, recast your attention here, and be willing to revisit your sense of what is consequential, decisive, or worth remarking in these instances that I am holding up for your regard and consideration. Wittgenstein thus shares with writers of fiction a sense of how to arrive at the parts or aspects of the world that in the end have valence and import: look and see (PI §66), and then start

---

Cavell (Chicago, IL: University of Chicago Press, 2017); and Yi-Ping Ong, *The Art of Being: Poetics of the Novel and Existentialist Philosophy* (Cambridge, MA: Harvard University Press, 2018).

[4] Harrison, *Inconvenient Fictions*, 11.   [5] Gibson, *Fiction and the Weave of Life*, 35, 31.

to tell and describe, and then suppose something and redescribe, and let's observe where we get and what we find.

The storiedness of the paths that philosophy travels in *Philosophical Investigations* thus stands as evidence of Wittgenstein's foundational interest in how fictions help us think, understand, explore, judge, and see – that is, his interest in the intrinsic world-directedness and world-boundedness of imaginative fictional forms. That fictional narratives can do such things at all and can change or transfigure our sense of the world is a potential power of fiction that Wittgenstein's later philosophy continually harnesses and puts to use. Insofar as fictional projection therefore *is* Wittgenstein's method, it reveals not only that he has overlapping investments with those who craft stories but also that his philosophy uniquely attunes us to what fiction *can do*, all the time, anyway, in all of its manifestations across literature and the arts. This chapter, therefore, will not only focus on how Wittgenstein imports the power of fiction to do philosophical work but also on the ways that his later philosophy underlines what fiction has always been up to and is constitutively capable of – what it always asks and has asked of its readers.

II.

In *Philosophical Investigations* Wittgenstein at every moment considers and examines an imaginative scenario – a concrete, suppositional, tentative, nonevidenced, extended, and evolving instance of this or that: shopping for apples, teaching addition, encountering a pot in a fairy tale, shouting imperatives while building a house, scribbling in a notebook while in pain. Scenarios like these develop in *Philosophical Investigations* through dialogue, so that the fictions they conjure take the form of dynamic storytelling. These small fictions carry nearly all of the philosophical weight in the text, yet their philosophical objective or yield is not self-evident and, importantly, is not intended to be. As Wittgenstein remarks, "Don't take it as a matter of course, but as a remarkable fact, that pictures and fictitious narratives give us pleasure, absorb us" (PI §524). In *Philosophical Investigations* he enfranchises the absorptive pull that fiction can exert to do – in effect, to take over for – the classic work of thought. This use of sketches and stories is a profoundly original way of thinking through philosophical problems, or of thinking about what to *do with* philosophical problems.

Grasping why fiction plays this unique role in *Philosophical Investigations* entails getting at something more consequential than how a philosopher uses stories in a specific, original, or idiosyncratic way. For genre often enables and bespeaks a greater perspective onto the world. And fictional narrative forms, whatever specific perspectives they materialize or evidence, necessarily picture human agents in evolving contexts of intention, understanding, judgment, and desire, and they embed human beings within social institutions, local communities, and historical practices. "What we are supplying," comments Wittgenstein, "are really remarks on the natural history of human beings" (PI §415). We might observe along with David Schalkwyk, then, that *story*, as it comes forward in artifacts like narrative fiction, film, or performance, might itself be an instance of what Wittgenstein called "grammatical investigation"[6] – a way of tarrying with the possibilities of how things can happen, entertaining scopes of use, and watching things transpire and then follow. From a certain perspective one actually might be tempted to ask, How could Wittgenstein *not* have regularly imagined human beings continually doing things, trying things, talking to one another, understanding things, and misunderstanding things?

Wittgenstein's use of fiction thus evidences a specific philosophical perspective on language and action. Or one might say that his philosophical perspective on language and action in the world necessitates a form of exploration that offers what fiction and storytelling afford. Wittgenstein's sketches of fictional circumstances, happenings, and characters hold up the tightly bound interweave between words and activity that he called a "language-game," that is, "language and the activities into which it is woven" (PI §7). Because they are particularized and concrete, his sketches stall and thwart our wish to know something about language *generally* without a frame of context or circumstance, namely, our wish to describe language outside the homes of language-games.

We see in *Philosophical Investigations*, for instance, in the rhythm of the opening sequence of paragraphs in which Wittgenstein regularly returns to the characters of two builders, how our demand to understand a word's meaning generally, outside of a context of use, confuses the meaning that a word takes on when it functions within the context of

---

[6] See David Schalkwyk, "Fiction as 'Grammatical' Investigation: A Wittgensteinian Account," *Journal of Aesthetics and Art Criticism* 53(3): 287–298 (Summer 1995), doi:10.2307/431354.

human practices. In the opening paragraphs, Wittgenstein initially sets into motion a simple language-game between a pair of builders consisting solely of nouns and ostensive definitions that link word and object, so that blocks, pillars, slabs, and beams are called out in order to be passed along from one builder to the other (PI §2). Having established that a language-game like this is generally in line with what we call "naming" (PI §7), Wittgenstein then asks us to imagine an expansion of this fairly primitive use of words, and he adds demonstratives – *this* and *that* – to the range of vocabulary available to the suppositional builders (PI §8). Now there are different tools in the builders' toolboxes (PI §11), tools as unlike as a glue-pot and a screwdriver, and the concreteness of the difference between the two kinds of words – between *slab* and *this* – makes our philosophical question about them *as words* seem hollow and fall flat. When we ask the general question, "Now what do the words of this language *signify*?" (PI §10), we see that we are deeply misguided. Wittgenstein's shifting sketch underlines just how differently handy *slab* and *this* can be to the builders. As the sketch in this opening sequence develops and moves forward, it becomes unclear what anyone might have wanted to know in asking how both words "signify."

The evolving episode imagining conversations between builders in this way forces the question of what we ever imagined *slab* and *this* to have in common anyway. Aren't we essentially confused when we ask after concepts like *meaning* or *signification*? As Wittgenstein puts it, "the general concept of the meaning of a word surrounds the working of language with a haze which makes clear vision impossible." In his sketch of the builders, unimagining *slab* and *this* to be cognates, cousins, or analogous tools – unassimilating them – is what helps to "disperse the fog" (PI §5). To aid our imagination in seeing the words as essentially different tools, Wittgenstein brings us back to what he calls the rough ground (PI §107) through the details of an imaginative scene. He thereby calls into question what our initial impulse to assimilate these unlike things – *slab* and *this*, glue and screwdriver – seeks to accomplish. There is no general truth claim about language in this instance that Wittgenstein wishes either to confirm or to deny, for example, a claim like the following: "If we say, 'Every word in the language signifies something'" (PI §13). Instead, Wittgenstein presents us with an evolving collection of concrete particulars, reiterations of a scene that involve a recurrent cast of characters continuously exposed to or thrown into changing sets of needs, obligations, circumstances, and capacities. So that insofar as we as readers are curious about something we call "language," Wittgenstein forces us to see that our professed curiosity remains irresponsible or, better, overwhelmingly incomplete without the inclusion of numerous accompanying, adjacent, and attendant curiosities about action, intention, character, environment, and many other things that together attune us to the complex shape of human life. In other words, it is not clear what would count as an instance of what we keep calling language, since so much else is needed to make any sense of how we write, speak, act, and live.[7]

The stories and sketches in *Philosophical Investigations*, and the perspective on language and life that they register, thus oppose and actively impede what Richard Eldridge has called the "underdescription" of human life.[8] Wittgenstein's stories describe, and then they redescribe, and at each step this necessitates pulling us not toward a new insight but toward further particulars – details of circumstance, need, strategy, desire, intent, ability, tools available, materials at hand, practices at work, and all of the ways we navigate these things in our life with others. "The selecting of details," writes Charles Altieri, "is how imagination produces a world in which it solicits our responding imaginative activity."[9] Particulars in *Philosophical Investigations* certainly help us think about the world, but they also help us to see how the temptation toward generalities too often impedes our thinking about the world.

---

[7] For Stanley Cavell, whose readings of *Philosophical Investigations* repeatedly revisit this intimate interweave between language and world, Wittgenstein everywhere refuses a general account of language on just these grounds. Wittgenstein observes, for example: We are under the illusion that what is peculiar, profound and essential to us in our investigation resides in its trying to grasp the incomparable essence of language. That is, the order existing between the concepts of proposition, word, inference, truth, experience, and so forth. This order is a *super*-order between – so to speak – *super*-concepts. (PI §97)
Wittgenstein asks here, What might serve as an instance of *that* language, that is, the "essence of language"? How is *all* language learned? What *is* a language game? At every step, Wittgenstein refuses such questions. This is a radical challenge to the entire apparatus of operative concepts that guides inquiry into "language" understood as words, signs, or any linguistic unit. Wittgenstein's challenge cuts off that inquiry at its opening move: the objection is to the unit of meaning understood as the word or sign. For an insightful discussion of the idea of the sign and the history of literary theory and criticism in relation to Wittgenstein and his lineage, see esp. Moi, *Revolution of the Ordinary*, "Part II: Differences," 113–174.

[8] Richard Eldridge, *Leading a Human Life*, 8. In this context, Eldridge reads *Philosophical Investigations* as essentially dramatic in its structure: "Through its drama, it aims at making it impossible for us to forget the entanglement of conceptual consciousness with memory, desire, social relations, and aspirations to expressive freedom."

[9] Altieri, *Reckoning with the Imagination*, 59.

In this sense the structure of paragraph and aphorism of *Philosophical Investigations*, one that works rhythmically to recall and regularly reinterest us in ordinary details and particulars, can at first glance appear to be in tension with Wittgenstein's commitment to fictional story forms. Yet the tension between the larger arcs of Wittgenstein's sketches and the self-enclosed form of philosophical aphorism actually brings into view the important contrast between terms like *fiction* or *story* and the more sophisticated concept of *narrative* often used in the fields of literary studies and philosophy to call up an idea with different contours. For while *narrative* captures the shape of fictional forms that pivot on a sense of direction or cohesion that is at least in part overarching, *story* encompasses fictions that are also tentative, evolving, fragmentary, intentionally brief, or perhaps unending and unfinished – that is, fictional forms in which the accumulation and accretion of detail proceeds without an overarching directedness. Robert Chodat's valuable readings of strands in both disciplines that invite recourse to the semitechnical term *narrative* (and related terminology like *narrativity*, *narratology*, *the narrative self*, or *the narrative turn*) illuminate just how little Wittgenstein's own investments align with a desire to locate or isolate something like a narrative impulse.[10] The stories in *Philosophical Investigations*, in fact, resist and defy even the most basic sequence of beginning, middle, and final resolution and release, one that the concept of narrative usually necessitates, however loosely or unrigorously. This is an important point about Wittgenstein's method. His manner of philosophizing, which he once characterized as "poetic composition" (CV 24e), is not linked in consequential ways to a structure we would describe as "narrative" and instead progresses forward with a sense of caution or reluctance in arriving at resolutions or answers. As his thinking moves in *Philosophical Investigations*, Wittgenstein is always ready to sacrifice precisely arc or philosophical plot, and he invariably prioritizes, instead, laying out and as it were letting us witness increasingly individuated cases of emplottedness, more and more concrete entanglements of words and world that in fact frustrate and obstruct a greater plotlike progress. First the builders know only nouns, then they also know demonstratives, and the sketch thus thickens and thickens. The details accumulate without tension, climax, or telos but not with randomness or looseness

---

[10] Robert Chodat, "Is Narrative a Something or a Nothing?" in *Wittgenstein on Aesthetic Understanding*, ed. Garry Hagberg (London: Palgrave Macmillan, 2017), 99–130; see esp. 101–106.

either, so that what Altieri insightfully calls "a texture of invention" is felt at every step in how they are assimilated and arranged.[11] The terms *fiction* and *story* therefore underscore with a different emphasis than might the term *narrative* one simple aspect of Wittgenstein's manner of sketching and then resketching examples: his stories extend over time. But in Wittgenstein's estimation, time does not evidently lend life shape and coherence but rather provides increasingly complex and interesting occasions for pursuing ways of making sense of things, inventing questions, and moving toward tentative or momentary answers. Fiction or story, in this way, is an open-ended method that allows Wittgenstein to investigate and prod the crossroads between our ideas, our identities, and our world.

An extended temporal form, therefore, allows Wittgenstein to pursue a particular philosophical idea about language and meaning, one which a static or synchronous manner of sketching or describing would not have supported. When we last left Wittgenstein's builders at PI §10, they still had a future in the *Investigations*, not yet fully broadened and protracted in the text across philosophical paragraphs. Their fate as figures was still unknown to us and part of an open landscape in which Wittgenstein might have subjected them to any number of various conditions of meaning-making and let us observe how these conditions play out. Will the builders learn numerals? Or begin to communicate about colors? Will they start building bridges or tunnels? Perhaps new kinds of tangles lie in subterranean and suspended forms of built construction. Will the builders eventually come to discover that *this* and *that* are overall very handy outside the life of building things? What if they become poets and start speaking of slabs of time or beams of light? "Uttering a word," writes Wittgenstein, "is like striking a note on the keyboard of the imagination" (PI §6). Surely, as Rush Rhees knew, Wittgenstein cannot let his builders continue building the same structure with the same blocks, pillars, slabs, and beams forever, for this is not actually a language.[12] When will *slab* come in handy again? The words the builders have learned and the contexts in which those words find homes begin in *Philosophical Investigations* to stretch and jump ahead. There is control in the leaps forward that Wittgenstein makes between paragraphs as the builders' uses stretch and extend, for not just anything

---

[11] Altieri, *Reckoning with the Imagination*, 8.
[12] See Rush Rhees, "Wittgenstein's Builders," *Proceedings of the Aristotelian Society* 60 (1): 171–186 (June 1960), doi:10.1093/aristotelian/60.1.171.

can count as a slab and not every instance falls into accord with the word's possible usages. On the other hand, the unexplored contexts and places for us and for the builders to talk about slabs are in actuality unending.

Indeed, as Wittgenstein pulls forward, widening and reorganizing the scenario across paragraphs, he asks us to picture a different concrete possibility. We are to imagine that the spoken imperative "Five slabs!" (as in "Bring me five slabs!") suddenly becomes objective account-keeping as one of the builders metamorphoses into a manager or stockist whose factual report of materials on hand might read, "Five slabs" (PI §21). Our imaginations are further prodded as Wittgenstein speculates about a foreigner, a non-native speaker, who articulates the syllables in the sentence "Bring me a slab" unusually quickly and elides the pauses between the four words, so that it might sound as if the speaker were uttering only one word, perhaps the approximate equivalent of "building stone" in their native language (PI §20). There are no rules for how the builders apply words in future contexts nor for how the sequence of shifting sketches in the *Investigations* proceeds, and each variation Wittgenstein introduces demands that we reconsider or reconceptualize some idea about the workings of language anew. At the same time, the builders' as-yet-unsurveyed applications are bounded by what Martin Stone has called "normative reach," that is, the constrained but still open reaching into new circumstances that reactivates a word and brings it newly into play as we learn to "go on" in language and in the world together.[13]

Importantly, moving forward in life with language for Wittgenstein is not like proceeding according to a rule or prescribed criteria. He stages the following monologue on the topic of rule-following:

What do I call "the rule according to which he proceeds"? – The hypothesis that satisfactorily describes his use of words, which we observe; or the rule which he looks up when he uses signs; or the one which he gives us in reply if we ask him what his rule is? – But what if observation does not clearly reveal any rule, and the question brings none to light? – For he did indeed give me an explanation when I asked him what he meant by "N," but he was prepared to withdraw this

---

[13] Martin Stone, "Wittgenstein on Deconstruction," in *The New Wittgenstein*, ed. Alice Crary and Rupert Read (London and New York: Routledge, 2000), 83–117; here 87. See also Cavell's reflections on this point throughout "The Availability of Wittgenstein's Later Philosophy" (in *Must We Mean What We Say? A Book of Essays*, 2nd ed. [Cambridge: Cambridge University Press, 2002], 44–72) and "Excursus on Wittgenstein's Vision of Language" (in *The Claim of Reason*, 168–190, reprinted in *The New Wittgenstein*, 21–37).

explanation and alter it. – So how am I to determine the rule according to which he is playing? He does not know it himself. – Or, more correctly, what is left for the expression "the rule according to which he proceeds" to say? (PI §82)

As the play of voices and perspectives in this passage suggests, meaning for Wittgenstein is neither like a signpost that stands pointing forward with unmistakable direction (PI §85) nor like rails laid to infinity on the ground in a straight line (PI §218). Our trying to go on in language is much trickier than that. "'Now I know how to go on!'," writes Wittgenstein, "is an exclamation; it corresponds to an instinctive sound, a glad start. Of course, it does not follow from my feeling that I won't find I'm stuck when I do try to go on" (PI §323). The speaker who exclaims confidently in this paragraph that she knows how to go on, as Wittgenstein underlines, expresses a good feeling, a sense of confidence in her know-how, and she is not making a claim about having what we call knowledge. We do in fact get stuck when we try to go on, since we cannot have learned all its uses and applications when we learned a word. But the only test of our ability to go on, of our adequacy or artistry, is a happy future use, an application that evidences our learning and getting that *this* is a good moment to use this or that expression. Meaning has to be able to evolve and develop, and we are responsible for that development as we "go on" and continue expressing ourselves and speaking with one another in ever-shifting and new contexts. Here is Richard Eldridge again:

An evolving orientation, involving possibilities of motion and resistance, toward things, toward others, and toward oneself, is bound up with the structure of conceptual consciousness and its animation in relation to practice. This is not a matter of a given *archetype* (either in mind or nature) and not a matter of an arbitrary convention and nor a matter of something simply and transparently fixed in "what we do," but instead a part of a process, a life with and in language and conceptual consciousness. Something – a natural power – is brought into effective articulation and life, within this process of accommodation and resistance, within oneself, with others in practice.[14]

Insofar as our understanding something thus requires not just quiet knowledge but the real effort of open articulation – stops and starts, getting stuck, picking up again – we might think of *story* as the medium that allows us to explore the speculative reaching of our forms of articulation and of our entanglements. Meaning, like intention, precisely

[14] Eldridge, *Leading a Human Life*, 237.

reaches forward without anything we can point to as direct, logical, or metaphysical cause, and it is thus the open realm of story that lets us envisage the possibilities and consequences of the forward reaching of our meanings, subject at once to bounds and limits *and* to human freedom in use and action. For like our intentions and actions, meanings don't have – to recall Wittgenstein's own phrasing – a cause but instead what he called a natural history, a way things move and evolve without logic, but with a sense and direction we will always try to make out and to make sense of. And so we need stories to be able to follow our own forms of understanding in the broadest sense into the future realities into which they project and ultimately settle.

We can thus think of story as a kind of grammatical investigation of the possibilities that emanate from a present-tense intertwine of self and world. Insofar as stories capture selves in the world temporally outstretching in this way, story as a form is also uniquely capable of exhibiting the self's interior life (its judgments, intentions, desires, hopes) from an outward perspective. Stories bespeak a worldview that cannot but picture human souls moving or living as human bodies in the world – and they are thus their pictures.[15]

Wittgenstein writes in *Philosophical Investigations* that he is concerned with "the spatial and temporal phenomenon of language" and not some "non-spatial, non-temporal phantasm" (PI §108). This specter of nonmaterial language famously preoccupies him and figures in the text as the illusory activity of pointing to inner experience or interior sensations (PI §275). Thus, in the *Investigations* – as in so many kinds of fiction, film, and drama – speaking, looking, going, acting, and reacting (or failures to speak, look, go, act, or react) take the place of unseen interior lightbulbs or inward sparks. These human activities are the markers of things like understanding, judging, feeling, sympathizing, loving, hating, or not caring at all. This does not mean that Wittgenstein replaces inner life with outward forms but, instead, that the sketch or story in *Philosophical Investigations* stays faithful at every point to picturing what Yi-Ping Ong calls an "inextricability of character and situation."[16] The emphasis in Wittgenstein's sketches (as in the tradition of realism in the novel that Ong takes up) falls on the revelation of the world understood *as*

---

[15] On this point, David Schalkwyk's readings of literary texts in relation to the topic of Wittgenstein and privacy are especially insightful. See "Wittgenstein's Philosophizing and Literary Theorizing," esp. 70–71.

[16] Ong, *Art of Being*, 165.

developing, encircling situatedness. Meaning in Wittgenstein's worldview reaches not only forward but also outward. The sketches that populate and anchor the *Investigations* thus have an extraordinary capacity: they represent the first-person perspective of a human agent – that is, the point of view of living a life – and, at the same time, an other-than-first-person reflective distance on that life. The latter, like the point of view of a novelist, attends to numerous adjacent curiosities (about environment, action, coincidence, the parallel lives of others, the distant lives of others) that make sense of and illuminate the shape of that singular life. The philosophical yield of Wittgenstein's small fictions thus lies in their ability to contain or enclasp the contours of how meaning takes shape not in the space inside of us but in the spaces between us in the world and between one another.

III.

The ways that Wittgenstein's stories aspire to help us get clear on the concrete shape of our world and on the horizons of value that give it that shape – how they are what I called reality- or actuality-seeking – remind us that this power of helping us simply *see* inhabits fictions of all kinds. This attention to the essential world-directedness of fictional forms has the potential to revitalize perennial questions in the study of literary fiction, the novel, film, and performance, and it can reorganize how we think about the ways literature engages with the world and what it is that fictions do. In provoking us on the topic of what fictions and stories do, Wittgenstein's philosophy necessarily also prods us on the topic of what literature asks of us as readers. For when fiction shows us something about ourselves, or about the world, or about our place in it, it does this without handing us any propositional content. It has to *show* us that thing – give it to us, as contemporary and historical readers, as an imaginative picture of the world and an idea about the world at once.

Philosophical Investigations confronts the limitations of philosophical argument – or what I have called "propositional content" – with a form of fictional exploration, one in many ways akin to literary, cinematic, and other artistic story forms. The collecting, heaping, and arranging of details into what we call story, as we have seen, demands both a palpable texture of arrangement and at the same time a commitment to a continually developing collection of particulars and individuated cases of situatedness. And the latter can frustrate and obstruct narrative progression or arc. As Wittgenstein's sketches move forward and his casts "go on" in language, the scenarios he builds impress themselves as meaningful grammatical investigations – in other words, as more than loosely orchestrated anecdotes – because of the ceaseless pull of the particular, both an imaginative and intellectual pull, that unsettles whatever philosophical plots we might have developing in our minds. With each rhythmic fictitious appeal – now the builders can count, now they are pointing to things, now one of them doesn't speak our language – the questions that seemed pressing to us are shaken out of urgency, and our philosophical curiosity is shuffled around anew. Each of Wittgenstein's particulars has the potential to unsettle a larger sense of things.

There are novelists whose crafts in storytelling are wedded to the revelatory pull of the particular and the arranged clutter and complexity of everyday life in analogous ways. They are also the novelists who tend overtly to fight or outwrite the lines of traditional narrative arc. Virginia Woolf's complex and striking reflections on marriage within *Mrs. Dalloway*, for example, often play with detail in ways that give us entry into an everyday world whose parameters simply will not give or yield an expected plot – especially not a marriage plot – and whose texture and atmosphere, in fact, feel arranged against the grain of any plots we might invoke. This quality of Woolf's novel, incidentally, is similar to what Cora Diamond in a different context calls "the difficult of reality" when she describes how the world can outpace or resist the ways we try to arrange it and give it shape when we strive for forms of understanding. As Diamond helps us see, it is not simply that the world defies abstract conceptualization but that it continually teaches us about itself as it reshuffles our forms of understanding, sometimes having to force difficult lessons.[17]

In Woolf's novel, on that particular day in June in 1923, Clarissa Dalloway is vaguely occupied by the thought of her relationship to Richard Dalloway, and she reflects, undirectedly, on the emptiness of her marriage and as she walks through the streets of London, getting the flowers herself and later preparing for her party. In the remainder of the novel Woolf seems to wonder aloud and ask a revolutionary question about Clarissa: what if on that day in June when her hollow marriage

---

[17] Cora Diamond, "The Difficulty of Reality and the Difficulty of Philosophy," *Partial Answers: Journal of Literature and the History of Ideas* 1 (2): 1–26 (June 2003), doi:10.1353/pan.0.0090.

occupies her mind like this – what if on that very day the woman who in her youth gave Clarissa "the most exquisite moment of her whole life" with the gift of a kiss, Sally Seton, what if she unexpectedly finds her way into the novel and into Clarissa's life and attends the party Clarissa is planning?[18] Sally Seton does, of course, reappear and wander, now decades later, into Woolf's novel and Clarissa's life, but she is now "older, happier, less lovely." In a detail that screeches in the text like nails on a chalkboard as it follows so many of Woolf's beautiful reflections on love between women, Sally Seton declares loudly several times that she has become the mother of "five enormous boys." As she enters the novel's present tense in London, now fifty-five years old and no longer just a character in Clarissa's recollections of early summers spent at Bourton, the Sally who gave Clarissa the gift of a miraculous kiss also becomes strange to us on the printed page when she is introduced by Woolf as the unfamiliar "Lady Rosseter." Sally kisses Clarissa in the drawing room as she arrives at the party, a new kind of kiss coincident with her reappearance in the present tense of the novel, now once on each cheek politely in a manner that Woolf describes as overeffusive but not at all actually vibrant.[19]

There is no marriage plot or variation of marriage plot anywhere in sight in Mrs. Dalloway. Every detail about Sally Seton (and, analogously, also Peter Walsh) conspires to confirm that Clarissa Dalloway's way of finding freedom in love consists precisely of the independence that her toneless, uninteresting marriage to Richard Dalloway permits and authorizes. What might read as quiet tragedy in an Austen novel – lovelessness, a marriage without respect and esteem – is in Woolf's text the unexpected source of freedom and life. Marriage in the committed sense nearly appears to be incompatible with the best ways Clarissa Dalloway occupies life with others. What a different day in June it would have been – what a different life – had Sally Seton or Peter Walsh, those whom she might actually have loved, been waiting for her to come home from her morning excursion to the florist. How oppressive! Would she even have been permitted to go alone? Woolf, in fact, indicates at several points that Clarissa actually treasures her autonomy from real feeling, and the novel itself, in all of the rich and wonderful interior movements it traces and records in Woolf's demanding and stunning sentences, attests to the internal range and depth of Clarissa's character. This

---

[18] Virginia Woolf, Mrs. Dalloway (New York: Harcourt, 1981), 35.   [19] Ibid., 171, 181.

palpable depth has been afforded to the character Clarissa Dalloway by autonomy from the kind of love-plots novels generally like to trace. In *Mrs. Dalloway*, realities do grate against plotlike possibilities – Sally does not enter the novel to redeem Clarissa, or Peter to rescue her – and because they do, the world does come alive and indeed opens up, "this moment of June," the sky, streets, people, sounds – the things Clarissa can afford in earnest to take in and see. Woolf tells us right away about Clarissa that these things are "what she loved."[20] Perhaps this is one way to understand the preoccupation with particularity (in actions, events, characters, and environments) in the modernist novel more broadly. Woolf's details, the things Clarissa "loved," do not cohere or come together under a larger sense of directedness, and fiction in her hands refuses to make a whole.

In the novel that I have long suspected Woolf had in mind continuously when she wrote *Mrs. Dalloway*, Jane Austen's *Persuasion*, the pull of the particular overrides narrative progression almost completely, so that it is actually difficult to capture just how little happening happens in this text. No wonder Woolf admired Austen so much. This sense of resistance to conventional plot that supports an alternative allegiance to the particulars of the everyday is especially stark if we consider *Persuasion* next to the spirited and energetic stories that structure some of Austen's earlier novels such as *Pride and Prejudice* or *Emma*. In these texts, Austen's commitment to the marriage plot is evident in the ease and real pleasure of her executions. Plot in Austen's final novel, *Persuasion*, is made up of a different substance than it is her more direct renditions of final happy marriage. Austen, in *Persuasion*, is concerned with excavating the moral weight of ordinary events, unextraordinary actions, and everyday dialogue to the exclusion of a concern with her heroine's classic development.

In *Persuasion*, Austen leaves offstage everything we could possibly want to witness about the love affair between her protagonists, Anne Elliot and Captain Wentworth, since she relegates the decisive summer of passion eight years ago to a hasty paragraph in the opening chapters of the novel. Instead of handing us the pleasures of a love story, Austen overlays that long-ago tumultuous summer, still hidden entirely in its exuberance from our view as readers, like a transparency onto Anne Elliot's painfully drained and mundane present reality – in the same way that Woolf will overlay the summers spent at Bourton onto Clarissa's

---

[20] Ibid., 24.

present-tense London. The heroine in *Persuasion*, Anne Elliot, who is the most muted, melancholy, and inwardly reflective of all of Austen's characters, actually threatens to evaporate within the first chapters of the novel as her own cares and occupations receive so little acknowledgment from the characters around her. Anne only ever listens to others, nurses others, tends to others, and otherwise seems to exist for their sake and utility. She is barely there.

What will it take, then, for Austen to fashion a plot in which such a character finds her way into a satisfying union with another? What has to happen so that the respect and esteem that Anne Elliot and Frederick Wentworth mutually hold for one another, undisclosed and acknowledged dangerously belatedly, can become a marriage? One might say that Anne Elliot first has to wake up to the world generally rather than receding into it before she can become aware of – simply *see* – Wentworth's real feelings for her. Sighs, glances, walks, evasions, compliments, retorts, and – in a final riveting climax – a pen dropping from a letter-writer's hand: these are the things, the substances of Regency life, that Anne must learn to see are saturated with meaning. Anne must do this in order to arrive at the accurate understanding that Wentworth's love for her has not wavered. If she cannot learn to read a glance or the negative gesture of an inadvertently dropped pen, she is doomed to never see love. But Anne must also come-to in the world more generally, waking up to a world of everyday exchanges that flow with significance. That is, Anne's recognizing that the glance and the pen matter – or, indeed, that they are decisive – entails more than the recognizing the nuances of social, personal, and bodily codes. Anne must come out of her shell overall, a shell built of a too-rich and perpetually attended interior life, and begin to enter the spaces of action and activity that Austen has laid out in the novel by waking up to the actual world. As she learns to act and look around and see, it is as though we as readers do too, suddenly moved alongside her by a prolonged look, an unsolicited gesture, or a hand's visibly shaky and unsecure grasp of a writing instrument. In this way, Austen also helps us see the world as she attunes us to the increasingly meaningful and consequential texture of Anne Elliot's everyday.

Wittgenstein's thinking about uses of fiction can help us understand the difference between the ideas Woolf and Austen hold as novelists about what counts as a detail or particular in the texture of everyday living. This tells us something about how each understood the ability of writing to draw us toward and into the shape of life, but it also tells us something about how each novelist understood her concrete historical world. Woolf's skies and cars and streets of London are a flood of impressions and mostly unassimilated present-tense feelings and reflections, while Austen's walks and teas and glances as a rule reverberate with an undercurrent of moral, social, and personal meaning. Wittgenstein helps us recognize how Austen's late-Romantic bildungsroman anticipates Woolf's modernist experiment in its allegiance to the particular. It can also help us to begin to appreciate the different kinds of threats to traditional plot that *Persuasion* and *Mrs. Dalloway* constitute in the history of the novel.

It is difficult to point concretely to the ways that fiction in its essential world-boundedness attunes us to our world. One of the reasons this is so stems from the fact that many conversations at the crossroads of literature and philosophy disallow modes of reading in which we can attribute to stories things like showing us, attuning us, changing us, or inspiring us. But to help we can turn to an emerging body of criticism and thought whose investments encourage us to see the world *in* fiction rather than segregating or isolating the fictional from the real.[21] Whether it is Stanley Cavell's image of oneself being read by a text, Toril Moi's metaphors of reading as adventure, Cora Diamond's locating the moral interest of a text as everywhere in it, John Gibson's appeal to reading for life, or Bernard Harrison's discussions of texts that point to and criticize us – all of these pictures of reading insist that forms of fiction grant us an encounter not with an otherworldly reality but with our own world.[22] The parameters or outcomes of encounters like these with stories, novels, films, and performances cannot be drawn or predicted in advance. But we can return to the sentiment that animates the epigraph I have chosen for this chapter from an early fragment of Wittgenstein's to keep recalling and highlighting the reach of what we can learn from fiction: "Nothing is more important for teaching us to understand the concepts we have than constructing fictitious ones" (CV 49e).

---

[21] On this point, see especially David Schalkwyk's discussion of the "deeply ontologizing notions" (41) of many contemporary theories of fiction that insist on the other-worldly character of fictional forms; see his "Language, Reference, and the Objects of Fiction: A Wittgensteinian Critique," *symploke* 2 (1): 9–47 (Winter 1994), https://www.jstor.org/stable/40550334.

[22] Stanley Cavell, *The Claim of Reason and Themes out of School: Effects and Causes* (Chicago, IL: University of Chicago Press, 1984); Moi, "The Adventure of Reading"; Cora Diamond, "Having a Rough Story about What Moral Philosophy Is," in *The Literary Wittgenstein*, eds. John Gibson and Wolfgang Huemer (London, Routledge, 2004), 133–145; John Gibson, "Reading for Life," in *The Literary Wittgenstein*, 109–124; and Bernard Harrison, *Inconvenient Fictions*.

7 Wittgenstein and Lyric
Hannah Vandegrift Eldridge

Abstract: The impact of Wittgenstein's work on lyric poets, literary critics, and philosophers has been well documented. Philosophers and literary scholars, including Charles Altieri Stanley Cavell, Richard Eldridge, Michael Fischer, Walter Jost, and Joshua Wilner, have drawn on Wittgenstein to consider poetry from the Romantics to the present. Numerous poets from the mid-twentieth century on – among them Barbara Köhler, Marjorie Perloff, Lyn Hejinian, John Koethe, Charles Bernstein, and Ingeborg Bachmann – discuss or reference Wittgenstein, to say nothing of the authors like Perloff, David Rozema, Christopher Norris, or Benjamin Tilghman who contend that Wittgenstein's writing is itself "poetic." This chapter takes a different approach: it argues that Wittgenstein's work illuminates the central questions of the theory of the lyric, namely questions about what lyric poetry is and what it does. As questions of essence and existence, these are the kinds of question Wittgenstein helps us understand – not, primarily, by answering them but by prompting us to consider why and how we ask them. Moreover, Wittgenstein's attention to the ways poems use language and what we do with them shows how both poetry and the ways we respond to poems rest on his view of language as emerging from and constituting a form of life.

Keywords: Lyric Poetry, The Lyric I, Romanticism, Poetic Meaning, Language and Forms of Life, Poetic Form, Presentation versus Representation, Friedrich Hölderlin, Paul Celan.

The impact of Wittgenstein's work on lyric poets, literary critics, and philosophers who attend to the lyric has been well documented. Readers and scholars of poetry have been among Wittgenstein's most ardent admirers within literary studies, often for the rigorous respect his later work pays to the particularities of grammar and voice. Romantic poets have been discussed at length by Stanley Cavell, Richard Eldridge, Joshua Wilner, and Michael Fischer. Walter Jost's Wittgenstein is aligned with twentieth-century poets such as Robert Frost and Elizabeth Bishop; Charles Altieri's Wittgenstein is aligned with Wallace Stevens. Numerous poets from the mid-twentieth century to the present – among them Barbara Köhler, Marjorie Perloff, Lyn Hejinian, John Koethe, Charles Bernstein, Jan Zwicky, and Ingeborg Bachmann – discuss or reference Wittgenstein, to say nothing of the authors like Perloff, David Rozema, Christopher Norris, or Benjamin Tilghman who contend that Wittgenstein's writing is itself "poetic." In what follows, I take a different approach and outline the ways in which Wittgenstein's work illuminates the central questions of the theory of the lyric, namely: questions about what lyric poetry is and what it does. As questions of essence and existence, these are the kinds of question Wittgenstein helps to understand – not, primarily, by answering them, but by prompting us to consider why and how we ask them. Moreover, Wittgenstein's attention to what we do with poems and how they use language shows how poetry itself and the ways we talk about and respond to poems rest on his view of language as emerging from and constituting a form of life.

Wittgenstein thus plays two roles in my arguments: first, as a thinker whose ways of thinking help me articulate why we should not just give up on "lyric" as a category and get on with the business of talking about poems, and second, as a thinker whose persistent questioning with and in language helps explain the importance and effects of poetry often called "lyric." In what follows, I turn deliberately to work by theorists and scholars of the lyric who do not in general take up a Wittgensteinian or a more generally "philosophical" perspective to show how Wittgenstein illuminates the questions lyric studies poses itself, not only the questions about poetry that philosophers (Wittgensteinian or not) ask.

The question of whether anything called "lyric" exists has dominated one prominent line of analysis in literary studies' discussions of poetry. Scholars in this vein suggest abandoning "lyric" as an overarching category in favor of attention to the multiplicity of forms, genres, and texts that are only lumped together as so-called "lyric" by modern criticism and theory. Virginia Jackson, the most prominent exponent of this line of argument, coeditor of *The Lyric Theory Reader* and the author of the article on "Lyric" in the most recent edition of the *Princeton Encyclopedia of Poetry and Poetics*, points out quite correctly that:

In Western poetics, almost all poetry is now characterized as *lyric*, but this has not always been the case. Over the last three centuries, *lyric* has shifted its meaning from adjective to noun, from a quality in poetry to a category that can seem to include nearly all verse. The ancient, medieval, and early modern verse we now think of as lyric was made up of a variety of songs or short occasional poems. Since the 18th century, brevity, subjectivity, passion, and sensuality have been the qualities associated with poems called *lyric*; thus, in modernity, the term is used for a kind of poetry that expresses personal feeling (G. W. F. Hegel) in a concentrated and harmoniously arranged form (E. A. Poe, S. T. Coleridge) and that is indirectly addressed to the private reader (William Wordsworth, John Stuart Mill).[1]

She thus argues that the "idea of lyric" is a "modern invention," and considers but eventually rejects the possibility that "lyric" might be a name applied after the fact (but nonetheless appropriately) to poetry that had modern lyric features but existed without a name. This solution, in her view, cannot hold up because the modern "notion of subjectivity, emotion, and compression in poetry – in sum, the personal lyric – did not match ideas about poetry (or persons) in antiquity" (826).

Instead, "before the early modern period, one often finds that *lyric* is a rather abstract term for the miscellaneous and historically specific genres that now seem to us lyrical in retrospect" (827). Jackson ultimately rejects "our current sense of the lyric" as "a persistent confusion – among verse genres, between historical genres and natural "forms," between adjective and noun, between cognitive and affective registers, between grammar and rhetoric, between privacy and publicity, and among various ideas about poetry" (826). This confusion has been, as Jackson acknowledges, "enormously generative for both poets and critics" (826), but because it ultimately obscures important historical, generic, and individual differences, we are better off without it. I find much of the work produced by this approach enormously compelling, particularly in its attention to formal detail and the cultural-political work done by those forms in their situated historical moments; this work can make one wonder why we bother with "the lyric" at all.

Here, the Wittgensteinian habit of thought that asks *why* we theorize, in this case about "the lyric," and his exfoliations of the drive to theorizing as itself significant of our mindedness becomes helpful: it is important to our experience of poetry to talk about "the lyric" precisely

---

[1] Virginia Jackson, "Lyric," in *The Princeton Encyclopedia of Poetry and Poetics*, 4th ed., ed. Roland Greene (Princeton, NJ: Princeton University Press, 2012), 826. Henceforth cited parenthetically.

because we *do* talk about and people *have* kept theorizing about it, and that seems to tell us something important about our lives with poems. In a review article titled "What is This Thing Called Lyric?," Stephanie Burt takes precisely this approach, beginning by offering an extensive collection of other scholars' definitions in response to the question "What can the word "lyric" these days mean?"[2] Burt notes objections to various definitions and to the notion of "the lyric" as an overarching genre, and then shifts attention to what we say about "lyric" and the emergence and usage of the word. Although readers (critics, literary scholars, philosophers) cannot define lyric "using internal features alone," it seems possible to "say what succeeds, aesthetically or emotionally, for us, when we read what we have learned to call 'poetry,' and what we have tried to call 'lyric,' making our evaluations – and then, and therefore, our definitions – explicit" (429). In response to objections along the lines of Jackson's, that lyric is a term applied only after the fact by critics and theorists, Burt compares the use-history of "lyric" to other words: "Lyric poetry was not just the same in 1850 or 1400 as in 1950, but neither was an apple, or an earlobe; nevertheless, we hypothesize that apples and earlobes were present in 1400 and in 1850 and that some people enjoyed them in some way – though 'earlobe,' the word, dates only to 1859. Did John Donne have earlobes? Did John Donne write lyric poems?" (429) She acknowledges that one can always object that our best efforts at understanding "what historically specified groups of people have meant by a term" (429) run up against the opacity of other minds: "We cannot know whether early modern readers understood Sidney's sadness as we think

---

[2] To wit: "A poem with one speaker; a poem in which the poet speaks to herself; 'short, intense and exquisite redactions of impassioned speech' (a notion with 'recognizable beginnings in the early Renaissance') (Roland Greene); a poem involving apostrophe, 'a turning aside from whatever is taken to be the real or normal addressee' (Jonathan Culler); ancient Greek poems accompanied by lyre; 'a genre of song,' 'by definition musical' (Robert von Hallberg); poems that can be sung; poems that resemble song; 'the voicing of one moment's state of feeling' (Mark Booth); 'any fairly short, non-narrative poem presenting a single speaker who expresses a state of mind or a process of thought and feeling' (M. H. Abrams); work that is 'personal, subjective, short, meditative, emotive, private, musical' (Dean Rader); 'a special kind of personal utterance' whose subcategories include 'hymn, laud, ode and nocturne' (Gabrielle Starr); verse, or poetic language, 'made abstract,' so that it does not represent a socially specifiable individual but instead makes available emotions and a psychological position, 'an utterance for us to utter as ours,'" much as sheet music can be played by any sufficiently skilled musician (Helen Vendler); a poem that descends from, or resembles, other poems often called lyric." S. Burt, "What Is This Thing Called Lyric?," *Modern Philology* 113 (3): 422 (February 2016), https://doi.org/10.1086/684097, 424–425. Henceforth cited parenthetically.

we understand Sidney's sadness, or John Ashbery's sadness, for the same reason that I cannot truly know whether you see what I see when I see 'red'" (430).

Burt suggests instead that we "look at what actual readers have said" (430); there exists good evidence that people talked about and interacted with works in ways that we talk about and interact with what we call lyric (430–431), in contexts from troubadour culture to twelfth-century China to Ancient Egypt (431–432). No provable definition can classify what we will identify as lyric prior to such experiences; rather, definition follows and struggles to keep up with reading, hearing, and speaking: "We think that we know what poetry (or good poetry) and lyric poetry (or lyric work, or good lyric work) are because we have already read some. And we are not alone. Our habits and tastes and not-yet explicit reactions ... tell us how to use a word correctly even if we cannot say why that usage is correct" (432).[3] For this reason, "we cannot learn how to use those definitions, what kind of work they do, by looking only at explicit theories that people developed in order to explain the kinds of experience that they already believed they had had" (432–433). Burt recognizes that we cannot possibly prove that we know what happened in another mind that produced something we call "lyric" and contends that, nonetheless, we can identify and identify with ways of talking about poems that chime with how we use the word.[4] Both by way of communities of speaking and saying and by way of the problem of other

---

[3] In response to the notion that "lyric" is a matter exclusively of arbitrary readerly convention, Burt addresses Stanley Fish's famous "experiment" in which Fish supposedly "proved" that "poetry" is an arbitrary convention by getting his students to read a list of names as "a Renaissance lyric poem" (435). Burt points out that "Fish got his students to interpret "Jacobs-Rosenbaum" as if it were Donne, but does not say that he got them to like or admire it. "Definitions of poetry are recipes," Fish continued, "for by directing readers what to look for in a poem, they instruct them in ways of looking that will produce what they expect to see" cit. Burt 436. Actual recipes instruct us in ways of cooking that will produce what we expect to eat; and, like recipes for producing poems (or kinds of poems: odes, mad songs, "lyric"), recipes for food require ingredients, and recipes can fail" (435–436).

[4] Burt's explicit recourse to Wittgenstein is, in fact, less persuasive than the general Wittgensteinian character of her investigation of our language use; she refers to "Wittgenstein's elaborations on 'I know that I am a human being' [*On Certainty* 2e]," of which she contends "Such claims solicit, and receive, sophisticated defenses in philosophy departments" (435). Whether or not claims like this one are in fact the daily bread of philosophy departments, and whether philosophers are the primary arbiters of "the view that persons exist" (35), to take Wittgenstein's remark "I know that I am a human being" as a straightforward argumentative claim, seems to me an oversimplification.

minds, Burt's account links the lyric to persons; she asks us to enter into the language-game of giving an "account of how poems – lyric poems – evoke individuals" (438).

John Koethe raises the question of the mutual imbrication of lyric and subjectivity in and for Wittgenstein as he probes Wittgenstein's "affinities with literary modernism."[5] While Koethe notes that Wittgenstein shares with modernists (and their romantic forebears) a "dismantling of the Cartesian conception of self and mentality" (96), a "manner ... of writing" (97), and a "deflationist attitude towards the theoretical" (97), he notes a "disparity between doctrine and sensibility" (99) in Wittgenstein that complicates these characteristics. Koethe acknowledges that Wittgenstein sometimes *sounds* as though he wants us to just stop theorizing about representation, or subjectivity, or private language, but makes a compelling case that this is a misreading:

> Wittgenstein perhaps encourages the idea that it's easy to rid ourselves of illusions like this by blaming them on "language," or on a misconstrual of the "grammar" of our ways of describing, say, our sensations (for example, on the model of "object and designation"), as though we could dispel them merely by adopting a different way of talking. This is misleading: when he says "they lay in our language" what he means, I take it, is that we feel compelled to conceptualize our experience in certain ways, and that we find it difficult, if not impossible, to arrive at alternative ways of conceptualizing it. (100)

I cite Koethe's remarks at length here because they help us draw attention to the ways Wittgenstein anticipates two strands in contemporary discussions of lyric. Koethe's tension between "doctrine" (what Wittgenstein's writings are roughly taken to say) and "sensibility" (their mode, tone, and composition) helps show that Jackson's and Burt's treatments of "the lyric" are two kinds of Wittgensteinian gesture, which we might call Rortyian and Cavellian, respectively.[6] Jackson mirrors the doctrine, in which we recognize that "lyric" is a misleading conception and "walk away from it," just as "the attentive reader of

---

[5] John Koethe, "Wittgenstein and Lyric Subjectivity," *Literary Imagination* 10 (1): 96–101 (2007), 100. Henceforth cited parenthetically.

[6] Koethe criticizes "philosophers like Richard Rorty" for taking Wittgenstein's answer to (e.g.) the question "How do we manage to represent the world in language and thought?" to be a "simplistic" 'We don't'" (100). Richard Eldridge has registered a similar critique: Rorty misreads "the Wittgenstein of the *Investigations* insofar as he thinks that Wittgenstein there urges us to stop thinking about essences and natures altogether, as though we could stop" (Richard Eldridge, "Philosophy and the Achievement of Community: Rorty, Cavell, and Criticism," *Metaphilosophy* 14 (2): 124 (April 1983).

[Wittgenstein's] later work is supposed to come to see through the Cartesian model of the mind and walk away from it, as Wittgenstein himself was supposedly able to do" (Koethe, 100). Burt's interrogation of the category of "lyric" registers the "sensibility," in which we cannot simply step outside our concepts, as misleading as they might be (and as the concept of "lyric" occasionally has been). Stanley Cavell is perhaps the most persistent defender of the idea that the very fact of our being drawn to "pictures" and "grammars" – like interiority or Cartesian dualist subjectivity – is a constitutive characteristic of human mindedness, what Wittgenstein calls the "running against the walls of our cage" as "a document of a tendency of the human mind which I personally cannot help respecting deeply."[7]

While it might seem overblown to cast a (seemingly) literary-theoretical debate in terms of existential categories like human existence and finitude, as Burt notes, "Apparently, if you want to believe in 'lyric,' in the most important current senses for the term, you have to believe that there are persons too ... To ask about the boundaries of lyric is to ask (as Turing also asked) what a person is, how we know, and why we care" (437). The rapidity with which theorists of the lyric turn to the category of the subject suggest that, at a minimum, what you say about the lyric will show something about what you have to say about subjectivity. Indeed, it might be that the idea of the lyric – in its guise as the genre of interior subjectivity characterized by Hegel – received a name when it did because philosophy and poetry needed a way to say something about the relation between subjectivity and language that is not exhausted by the representation of subjects in language.

If we bear in mind the tension between the doctrine of attending to the poems and practices that can be obscured by lyric and the centrality of lyric to the thinking through of subjectivity and language, what are the questions, definitions, or investigations that unfold when we continue to theorize about lyric? A 2017 issue of the *Journal of Literary Theory* on the topic of "Theories of the Lyric," sets itself the task of bringing together a field that is "fragmented along linguistic, national and disciplinary lines."[8] The volume's authors take up questions of fictionality,

---

[7] Ludwig Wittgenstein, "A Lecture on Ethics," *The Philosophical Review* 74 (1): 12 (1965). Cavell articulates this tendency in *In Quest of the Ordinary: Lines of Skepticism and Romanticism* (Chicago, IL: University of Chicago Press, 1988) as "the human wish to deny the condition of human existence" as finite and limited (5).
[8] Claudia Hillebrandt, Sonja Klimek, Ralph Müller, William Waters, and Rüdiger Zymner, "Theories of Lyric," *Journal of Literary Theory* 11 (1): 1–11 (2017).

distinctions from narrative or dramatic genres, speakers, relations to music and sound historical development, and interpretive practices. Are lyric poems fictional? What makes lyric different from novels or plays? Who speaks in the poem? Is there such a thing as a lyrical "I"? Are poems songs? Who wrote the first lyric poem? Is poetry still lyric? How do we read poems? Do they affect us differently or specially?

In response to these questions, numerous authors both in the issue and beyond articulate overlapping sets of varying numbers of lyrical traits or characteristics. In his ambitious *Theory of the Lyric* (2015), Jonathan Culler works from readings of exemplary poems to draw out features that "do not constitute a checklist for deciding what is a lyric but rather a system of possibilities that underlie the tradition and ought to be borne in mind when reading poems that may have a relation to that tradition."[9] He breaks down this system of possibilities into "four parameters": the "enunciative apparatus of the lyric" which focuses on voice and employs "effects ... of aurality" (36) and, second, "lyric's attempt to be itself an event rather than the representation of an event" (36), making it a *presentation* rather than representation of what Culler calls "truths about the world" (36). Third, Culler describes the lyric as "ritualistic" rather than exclusively fictional, related to formal patterning, repetition, and invocation rather than fictional worlds (37); finally, he describes the lyric's "explicitly hyperbolic quality," whereby "lyrics hyperbolically risk animating the world, investing mundane objects or occurrences with meaning" (38). Although Culler resists a straightforward definition of the lyric, he insists on the importance of maintaining the idea of lyric as a genre, or better a macrogenre that encompasses the numerous subforms (elegy, ode, hymn, ballad) that have been deployed in the history of the lyric. Moreover, even the numerous poetic or literary movements that have positioned themselves as opposing the lyric or lyricism need the category to react against (77). Culler closes with an almost-definition, understanding "lyric as epideixis – public discourse about meaning and value – made distinctive by its ritualistic elements" (350).

Building on Culler's argument by attending to interpretive practices and adjacent genres, Jahan Ramazani notes that although "lyric differs from more empirical and mimetic genres by virtue of the density of its

---

[9] Jonathan Culler, *Theory of the Lyric* (Cambridge, MA: Harvard University Press, 2015), 6. Henceforth cited parenthetically.

verbal and formal mediation of the world," it nonetheless "can't be defined by one or even many formal features that are exclusive to it."[10] Instead, he suggests, "lyric can be described as a range of nonexclusive formal strategies encoded in texts and the communities that produce and receive them" (97). The combination of texts and communities, production and reception exist, of course, in specific historical moments but often persist and extend outside them: "lyric and affiliated subgenres and modes live historically but survive transhistorically, albeit often dramatically refashioned" (97). In doing so, lyric also crosses national and linguistic boundaries ("lyric is transnational") and thus "needs to be studied at both the micro and macro levels – both its language-specific intricacies and textures, and its participation in broader patterns of genre, history, and cultural migration" (97). Ramazani calls for a "transnational poetics" that is "attentive to cross-cultural hybridization, creolization, and vernacularization in lyric"; this attention can help remind the European-American academy, in particular, that "lyric is intergeneric, best understood in its dialogue" with genres like prayer and news (97). Indeed, lyric may be particularly suited to crossing cultural and linguistic boundaries because it is "neither merely personal nor entirely impersonal, making it readily appropriable," inviting readers to speak through and with the voices and personae it unfolds (97).

Klaus Hempfer theorizes the epistemological status of work like Ramazani's and Culler's that eschews definition for description using the concept of the prototype. Prototypes differ from categories or classifications in that they focus on the core of a set of characteristics of a genre, rather than the boundaries.[11] Prototypes of categories describe "clearest cases of category membership" (411), and membership in those categories is a matter of degree of similarity to the prototype, not a binary between membership/non-membership in the category (411). To extend prototype theory to literary genre, Hempfer draws on Wittgenstein's notion of family resemblances and his remark that the most important concepts in ethics and aesthetics, as in ordinary

---

[10] Jahan Ramazani, "Lyric Poetry: Intergeneric, Transnational, Translingual?," *Journal of Literary Theory* 11 (1): 97 (2017), https://doi.org/10.1515/jlt-2017-0011. Henceforth cited parenthetically.

[11] Klaus Hempfer, "Some Aspects of a Theory of Genre," in *Linguistics and Literary Studies / Linguistik und Literaturwissenschaft Interfaces, Encounters, Transfers / Begegnungen, Interferenzen und Kooperationen*, eds. Monika Fludernik and Daniel Jacob (Berlin: de Gruyter, 2014), 406. Henceforth cited parenthetically.

language, have blurred edges (410). Unlike family resemblances, which Wittgenstein famously describes as "like a rope whose strength does not reside in the fact that some one fibre runs through its whole length, but in the overlapping of many fibres" (PI §28e) in the prototype there are "core" features that do occur in all instances belonging to the category (412). Hempfer acknowledges that the lyric prototype is particularly difficult to identify, and he commits himself only to asserting that the prototype "must be defined in such an 'abstract' manner so as not to coincide with any specific historical lyrical form" and, moreover, "must not contain any mutually exclusive attributes" (415). While Hempfer's prototype description doesn't give much sense of what a "lyric prototype" would look like, work like Ramazani's and Culler's, not to mention the lists of microgenres provided by Jackson and the multitude of definitions Burt contemplates, begins to suggest some characteristics of the "family" of the lyric.

Hempfer is not the only theorist of the lyric to link genre to family resemblances, but his recourse to Wittgenstein's term foregrounds a difficulty for literary-theoretical appropriations of Wittgenstein's writing, one to which my argument here is not immune: the tendency to distill Wittgenstein's complex and self-questioning series of writings into "Wittgenstein's concept of family resemblances" or, in my case, "Wittgenstein's view of language." As Koethe notes, "the manner of Wittgenstein's writing" as "aphoristic, disjunctive and nonlinear," creating a "cacophony of multiple voices and shifting perspectives" marks (one of) his affinities with literary modernism (97) and at the same time hinders any such distillation. These attributes are in keeping with Wittgenstein's own notorious remark, in *Culture and Value*, that "Philosophie dürfte man eigentlich nur *dichten*" ("philosophy ought really to be written only as a *poetic composition*") (CV 24e), the source of the various assertions I noted that Wittgenstein's writing *is* poetic. We ought, certainly, to be cautious in taking any single argumentative proposition as Wittgenstein's unified and final view on X, and when I refer to thoughts like "language as use rather than reference," I hope to indicate less a single discursive position than a series of stances into which we are invited by his persistent investigations of how we talk to and with each other.

At the same time, however, I take issue with the assertion that Wittgenstein's writing *is* straightforwardly poetic, or, to go even further, that a line of Wittgenstein is no easier to describe than a line of poetry. First, as Koethe notes in a different article,

Despite the concluding pronouncement of the *Tractatus* that its sentences are nonsense, and despite Wittgenstein's repeated insistence that the *Investigations* merely reminds us of obvious facts and embodies no philosophical theses or arguments, I would maintain that the former is a deeply systematic and constructive work, and that the latter continues to embody the semantic (and psychological) nonfactualism of the earlier book, in support of a community-based conception of language.[12]

Moreover, the very kind of attentiveness to our own habits of reading and talking about poems that Wittgenstein calls for – and which I discuss in more detail later in this chapter – suggest that we should ask if we *do*, in fact, do the same things with a line of Wittgenstein and a line of, say, Hölderlin. I am determined to hold on to the experiential difference between reading "Weh mir, wo nehm' ich, wenn / Es Winter ist, die Blumen"[13] and "Now think of the following use of language: I send someone shopping. I give him a slip of paper marked 'five red apples'" (PI §1) or the German original. The relation between formal shaping – in the case of Hölderlin's poem the alliteration and assonance, the startling enjambment of "wenn / Es" – and communicative content is different. I take special care to mark the end of Hölderlin's lines in quoting him, whereas I am not concerned with the lineation of what the *Philosophical Investigations* prints as a joined-up paragraph. (There are, of course, times where line breaks in Wittgenstein *do* matter, as when he uses line breaks to indicate voice shifts.) Moreover, the distinction would become clearer the more I cited of each work: the relation between the line and a half of "Half of Life" cited here and its compressed and paratactic fourteen-line entirety versus the two lines of section 1 and the entirety of the *Investigations* seems to me importantly different.

The differences – as with many of our categories – between philosophy, literature, and lyric are surely not absolute: one might envision a gradient with (say) Frege on one end, Wordsworth (perhaps) at the other, and authors like Wittgenstein and Musil in the squashy middle. But if we take Wittgenstein seriously in asking how we talk about poems, literature, or art works more generally and in paying attention to the distinctions we draw, we enter the ambit of his own remarks on aesthetics and

---

[12] John Koethe, "Perplexity and Plausibility: On Philosophy, Lyrical and Discursive," *Common Knowledge* 20 (1): 55–61 (December 25, 2013).
[13] Friedrich Hölderlin, *Sämtliche Werke und Briefe in drei Bänden*, vol. 1, 445. "But oh, where shall I find when / Winter comes, the flowers" (Friedrich Hölderlin, *Selected Poems and Fragments*, trans. Michael Hamburger, 4th ed. (London: Anvil Press Poetry, 2004), 171; (translation modified).

his rather more limited explicit discussions of lyric poetry and poets. Wittgenstein's discussion of aesthetics is a discussion – better, a critique – of a language-game, of how the philosophy of art has forgotten how we use language in its efforts to define "beautiful" or "good." He explains, "We don't start from certain words, but from certain occasions or activities" (LC 3); reading poetry is just such an activity.

Wittgenstein invites us to "Take the question: 'How should poetry be read? What is the correct way of reading it?'" and suggests proper metrical stress – in the case of Klopstock, almost overemphasis – as one context for such questions (LC 4). I take it that the main point here is not the relatively mundane one that following a poet's reading suggestions enlivens his verse[14]; rather, Wittgenstein focuses on his own responses to the sudden and new experience of the poem, which he distinguishes from the use of "aesthetic adjectives": "The important fact was that I read [the Klopstock poems] again and again. When I read these poems I made gestures and facial expressions which were what would be called gestures of approval. But the important thing was that I read the poems entirely differently, more intensely, and I said to others: 'Look! This is how they should be read.' Aesthetic adjectives hardly played any rôle" (LC 4–5). In our form of life with poems, we do not go around sticking on labels from aesthetics ("good," "beautiful," "sublime"); we continue to read and we call others' attention to what we have heard, or seen, or felt.[15]

Wittgenstein reminds us that it is often not easy to say what we do with poetry or what has arrested our attention and brought us back to a work. He wonders whether we read because of "associations" or ideas extracted out of poems, and he admits it would be possible to read this way: "You *could* select either of two poems to remind you of death, say.

---

[14] "There are cases of poetry which should be almost scanned – where the metre is as clear as crystal – others where the metre is entirely in the background. I had an experience with the 18th century poet Klopstock. I found that the way to read him was to stress his metre abnormally. Klopstock put u _ u (etc.) in front of his poems" (LC 4).

[15] This does not mean that Wittgenstein collapses all differences of style, poet, or epoch into subjective response; reflecting in puzzlement on his own remark that there are shared peculiarities of style between Johannes Brahms and Gottfried Keller, he notes that "One can actually judge when a piece of poetry was written by hearing it, by the style. You could imagine this was impossible, if people in 1850 wrote the same way as in 1750, but you could still imagine people saying: 'I am sure this was written in 1850.' Cf. [a man on a railway journey to Liverpool saying.] 'I am sure Exeter is in that direction'" (LC 32).

But supposing you had read a poem and admired it, could you say: 'Oh, read the other it will do the same'?" (LC 35). The question, then is what *do* we do with poetry: "How do we use poetry? Does it play this role – that we say such a thing as: 'Here is something just as good...'? [...] We *don't* read poetry to get associations. We don't happen to, but we might" (LC 35). Sometimes, in fact, we do seem to use poetry this way, as the existence of both print and internet compilations of "poems about love" for weddings, or '"mourning poems" for funerals indicate. I would argue that the reason we seek out and perform poems at moments of ritual importance, however, might well have less to do with the associations they evoke than with other features of the lyric, particularly the kind of formal shaping and material texture I gestured toward very briefly in citing Hölderlin.

At times, the very effectiveness of formal-material features – just *this* line ending, just *that* rhyme – can provoke bafflement at what Wittgenstein sketches as the "indescribable," something that arrests us in a fullness of experience not explained by the referential content of any "association." In the lecture notes of a course on description (*not* aesthetics), he remarks "One of the most interesting points which the question of not being able to describe is connected with, [is that] the impression which a certain verse or bar in music gives you is indescribable. 'I don't know what it is...Look at this transition. ... What is it?...'" (LC 37). Wittgenstein insists again that this is not a case of adjectival labeling (we don't say "This is indescribable" in response to an impressive poem); rather, the feeling of something's being indescribable comes from "a case that saying one is incapable of describing comes from being intrigued and *wanting* to describe, asking oneself: 'What is this? What's he doing, wanting to do here? – Gosh, if only I could say what he's doing here'" (LC 37). The questions "What is this?" and "What's he doing here?" (gender equality is not something for which we should look to Wittgenstein) open onto the ongoing questioning that preoccupies contemporary theories of the lyric and scholars of poetry: What *does* poetry do, and how does it work?

The questions and suggestions Wittgenstein raises about our lives with language, I argue, do a better job than virtually anything else on offer in explaining how poetry, as language, does what it does, in particular with regard to subjectivity, world-orientation, and the revivifying of language in moments of alienation and oppression. As Wolfgang Huemer explains, Wittgenstein's view shifts from the *Tractatus* to the work in and after the *Philosophical Investigations*: in the former Wittgenstein remains focused on issues of representation, asking "how words can depict the world" and views "language ... as an abstract system," whereas in the *Philosophical Investigations* and after, he looks at "language as ... a social practice" and attends to use rather than reference.[16] His considerations of meaning as use resist a cultural conviction as old as Plato, the conviction that language is or ought to be a system of *reference* to a reality that somehow exists by itself, apart from being perceived and talked about, and that names of objects, in particular, can be true or false of reality.[17] Wittgenstein, conversely, focuses on use and practice, explaining that "a meaning of a word is a kind of employment of it. For it is what we learn when the word is incorporated into our language" (OC §10) He adds, "children do not learn that books exist, that armchairs exist, etc. etc., – they learn to fetch books, sit in armchairs, etc. etc. (OC §62). Or, as Stanley Cavell has put it, "we learn language and learn the world *together*."[18] None of their sentences is a straightforward argumentative claim – what is a *kind* of employment? How *incorporated*? What does it mean to *learn* the world versus learn *about* the world? – but they suggest a powerful mutual imbrication of words and world that is not a relationship of one-to-one correspondence.

These remarks share at least some attributes with stances more widely adopted in literary studies, as the L=A=N=G=U=A=G=E poet Charles Bernstein notes in a review of Cavell's work on Wittgenstein. He points

---

[16] Wolfgang Huemer, "Introduction: Wittgenstein, Language, and Philosophy of Literature," in *The Literary Wittgenstein*, eds. John Gibson and Wolfgang Huemer (London: Routledge, 2004), 1–13, 1.

[17] For a full reading of this conviction, see Bernard Harrison, "Imagined Worlds and the Real One: Plato, Wittgenstein, and Mimesis," in Gibson and Huemer, *The Literary Wittgenstein*, 94. Harrison explains this conviction as one that language is "empty of reality, a mere notation." In this picture, reality "just does divide up into certain categories of nameable elements, and it is the business of philosophical inquiry ... to determine the identity and nature of those categories of elements" (94).

[18] Stanley Cavell, "Must We Mean What We Say?," in *Must We Mean What We Say? A Book of Essays*, updated ed. (Cambridge: Cambridge University Press, 2002), 1–43; here 19. See also Martin Stone, "On the Old Saw, 'Every Reading of a Text is an Interpretation': Some Remarks," in Gibson and Huemer, *The Literary Wittgenstein*, 200ff. Some readers, such as Marjorie Perloff, collapse the *Tractatus* and the *Investigations* and see Wittgenstein's view of language as emphasizing the unreliability of reference without the focus on use: Perloff's stance toward Wittgenstein is characterized by remarks like "a trip [through the *Philosophical Investigations*] will gradually make it impossible for us to trust, ever again, the full authority of a given word or group of words to *name* a particular thing" Marjorie Perloff, *Wittgenstein's Ladder: Poetic Language and the Strangeness of the Ordinary* (Chicago, IL: University of Chicago Press, 1996), 68.

out that Cavell (and Wittgenstein, in Cavell's reading) and Jacques Derrida are similar "in respect to getting rid of the idea that words refer to metaphysical absolutes, to universals, to 'transcendental signifieds,' rather than being part of a grammar of shared conventions, a grammatology."[19] But they differ radically in their responses to the absence of such transcendental signifieds: "What Derrida ends up transforming to houses of cards – shimmering traces of life, as insubstantial as elusive – Wittgenstein locates as *meaning*, with the full range of intention, responsibility, coherence, and possibility for revolt against or madness without" (Bernstein, 304). Picking up the idea that we learn language in practice and use, Bernstein remarks that "learning a language is not learning the names of things outside language, as if it were simply a matter of matching up signifiers with signifieds, as if signifieds already existed and we were just learning new names for them.... Rather, we are initiated by language into a socious, which is for us the world" (Bernstein, 299). The relation between language, grammar, and form of life – which Cavell emphasizes is frightening in its lack of assurances and certainties – suggests the ways that the kinds of things the lyric does in language are also the kinds of things lyric does in the world. And so whatever lyric poetry discovers about language, it will also discover about the form of life from which it emerges. Changing language also entails changing a form of life.

Here, I think, is where we need to extend Wittgenstein's understanding of language, subjectivity, and forms of life beyond his own philosophizing in order to see how they illuminate our accounts of the lyric. Wittgenstein gives us the idea that doing something in language means doing something in a form of life, but he doesn't have much to say about the forms of life that inhere in and are changed by, say, transformations of sonnet form. I thus turn to a few particularly suggestive moments from recent scholarship on lyric poetry whose claims both extend and are deepened by a Wittgensteinian understanding of the mutual shaping of language and form of life – even as the authors in question do not necessarily see their work as taking part in a Wittgensteinian project and occasionally embrace standpoints contrary to any such project. I foreground the areas of sonic materiality, lyric intersubjectivity, and linguistic form both because Wittgenstein himself has less to say about

---

[19] Charles Bernstein, "Reading Cavell Reading Wittgenstein," *boundary 2* 9 (2): 304 (Winter 1981).

them and because they make distinctively lyric contributions to "all the whirl of organism Wittgenstein calls 'forms of life.'"[20]

In quite different ways, Sherri Irvin and Mutlu Konuk Blasing (to name just two examples) theorize sound in poetry as recasting and "recharging" our relation to language. Irvin, considering poems that seem to reject the transmission of any meaning altogether, argues that sound structures can "activate the resonances and associations evoked by the poem's words, rather than merely their referential content."[21] Doing so might productively "fray ... the connection between a word or expression and its main conventional meaning" (100). Blasing, taking a Lacanian approach to language, understands poetry, and its materiality in particular, as bringing to articulation the trauma of human initiation into the symbolic order of language: "Poetic conventions socially sanction a kind of language use that undoes, even as it reinstitutes, the illusion of meaning in language; they carry a history of communal acknowledgement of a shared trauma of individuation/socialization."[22] Poetry thus enables a "*willed* return" to language use, a deliberate rather than unconscious choice to enter into language (62–63). Curiously, even as she proposes a "lyric subject," Blasing conceives of her project as "outside humanism" (16); perhaps, if we understand the human of "humanism" as universal, transhistorical, and somehow a natural given, but if we follow Wittgenstein in understanding that learning language inducts us into a communal-social form of life, the fragility and transiency of the category of "the human" within that form of life becomes apparent. What Irvin and Blasing add, I suggest, is a sense that we can be arrested, either painfully or pleasurably, by the stuff that words are made of, and that this moment, too, can reshape a form of life.[23]

Susan Stewart and William Waters take up, among other things, the ways in which the lyric reaches toward others in its form of life. Waters

---

[20] Cavell, "The Availability of Wittgenstein's Later Philosophy," in *Must We Mean What We Say?*, 52.

[21] Sherri Irvin, "Unreadable Poems and How They Mean," in *The Philosophy of Poetry*, ed. John Gibson, (Oxford: Oxford University Press, 2015), 93.

[22] Mutlu Konuk Blasing, *Lyric Poetry. The Pain and the Pleasure of Words* (Princeton, NJ: Princeton University Press, 2007), 62.

[23] As I discuss in detail in the first chapter of *Lyric Orientations*, Stanley Cavell works out the relation between words and worlds beginning from the Wittgensteinian view of language and extending into the uses of language in American Transcendentalism; see Eldridge, *Lyric Orientations*, 28–33 and Stanley Cavell, *The Senses of Walden – An Expanded Edition* (Chicago, IL: Chicago University Press, 1992). Cavell attends less than I would to poetic form.

examines "poems that say you" as the most direct "way of talking about poetry as a form of contact," and suggests that the various forms of address and the responses they seem to demand might illuminate "why poetry is valuable, why it matters to us, and how we might come to feel answerable to it."[24] Address figures the intersubjective character of language as such: "address is not in the strict sense a grammatical category at all; it is the fiber of language's use and being" (Waters, 5). Stewart's account adds attention to the intersubjective character of meter as somatically effective speech: "as metered language, language that retains and projects the force of individual sense experience and yet reaches towards intersubjective meaning, poetry sustains and transforms the threshold between individual and social existence."[25] Both poetic form and its bodily efficacy mediate between individual, broader, and tradition: "Poetic form made of language relies on rhythm and musical effects that are known with our entire bodies, carried forward by poets working out of tradition and carried over by listeners receiving the work" (Stewart, 12). The poems that Waters and Stewart treat (and in Stewart's case, the poems she writes) sound and shape themselves within communities of language use, reminding us that not only the meanings of words are kinds of employment, but that both meaning and use take part in the affective, somatic, and conceptual responses to how words look and sound in just these lines and letters in this particulasr language.

Finally, Ingrid Nelson and Caroline Levine make two cases for the cultural-political work done by both canonical and innovative forms as particular types of structured language. Nelson draws explicitly on Wittgenstein's account of forms of life and of the way rules are embedded in practices to "put biopolitics in dialogue with literary formalism."[26] Levine has entered perhaps the most powerful argument in recent years for formalism as a politically attuned and effective mode of study and criticism, as it helps readers to critique forms in and of

---

[24] William Waters, *Poetry's Touch. On Lyric Address* (Ithaca, NY: Cornell University Press, 2003), 1–2.

[25] Susan Stewart, *Poetry and the Fate of the Senses* (Chicago, IL: Chicago University Press, 2002), 2.

[26] Ingrid Nelson, "Poetics of the Rule: Form, Biopolitics, Lyric," *New Literary History* 50 (1): 65 (Winter 2019). The extent to which Wittgenstein's "form of life" needs Nelson's addition of Giorgio Agamben to address biopolitics, as though biopolitics and its theorizations were not already part of a form of life, is debatable.

power structures and hierarchies.[27] She presents five ways forms work: (i) "forms constrain," (ii) "forms differ," (iii) "various forms overlap and intersect," (iv) "forms travel," and (v) "forms do political work in particular contexts" (4–5). Literary forms, Levine contends (and of which I would suggest lyric forms are amongst the most virtuosic and salient examples), do not align in any simple way with the world: "Literature is not made of the material world it describes or invokes but of language, which lays claim to its own forms – syntactical, narrative, rhythmic, rhetorical – and its own materiality – the spoken word, the printed page" (10). Drawing on Wittgenstein, I suggest, helps to show that the non-identity of these literary-material and world-material forms in no way precludes their interaction (something with which Levine would agree); rather, the differences between them mean that lyric form can index the infelicities or injustices of a form of life, bringing them into relief in and as language.

In closing, I turn to a poem by Paul Celan that works in and against traditions of the lyric:

FADENSONNEN [28]	THREADSUNS
über der grauschwarzen Ödnis.	above the grey-black wasteland.
Ein baum-	A tree-
hoher Gedanke	tall thought
greift sich den Lichtton: es sind	grasps for the light-tone: there are
noch Lieder zu singen jenseits	still songs to sing beyond
der Menschen.	the human.

"Fadensonnen" ("Thread-suns" or "Fathom-suns"), published in the volume *Atemwende* (*Breathturn*) in 1967, challenges lyricism and meaning in its almost laconic minimalism; although it names "songs," it lacks the obvious melody or rhythm that have canonically justified the lyric genre's proximity to music. Of its twenty-one words, four are composite neologisms, a feature of poetic (particularly sublime) speech in German since the eighteenth century. Celan mobilizes this trope in a very particular way in much of his poetry, both combining words and breaking them down into their component parts, sometimes in expected, sometimes unexpected places (as he does here in making and splitting the

---

[27] Caroline Levine, *Forms: Whole, Rhythm, Hierarchy, Network* (Princeton, NJ: Princeton University Press, 2015), 3. Henceforth cited parenthetically.
[28] Paul Celan, *Die Gedichte. Kommentierte Gesamtausgabe*, ed. Barbara Wiedemann (Frankfurt: Suhrkamp Verlag, 2005), 179. My translation.

compound "tree-/tall" across the line). In his combinations of familiar terms into words whose combined meaning we cannot quite pin down, Celan, I suggest, "fray[s] ... the connection between a word or expression and its main conventional meaning" as Irvin describes (Irvin, 100), even as the poem's apparent grammatical and syntactic simplicity seems to offer more direct "meaning" than the poems Irvin discusses. Does "Faden" in the title mean "fathoms" or "threads," and how would either combine with suns, in the plural? How would an immaterial thought take up physical space to be as tall as a tree, or to grasp? Is "light-tone" a synesthetic blending of hearing and seeing that invites us to imagine a unity of light and sound, or a reference to the highly technical "sound-on-film" recording process from the early days of sound film?[29]

The poem is notably paratactic: its first phrase, marked off by a period, describes a blasted landscape under multiple suns, but the absence of a verb renders the scene static and devoid of agency. The remainder of the poem consists of two grammatically complete sentences joined by a colon; Celan undermines this syntax by breaking it into four lines, none of which aligns with natural intonational contours. Both the limited agency of those lines (the subjects are "a ... thought" and the ambiguous "it," as in "it's raining") and the semantic content of the second phrase challenge the connection between language, lyric, and the human: if *there are* songs to be sung either temporally after or spatially past human beings, by whom are the songs sung? Do they have words? Do the words mean? Are they heard by anyone or anything? The poem thus asks us to imagine what music or language are in the absence of the "address" that Waters describes as "the fiber of language's use and being" (5).

In its decoupling of songs and the human, "Fadensonnen" evokes "sweet songs" of chiming poetic musicality in suggesting suprahuman or nonhuman musicality. In the context of Celan's oeuvre and his poetological statements, this inhuman music hints the *poésie pure* Celan was accused of writing and that he critiqued in Mallarmé.[30] Its forms are not

---

[29] Barbara Wiedemann's note on the poem explains the meaning of *Lichttonverfahren*, but whether most readers would hear the word as a terminus technicus or a neologism is unclear; Paul Celan, *Die Gedichte*, 723.

[30] On Celan's ambivalent relation to musicality, see Axel Englund, "Modes of Musicality in Paul Celan's *Die Niemandsrose*," *Seminar* 45 (2): 138–158 (2009). Hans-Egon Holthusen, a member of the SS turned literary scholar, claimed in an early review that Celan's works "escape[d] the bloody horror chamber of history, ... ris[ing] to the ethereal domain of pure poetry" (cited in Pierre Joris, "Introduction: 'Polysemy without Mask,'" in Paul Celan, *Selections*, ed. Pierre Joris [Berkeley, CA: University of California Press, 2005], 21).

metrical or even clearly rhythmical, and thus the ways the poem might, as Stewart suggests, reach towards others and mobilize the body are highly attenuated: indeed, the interruptive line breaks make articulation halt and lurch, even as sound clusters ("grauschwarzen," "Gedanke," "greift"; "Lichtton," "Lieder") group the lines into two sets (that, once again, do not align with punctuation or syntax). This does not mean, of course, that "Fadensonnen" is devoid of rhythm or form. Celan makes effective use of the interaction – here, conflict – between line-endings and semantic-syntactical phrases to call attention to the particular arrangement of these words and these sounds on this page, the "syntactical narrative, rhythmic, [and] rhetorical" forms that draw on the materiality of "the spoken word" and "the printed page," all of which Levine characterizes as forms that are literature's own, not (or not only) those of the "material world it describes or invokes" (10). Thus, for example, the line break between "beyond" and "the human" uses the slight delay or pause of the break to allow the reader to experience a moment of uncertainty or possibility – beyond what? this time? this space? this crisis? – before the eerie conclusion that what "songs" move beyond is human beings, *Menschen*.

I have chosen a poem that positions itself in the tradition of lyric musicality, intersubjectivity, and materiality and yet, as one would expect from a poem written in the second half of the twentieth century, and in particular a poem written in German by a Jewish poet from Czernowitz in the wake of the Shoah, also calls those traditions into question. To demonstrate fully how this poem, against the background of Celan's verse practice and his theoretical concerns, works in atypical ways to both posit and interrogate categories like "song," "poem," and "human" would require a much more detailed elaboration than I can undertake here. I want, instead, to draw out just a few moments that underscore how approaching Celan's works from a Wittgenstein-inflected understanding of language as shaped by and shaping a form of life helps to understand the impact and effectiveness of the poem, that is, "being intrigued and *wanting* to describe, asking oneself: 'What is this? What's he doing, wanting to do here? – Gosh, if only I could say what he's doing here'" (LC 37).

Celan repeatedly and persistently describes his poetry as seeking an encounter between an "I" and a "you," words that are notably and unusually absent in "Fadensonnen" as compared with much of his work. Their absence, together with the poem's discussion of being "beyond human beings" or "beyond the human," is significant; the poem enacts the lack of address and response, "I" and "you," of an originally symbolist/aestheticist (later Heideggerian) view of language that seeks to move "beyond" human speech and communities of speakers. But Celan does not reject either musicality or the tendency of poetry to strive for the suprahuman achievement of technique, which he describes in his famous *Meridian* speech as "art": "Art, you will remember, is a puppet-like, iambic, five-footed thing" (154). The speech describes the relation between art and "poetry," a name for "the majesty of the absurd which [bears witness to] the presence of human beings" (157), as a complex dialectic: the uncanny inhumanity of art becomes the strangeness that poetry must traverse in search of an encounter (166–167). Celan's description of poetry as encounter in and as otherness suggests a highly attenuated intersubjectivity in lyric: "the poem becomes conversation – often desperate conversation" (165).

What "Fadensonnen" exemplifies is that there cannot, in the form of life and language that Celan inhabited and invites us to inhabit, be any certainty that the strangeness of language and its musicality return to the human. Celan uses markedly *less* fragmented and shattered language here than he does in many of his poems,[31] but material-linguistic and imagistic cohesion come at the cost of discarding the human, the conversation between "I" and "you," and the desperation that both threatens and makes that conversation possible. Celan's poetry, I want to say, indexes the trauma of history in language; often his poems prompt us to ask what has happened to a form of life such that just this language becomes necessary, and in "Fadensonnen" we confront the possibility of severing language from form of life, leaving "songs" but not subjects. Understanding language, in Wittgenstein's sense, as not

---

[31] For example, the poem "The Syllable Pain" ("Die Silbe Schmerz") ends: "a blind//L e t t h e r e b e // knotted itself in-/ to the serpentheaded free-/ ropes – : a/ knot/ (and counter- and contra- and yet- and twin- and thou-/ sandknot), which/ the [carnival-eyed] brood/ of martenstars in the abyss/ spell-, spell-, spelled/ out, out" (Celan, *Selections*, 92, my modifications to the translation in brackets); the splitting of words onto very short lines is even more striking in the original: "ein blindes// E s s e i // knüpfte sich in/ die schlangenköpfigen Frei-/ Taue – : ein/ Knoten/ (und Wider- und Gegen- und Aber- und Zwillings- und Tau-/ sendknoten), an dem/ die fastnachtsäugige Brut/ der Mardersterne im Abgrund/ buch-, buch-, buch-/ stabierte, stabierte" (160). Other poems that handle language similarly include "Engführung" (113–118), "Chymisch" (*Die Gedichte*, 134), "Benedicta" (145), and "Huhediblu," (156–157). It might be possible to identify fragmented or shattered and laconic modes or tendencies in Celan, as different strategies for responding in lyric language to a mutilated form of life; one would have to identify features and limit cases of each type and could then trace their appearance and relation across his oeuvre.

only emerging from but shaping, and sometimes challenging, a form of life shows how Celan's poetry – and lyric poetry in general – can become a paradigmatic place for sustained, original, and creative testing and contesting of both language and form of life.

* * *

As my overviews of theories of the lyric and of recent work on lyric materiality, intersubjectivity, and form have shown, Wittgenstein does not provide us with a theory of the lyric; nor does he offer arguments about or readings of particular poems or poets. But his attention to what we do with poems – how we talk about them, what we say to others, how they arouse interest, puzzlement, and attention – reminds us that one of the things we do with poems is theorize about the lyric, insofar as we find moments of linguistically formed and intensive subjective expression, try to define their particularities, and then seek to link them with other such moments in distant cultures, foreign languages, and new forms. Moreover, his view of language as emerging from and constituting a form of life complements investigations of materiality, intersubjectivity, and form by illuminating how the lyric's particularly dense and complex figurations of language probe the relation between language and the world, with the power to change both.

8 Life, Logic, Style
On Late Wittgenstein
Henry W. Pickford

Abstract: While readers have long recognized the innovative styles of Wittgenstein's writings, this chapter considers the philosophical significance of the concept, perception, and attribution of style in Wittgenstein's *Philosophical Investigations* and other works. Contrary to some interpreters, I argue in the first section that the later Wittgenstein continued to see philosophy as logic, but expanded his conception of what constituted "the logical" to include "forms of life," "life," "living," and so on. In the second section, I draw on recent work on the logical form of judgment about living organisms to describe distinctive logical features of such judgment including necessity, unity, generality and its relation to particularity, and temporality, and in the third section, I show that this logical form and its distinctive features can elucidate claims made about forms of life in *Philosophical Investigations*. In the final section, I show how Wittgenstein's concept of style exhibits the same logical features and thereby serves as a guiding metaphor for recognizing "the logical" in our everyday life-activities.

Keywords: Style, Concepts, Perception, Logic, Judgement, Generality and Particularity, Language-Games, *Lebensform*, Logic and the Everyday, Necessity, Unity.

To write the correct style means to set the wagon precisely on the rails.[1]

A reader familiar with Wittgenstein's later writings, and in particular the "rule-following considerations" in *Philosophical Investigations*, might well be taken aback by the image he uses in the epigraph to this chapter. In *Philosophical Investigations*, Wittgenstein uses the image of rails to

---

[1] Ludwig Wittgenstein, Bergen Nachlass, MS 117 225. Original: "Den richtigen Stil schreiben heißt, den Wagen gerade auf's Gleise setzen."

illustrate the inclination to think of one's possessing a concept as one's somehow already knowing all future applications of the rule for its correct application: "Whence the idea that the beginning of a series is a visible section of rails invisibly laid to infinity? Well, we might imagine rails instead of a rule. And infinitely long rails correspond to the unlimited application of a rule" (PI §218). However, this quotation suggests that the correct style can contribute to bringing about, or maintaining, the kind of understanding that is a topic of *Philosophical Investigations*. And this suggestion in turn means that Wittgenstein's understanding of the concept of *style* is of philosophical importance.

Reflection on Wittgenstein and style quickly diverges into at least two directions. In the *first* direction of inquiry, scholarship has shown how Wittgenstein embodies modernist principles in the aesthetic forms of his writings.[2] G. E. Moore suggested that the title of his first work, *Tractatus Logico-Philosophicus* is an explicit allusion to the *more geometrico* of Spinoza's *Tractatus Theologico-Politicus*, yet in his famous letter to his publisher Ludwig von Ficker, Wittgenstein avowed that the apodictic, even gnomically formulated text comprised merely the explicit part of the work, whereas the most important part, that devoted to what was most meaningful and significant in life – ethics, aesthetics, value – lies beyond the limits of language, itself perhaps an allusion to the theory that Plato's later works alluded to an unwritten, "esoteric" doctrine. Likewise, when Wittgenstein returned to the University of Cambridge and to philosophy, he self-consciously and arduously developed new styles of writing that baffled many philosophers when *Philosophical Investigations* and related works were published posthumously. It is Stanley Cavell's great service to suggest that Wittgenstein's later writings drew on literary genres that belong to and enrich the Western philosophical tradition. The back-and-forth of voices in *Philosophical Investigations*, sometimes ventriloquizing a claim made by his earlier philosophical self (e.g., concerning the putative general form of the proposition, PI §65) and then criticizing it, or interlocutors proffering, refining, and dismissing a line of thought only to return to it pages later,

---

[2] See, for instance, *The Literary Wittgenstein*, eds. John Gibson and Wolfgang Huemer (London: Routledge, 2004); *Wittgenstein and Modernism*, eds. Michael LeMahieu and Karen Zumhagen-Yekplé (Chicago, IL: University of Chicago Press, 2017); *Wittgenstein on Aesthetic Understanding* ed. Garry Hagberg (New York: Palgrave Macmillan, 2017). Cf. Wittgenstein: "Loos, Spengler, Freud and I all belong in the same class, that is characteristic for this age" (Bergen Nachlass, 183 29). Original: "Loos, Spengler, Freud und ich gehören alle in dieselbe Klasse die für diese Zeit charakteristisch ist."

suggest the drama of the dialectic staged in *dialogues* by Plato, Berkeley and others. Cavell also identifies the genre of *confession*, specifically its acknowledgment of temptation, as when a voice in *Philosophical Investigations* repeatedly reveals "I want to say ...," "I feel like saying ...," and so on, which silently invokes a philosophical tradition reaching from Augustine, Descartes, Rousseau, up to Freud, and to Cavell's own inimitable philosophical voice. These two genres that Cavell locates in the *Philosophical Investigations* – "the voice of temptation and the voice of correctness are the antagonists in Wittgenstein's dialogues" – induce self-scrutiny and self-assessment rather than belief by argument or justification. Cavell concludes:

> that is why there is virtually nothing in the *Investigations* which we should ordinarily call reasoning; Wittgenstein asserts nothing which could be proved, for what he asserts is either obvious (§126) – whether true or false – or else concerned with what conviction, whether by proof or evidence or authority, would consist in. Otherwise there are questions, jokes, parables, and propositions so striking (the way lines are in poetry) that they stun mere belief. . . . Belief is not enough. Either the suggestion penetrates past assessment and becomes part of the sensibility from which assessment proceeds, or it is philosophically useless.[3]

Cavell's judgment that Wittgenstein's later philosophy does not exhibit ordinary reasoning but rather aims to effect a change in sensibility might lead one to conclude that Wittgenstein had cast away concerns with logic as the canon of reasoning when he moved from the *Tractatus* to *Philosophical Investigations*, and this brings us to the *second direction* of reflection on style in Wittgenstein. For I shall suggest that – as intimated in the opening epigraph – the *concept*, perception, and attribution of style do real philosophical work for him, because the concept of style is informed by a certain kind of logic and reasoning central to his later thought.

This uninterrupted presence of logic in Wittgenstein is recognized by Juliet Floyd in her comprehensive and compelling analysis of *life-form* as a logical notion:

> In a broad sense, in Wittgenstein's philosophy the accent seems to approach more and more to *life* as time goes on. But logic, with its ideas of *form, possibility, necessity*, and its (endemic) metaphor of *chains of remarks* (or reasoning) (cf. PI Preface), is never left behind as part of the quarry. Wittgenstein still conceived

---

[3] Stanley Cavell, "The Availability of Wittgenstein's Later Philosophy," in *Must We Mean What We Say?*, updated ed. (Cambridge: Cambridge University Press, 2015), 65–66.

himself to be pursuing the nature of the logical, conceived of what he is doing *as* logic, sees philosophy *as* logic, until the end."[4]

Grammatical remarks, language-games, and ultimately forms of life are simplified and clarified procedures, routines "modules" etc., that are logical in the sense of providing rules for moving from one step to another, in arguing, in following a command, etc., and I follow this general picture of *the logical* as minimal recurrent patterns of words and actions that criss-cross in our everyday lives.[5] Her picture gains definition and relief in contrast to other studies of logic in the later Wittgenstein: for instance, Penelope Maddy claims that logic in the *Philosophical Investigations* is naturalized, an empirical object of study, despite Wittgenstein's explicit asseverations to the contrary.[6] This naturalistic view aligns in its empiricism with sociological and communitarian views of forms of life, where the de facto social practices of the linguistic community determine what are correct and incorrect applications of a rule.[7] The recoil from empiricist views of "the logical" in *Philosophical Investigations* can in turn propel interpreters into versions of transcendental idealism of one sort or another[8], despite Wittgenstein's claims that he is looking at "spatial and temporal phenomenon of language" (PI §108), and his declaration in *Remarks on the*

---

[4] Juliet Floyd, "Chains of Life: Turing, *Lebensform*, and the Emergence of Wittgenstein's Later Style," *Nordic Wittgenstein Review* 5(2): 7–89 (2016); here 34–35. My chapter is indebted in general to her reading of *Lebensform* in *Philosophical Investigations*, though I shift the emphasis of "the logical" from "modules," "procedures," even "apps" (at one point in her article) to the interwovenness of the logical with the natural. We are completely agreed, however, that logic in *Philosophical Investigations* is not rendered empirical. An important study that stakes out a "non-empiricist naturalism" in *Philosophical Investigations*, which I cannot address here, is Oskari Kuusela, *Wittgenstein on Logic as the Method of Philosophy* (Oxford: Oxford University Press, 2019).

[5] On this image in *Philosophical Investigations*, see Cora Diamond, "Criss-Cross Philosophy," in *Wittgenstein at Work: Method in the Philosophical Investigations* eds. Erich Ammereiler and Eugen Fischer (New York: Routledge, 2004), 201–220.

[6] Penelope Maddy, *The Logical Must: Wittgenstein on Logic* (Oxford: Oxford University Press, 2014).

[7] For example: Saul Kripke, *Wittgenstein on Rules and Private Language* (London: Wiley Blackwell, 1991); Meredith Williams, *Wittgenstein, Mind and Meaning: Towards a Social Conception of Mind* (New York: Routledge, 2002).

[8] For example: Bernard Williams, "Wittgenstein and Idealism," in *Moral Luck: Philosophical Papers 1973–1980* (Cambridge: Cambridge University Press, 1981), 144–163; Jonathan Lear, "Transcendental Anthropology" and "The Disappearing 'We'," in *Open Minded: Working Out the Logic of the Soul* (Cambridge, MA: Harvard University Press, 1998): 247–281 and 282–300.

Foundations of Mathematics: "Not empiricism and yet realism in philosophy, that is the hardest thing."

Whereas Floyd focuses on examining the occurrences of the term *lifeform* in *Philosophical Investigations*, I expand the focus, by considering further passages where "life," "living," "natural history," "human being" etc., are thematized, and read these passages from the perspective of the logical form of judgments about living organisms. In my remarks, I can only suggest what such a perspective might look like, and how it might resolve – or dissolve – the dilemma regarding the concept of form of life between empiricism and sociologism on the one hand, and versions of transcendental idealism on the other. The argument of my chapter falls into four broad parts. In the first section, I explicate "the logical" as it informs discussion of forms of life and related topics in *Philosophical Investigations*. In the second section, I briefly outline further features – necessity, unity, generality and its relation to particularity, and temporality – drawing on recent work on the logical form of judgments about living organisms, and, in the third section, I show how this logical form and its distinctive features can elucidate claims made about forms of life in *Philosophical Investigations*. In the final section, I show how Wittgenstein's concept of style serves as a guiding metaphor for recognizing 'the logical' in our everyday life-activities.

I. The Logical

Floyd's definition of *Lebensform* as "possibilities of life-structuring in life" suggests the sense of "the logical" at issue.[9] Describing (and recall that Wittgenstein repeatedly qualifies his aim as describing, reminding, at most substituting one expression for another, but *not* explaining) life-structuring activities involves concepts of order, sequence, possibility (and impossibility), necessity (and contingency), sameness (and difference); we can think of these concepts as minimal conceptual elements that constitute the idea of *logical form* here at work, together with notions of matching a form, agreeing with a rule, instantiating a form and other normative notions (of which *truth* is only one highly specialized normative notion). A *criterion* for example is a minimal element by which identity (sameness) can be established, and correctness (and error)

---

[9] Floyd. Chains of Life, 42.

determined (PI §51).[10] This way of seeing the structured activities of living is not straightforwardly empirical:

> What is the transition I make from "It will be like this" to "it *must* be like this"? I form a different concept. One involving something that was not there before. When I say: "If these derivations are the same, then it *must* be that ...," I am making something into a criterion of identity. So I am recasting my concept of identity. (RFM §§IV-29)[11]

The empirical concept of identity at work in the prediction "It will be like this" is at most statistical or probabilistic, what will likely happen to be the case; in this case the connection between what one predicts and what then happens is *accidental*. In the case of the statement "It *must* be like this" the connection is in some sense a *necessary* one. The kind of necessity, this nonempirical "logical must" (PI §437), partly constitutes "the logical" in *Philosophical Investigations*.

The terms he deploys – *grammar, language-game,* and *form of life* – function to elucidate aspects of "the logical" in our everyday lives, in the life-structurings we inhabit and perpetually reproduce.[12] A *grammatical* investigation reveals logical relations that characterize the kind of phenomenon ("grammar tells us what kind of object anything is" [PI §373; cf. §90])[13] and hence one discovers "a new conception. As if you had invented a new way of painting [*Malweise*], or again, a new meter [*Metrum*], or a new kind of song" (PI §401). A *language-game* is a simplified, isolated (PI §100) model of linguistic activity, demonstrating the minimal logical elements of regularity, sameness, sequencing, order, correctness, etc., to constitute a unity. The unity of the model, its "form," is only partially constituted by the possibilities, regularities, "rules" by which the linguistic activity is structured; rather even in the "primitive" games at the outset, actions are integral to the model as well: "I shall call

---

[10] On criteria, see Stanley Cavell, *The Claim of Reason* (New York: Oxford University Press, 1979/1999).

[11] "... it is as if the formation of a concept guided our experience into particular channels, so that one experience is now seen together with another in a new way" (RFM §§ IV–33); "The point is not to explain a language-game by means of our experiences, but to take account of a language-game" (PI §655).

[12] Often when Wittgenstein invokes mathematics as an object of comparison when considering an everyday phenomenon, he is invoking "the logical." Famously, the conclusion of the second part of *Philosophical Investigations*: "An investigation is possible in connection with mathematics which is entirely analogous to our investigation of psychology. It is just as little a *mathematical* investigation as the other is a psychological one" (PPF §372).

[13] Contrast the austere logical ontology of Frege: object, concept (function), thought.

the whole, consisting of language and the actions into which it is woven, the 'language-game'" (PI §7):

> The word "accord" and the word "rule" are *related* to one another, they are cousins. If I teach anyone the use of the one word, he learns the use of the other with it. (PI §224)

> The use of the word "rule" and the use of the word "same" are interwoven. (As are the use of "proposition" and the use of "true.") (PI §225)

A *form of life* in turn appears to widen the context within which a language-game is to be investigated: "And to imagine a language means to imagine a form of life" (PI §19).[14] It is as though Wittgenstein is expanding the scope of logical form, of "the logical," to encompass the wider context required for an adequate understanding of the phenomenon, the bit of reality, being investigated. Techniques, trained responses belong to the larger context of "an activity, or ... a form of life."

If we attend to *Philosophical Investigations* in this way, we become aware of other passages where he seems to reach for an even "wider context" still:

> "But doesn't what you say amount to this: that there is not pain, for example, without *pain-behavior*?" – It amounts to this: that only of a living human being and what resembles (behaves like) a living human being can one say: it has sensations; it sees; is blind; hears; is deaf; is conscious or unconscious. (PI §281)

> What gives us *so much as the idea* that living beings, things, can feel? ... (PI §283)

> Look at a stone and imagine it having sensations. – One says to oneself: How could one so much as get the idea of ascribing a *sensation* to a *thing*? One might as well ascribe it to a number! – And now look at a wriggling fly, and at once these difficulties vanish, and pain seems able to get a *foothold* here, where before everything was, so to speak, too *smooth* for it.

> And so, too, a corpse seems to us quite inaccessible to pain. – Our attitude to what is alive and to what is dead is not the same. All our reactions are different. – If anyone says: "That cannot simply come from the fact that living beings move in such-and-such a way and dead ones don't," then I want to intimate to him that this is a case of the transition "from quantity to quality." (PI §284)

The "wider context" here is conceptual, in that the *concepts* we use, and *attitudes* we adopt, the *actions* we undertake, cohere into a kind of unity, a kind of regularity, a kind of conceptual necessity that we can call the

---

[14] "The word 'language-*game*' is used here to emphasize the fact that the *speaking* of language is part of an activity, or of a form of life" (PI §23).

logical structuring of life. We bring sophisticated concepts like "sensation"(which might already be a partial "subliming" by metaphysically inclined philosophers) but also simple concepts like "wriggle," "wince," "startle" to things that look like, that we recognize, acknowledge as human beings, or living beings of certain kinds. These concepts, attitudes, actions, and activities constitute the language-game of "being in pain" (played differently in the first- and the third-person) within the form of life whose members should include what we grammatically designate a living being of a certain kind, beings of which we can predicate action-terms like wriggle and wince.

Of the language-games Wittgenstein lists starting at PI §23, some are highly sophisticated, involving elaborate rules and protocols that can extend over and intermittently between extended periods of time: "constructing an object from a description (a drawing)," "solving a problem in applied arithmetic," "forming and testing a hypothesis." Others appear to be what some philosophers might call basic actions: giving an order and acting on it, requesting, thanking, cursing, greeting, praying. All are logically articulable patterns of speaking, acting, doing, adopting attitudes, sufficient to qualify as unities or wholes of some sort. "The logical" for Wittgenstein consists of these "forms of living," patterned ways in which human beings are and can be, and his claim that "giving orders, asking questions, telling stories, having a chat, are as much a part of our natural history as walking, eating, drinking, playing" (PI §25) indicates an interweaving of the historical with the biological, for basic human functions like eating, drinking, reproducing, using language, etc. appear in different guises in different places and different times.[15]

---

[15] See Stanley Cavell, who identifies "the mutual implication of the natural and the social" in the relation between a vertical (biological) sense of *Lebensform* that individuates the human form of life (or life-form) from other species, and a horizontal (ethnological) dimension that individuates one specific sociocultural form of life from others: Stanley Cavell, "Declining Decline," in *This New Yet Unapproachable America: Lectures after Emerson and Wittgenstein* (Albuquerque, NM: Living Batch Press, 1989), 29–75; here 44. For a useful discussion of the debate in the literature regarding the natural vs. social bases for forms of life, see Danièle Moyal-Sharrock, "Wittgenstein on Forms of Life, Patterns of Life, and Ways of Living," *Nordic Wittgenstein Review* Special Issue: 21–42 (2015). Of superlative insight remains G .E. M. Anscombe, "The Question of Linguistic Idealism," in *From Parmenides to Wittgenstein* (= *Collected Philosophical Papers*, vol. 1) (Oxford: Basil Blackwell, 1981), 112–133; Cf. Wittgenstein: "The borders of empiricism are not unverified assumptions, or intuitively known to be correct; rather [they are] manners and modes of comparison and action" (Bergen Nachlass 163 20v) Original: "Die Grenzen der Empirie sind nicht unverbürgte Annahmen, oder intuitiv als richtig erkannte; sondern Arten und Weisen des Vergleichs und des Handelns"

If language-games and forms of life should indeed be understood as life-activities, then the logical form of judgments about the latter might provide insight into the logical form of judgments about the former.

II The Living

As Wittgenstein suggests the availability of certain logical elements for describing forms of life, the role of these logical elements might be elucidated by considering the logical structure of descriptions of living organisms. According to Philippa Foot and Michael Thompson, descriptions of the life-cycle or "life-activities" of a species of living organism exhibit a specific logical form of judgment that is expressed in what linguists call *generic sentences*.[16] The logical form of such judgments is unique in several respects.

The kind of *generality* expressed is not an instance of the concept of generality adopted by modern, Fregean, quantificational logic. The statement "Swallows build nests" does not translate *salva veritate* into existential quantification ("Some swallows/At least one swallow build[s] nests"), which is too weak: the judgment expresses a kind of generality, or perhaps a kind of necessity, that differs logically from a judgment such as "Some swallows have an odd number of feathers." Nor does it translate into universal quantification ("All swallows build nests"), which is too strong: some swallows, after all, do not ever manage to build nests. Moreover, the generality is not that of a covering law to instance (as in "objects fall to earth at 32 ft/sec^2"), or statistical preponderance to sample (as in "Most/The overwhelming majority of Americans believe in angels"): the judgments express neither an iron law of swallow behavior, nor some contingent statistical percentage of what a lot of swallows just happen to do.[17]

Similarly, the *truth conditions* of such judgments are not the same as for statements of Fregean or statistical generality. For instance, "Although

---

[16] Philippa Foot, *Natural Goodness* (Oxford: Oxford University Press, 2001). This section is indebted to Michael Thompson, "The Representation of Life," in *Life and Action* (Cambridge, MA: Harvard University Press, 2008), 25–82; but cf. also Julius Moravcsik, "Essences, Powers, and Generic Propositions," in *Unity, Identity, and Explanation in Aristotle's Metaphysics*, eds. T. Scaltsas, D. Charles, and M. L. Gill (Oxford: Clarendon Press, 1994), 229–244.

[17] For further explication of this type of generality, see Christian Martin, "Four Types of Conceptual Generality," *Graduate Faculty Philosophy Journal* 36 (2): 397–423 (2015).

'the mayfly' breeds shortly before dying, *most* mayflies die long before breeding."[18] Unlike universal quantification in Fregean logic and statistical generalizations, life-form judgments are peculiar in that they allow of *exceptions*, perhaps even massively so, without consequence for the judgment's truth value. Indeed, most actual instances can be exceptions, and yet the life-form judgment stands unimpugned. Rather than somehow quantifying over the members of a class, the judgments "express one's *interpretation* or *understanding* of the life-form shared by the members of that class."[19]

A specific kind of *unity* and *necessity* attaches to life-form judgments, for the judgment has implications even for instances of the natural kind that do not fall under the judgment, e.g., "Swallows build nests" has implications even for that vagabond swallow that does not build a nest, i.e., that it is an exception. "Most swallows build nests" cannot capture this kind of unity adhering to the natural kind *swallow*. That is, the natural history of a species (the set of life-form judgments about that species) is not composed of a set of more or less overlapping, restricted-quantified statements. Such a congeries loses track of the unity that ties the whole natural history together, of that which makes it the history of a single species, that makes it – the whole history – in some sense true of every member of the species, even though normally no single member will instantiate the predicates of all of the judgments. Another way of putting this point is that *the relation of general to particular* is unique: the members of a species that fulfill a life-form judgment do not exhaust the generality expressed by the judgment. The generality expressed by the judgment is not merely the sum of members that exemplify it; rather members *manifest* or *instantiate* the generality. While a whole is exhausted by the sum of its parts, and a set is exhausted by the sum of its members, what is manifested is not exhausted by its manifestations or instantiations. In this sense, the species-form, as described by the life-form judgments specific to it, is *not* an empirical concept, although it is *manifested* in empirical instantiations of it, individual swallows. Each of them *manifests, generically* (that is, surely imperfectly in some respect or other) *exemplifying* the species-form.

The specific generality expressed in these life-activity judgments bears a specific temporal order, a *time-generality*. "The swallow builds a nest," when the subject is an actual swallow, is time-specific, describing in the

---

[18] Thompson, "The Representation of Life," 68.   [19] Ibid., 72.

present tense the current action of that singular swallow: as an instance, an instantiation, or actualization of the species-form swallow, this time-specific description is applicable to this actual individual's movements. The swallow is locatable in space and time, and its activity of nest-building is datable, has duration, begins and ends at specific times, can be expressed in perfective aspect: "Yesterday that swallow built a nest in the afternoon." "The swallow builds a nest," however, when the subject is the species-form or natural kind *swallow*, is time-general, it describes a nondatable habitual or characteristic life-activity of the species, which might or might not be actualized, instantiated, manifested in time-specific descriptions of specific swallows. Here the past tense indicates a habitual, characteristic life-activity as part of the species-form's life-cycle, expressed in the imperfective aspect: "The swallow used to build a nest but now it takes over a nest of another bird."

The specific generality expressed in these life-form judgments is a normative concept, that is, a good, i.e., well-functioning swallow is a swallow that builds nests, a swallow that manifests the natural history – the life-cycle – of its species-form. A swallow that does not build nests is in that respect a defective instance of its species.[20] Species-form generality therefore is conceptually linked to a kind of *normativity*: the species-form expresses as it were normative truths about the species in question, and members of the species who do not fulfill, or make true, such species-form judgments can be judged deficient with respect to that specific norm expressed by the relevant life-form judgment. In this sense the species-form bears the possibility of an immanent critique of its members.[21]

---

[20] Compare Frege: "'The horse is a four-legged animal' ... is probably best regarded as expressing a universal judgment, say ... 'all properly constituted horses are four-legged animals'": that is, the implicit restriction on universal quantification presupposes one's being able to judge what is a "properly constituted" horse; Gottlob Frege, "On Concept and Object," in *The Frege Reader*, ed. Michael Beaney (Oxford: Basil Blackwell): 181–193; here 184.

[21] Compare Anscombe in "Modern Moral Philosophy": "It might remain to look for 'norms' in human virtues: just as *man* has so many teeth, which is certainly not the average number of teeth men have, but is the number of teeth for the species, so perhaps the species *man*, regarded not just biologically, but from the point of view of the activity of thought and choice in regard to the various departments of life – powers and faculties and use of things needed – 'has' such-and-such virtues: and this 'man' with the complete set of virtues is the 'norm', as 'man' with, e.g., a complete set of teeth is a norm"; G.E.M. Anscombe, "Modern Moral Philosophy," in *Ethics, Religion and Politics* (= *Collected Philosophical Papers*, vol. 3) (Minneapolis, MN: University of Minnesota Press, 1981): 26–42; here 38.

The specific logical form of judgment about living organisms as species or life-forms – the logical features just outlined – entails that if such judgments have truth-apt purchase on the world, the nature of the world must be suited to that form of judgment. This amounts to justifying the metaphysics of species or *life-form* in virtue of the logical form of judgment proper to our interpretation or understanding of the world of living organisms. Note that the metaphysical concept of species was derived from its role as possible subject in this logical form of predication. This is a logical-metaphysical derivation of what counts as a life-form, i.e., that which bears specific life-form judgments that describe its characteristic life-activities.

III. The "Wider Context" and Form of Life

For the purposes of this chapter we gain insight into the relationship between "the logical" and life in *Philosophical Investigations* by doing what Wittgenstein exhorts us to do: compare models to reveal logical form (PI §122, cf. §78). Wittgenstein's descriptions of forms of life exhibit a similar logical structure to that of the species-form judgment, and recognizing the similar structure provides useful glosses to some points he makes about language-games and forms of life in *Philosophical Investigations*.[22]

The generality that attaches to generic statements, as opposed to the existential or universal generality of Fregean logic, applies to the phenomena Wittgenstein is describing. The concept of family resemblance (where members share some characteristics, but not all, and share them in such a way that a unity is maintained, e.g., the concept "game"), or the "continuous overlapping of fibers in the thread" (PI §§65–67; cf. "tapestry of life" [*Lebensteppich, Band des Lebens*] in PPF §2 and §362) highlights this concept of generality: exceptions in one respect or another do not impugn the truth of the description of the activity in question. Likewise, a concept must not be well-defined in all possible applications, as Frege holds. The boundary of a game is not well established:

One can say that the concept of a game is a concept with blurred edges. – "But is a blurred concept a *concept* at all?" – Is a photograph that is not sharp a picture of a

---

[22] Not all, because some parts of a language-game or form of life function as "hinges" or agreements in judgment (e.g., the meter stick in Paris); however, these are parts within life-activities (measuring, building, designing) that do exhibit the generic logical form we have outlined above.

person at all? Is it even always an advantage to replace a picture that is not sharp by one that is? Isn't one that isn't sharp often just what we need?

Frege compares a concept to a region, and says that a region without clear boundaries can't be called a region at all. This presumably means that we cannot do anything with it. – But is it senseless to say: "Stay roughly here?" (PI §71)

Wittgenstein concludes, "Are we to say that we do not really attach any meaning to this word, because we are not equipped with rules for every possible application of it?" (PI §80) and shortly thereafter considers the wayward philosopher's literal response to this rhetorical question, in suggesting that Ramsey invites misunderstanding by thinking that games in fact are or approximate "calculi which have fixed rules"; Wittgenstein rejects idealism in this sense of constructing ideal languages and thinking that "if anyone utters a sentence and *means* or *understands* it he is thereby operating a calculus according to definite rules" (PI §81). The fact that "the application of a word is not everywhere bounded by rules" rules out the kind of Fregean universality that underlies the picture of words or concepts as calculi.[23] Yet on the other hand Wittgenstein does not abandon the concept of game or rule, nor does he reduce them to *empirical* concepts. The problems he is investigating are philosophical: "These are, of course, not empirical problems; but they are solved through an insight into the workings of our language" (PI §109),[24] rather, "we misunderstand the role played by the ideal in our language" (PI §100). The kind of normativity and generality expressed in the logical form of judgment outlined in the previous section avoids both horns of this dilemma.

Bringing this logical form to Wittgenstein's discussions of language-games and forms of life perhaps clarifies certain of his philosophical claims. Amidst the "rule-following considerations" in *Philosophical Investigations*, one of the puzzles he examines is the "connection"(*Zusammenhang*) between a concept and its applications. He repeatedly cautions against the temptation – becoming captive of a picture – to *always* conceive understanding a concept or the meaning of an expression as a mental state or

---

[23] The applicability of concepts can vary widely across language-games: "There is, in general, complete agreement in the color statements of those who have been diagnosed normal. This characterizes the concept of a color statement. There is in general no such agreement over the question of whether an expression of feeling is genuine or not" (PPF §§351–352).

[24] "But surely a machine cannot think! – Is that an empirical statement? No. We say only of a human being and what is like one that it thinks. ... Regard the word 'to think' as an instrument!" (PI §360).

process, or a "mental mechanism" that mysteriously effects connections between concept and reality when applying the concept. The logic of state or process is time-specific datability: a beginning, duration, and finite end, where the past tense can occur in either perfective or imperfective aspect. In some circumstances this time-specific logic will be appropriate, as when Wittgenstein considers phrases such as "I was going to say" something specific at some point in the past.[25] Similarly, sometimes the description of concept acquisition as the achieving of mastery of a technique exhibits this same time-specific logic: I learned the Russian word for "homeland" in college, say. However, understanding as the mastery of a technique does not exhibit this logical structure: one says in the past tense, "I *used* to understand Russian." Understanding a language is expressed in the logical structure of time-general life-activity; Wittgenstein is perhaps thinking along these lines when he writes: "How do I recognize that this color is red? – One answer would be: 'I have learnt English'" (PI §381) or "You learned the *concept* 'pain' in learning language" (PI §384).

Mutatis mutandis, this same logical structure subtends the connections between an order and what would or does fulfill it, and other logically minimal life-structuring. The mistake that is made is to invoke processes – and their logical form of time-specificity – to explain the tempting but mysterious mental mechanism that generates and guarantees – like rails reaching to infinity – the multitude of actual and possible connections between thought and action, understanding and behavior:

> How does the philosophical problem about mental processes and states and about behaviorism arise? – The first step is the one that altogether escapes notice. We talk of processes and states and leave their nature undecided. Sometime perhaps we'll know more about them – we think. But that's just what commits us to a particular way of looking at the matter. For we have a certain conception of what it means to learn to know a process better. (The decisive movement in the conjuring trick has already been made, and it was the very one that seemed to us quite innocent.) – And now the analogy which was to make us understand our thoughts falls to pieces. So we have to deny the yet uncomprehended process in the yet unexplored medium. And now it looks as if we had denied mental processes. And naturally we don't want to deny them. (PI §308)

Thinking of such life-activities in terms of finite mental states and processes tacitly introduces the logical structure of time-specificity, and

---

[25] On this, see John McDowell, "Are Meaning, Understanding, etc., Definite States?," in *The Engaged Intellect* (Cambridge, MA: Harvard University Press, 2009), 79–95.

invites the questions Wittgenstein is seeking to exorcise from philosophy[26]: when does the process set in, how is the mental state individuated and introspectable, how does it confer correctness on behavior, etc. Conversely, descriptions of language-games and forms of life should be understood with the time-general logical structure of habitual, characteristic life-activities. That logic is not the logic of relating two potentially independent items – mental state or process here, outward behavior there – precisely the wayward problem of connections that Wittgenstein diagnoses. Rather the concept of generality at work here entails that the relation is not one of quasi-mechanical connection but rather manifestation of conceptual competencies and life-structurings described as language-games and forms of life.

And because these life-structurings are described in generic statements, what counts as a manifestation of the form of life will be open to variability, exceptions, etc., will be manifested by agreement in language, agreement in judgments:

"So you are saying that human agreement decides what is true and what is false?" – What is true or false is what human beings *say*; and it is in their *language* that human beings agree. This is agreement not in opinions, but rather in form of life. (PI §241)

It is not only agreement in definitions, but also (odd as it may sound) agreement in judgments that is required for communication by means of language. This seems to abolish logic, but does not do so. – It is one thing to describe methods of measurement, and another to obtain and state results of measurement. But what we call "measuring" is in part determined by a certain constancy in results of measurement. (PI §242)

The concepts *life/living, thinking/understanding,* and *measuring* (as a kind of activity rather than a particular event) can thus be seen to exhibit the same logical structure of life-activity: "This is what we do," that is, "What people accept as a justification shows how they think and live" (PI §325). The relation of manifestation also illuminates Wittgenstein's thoughts regarding the connection between order and action:

"I'm leaving the room because you tell me to."
"I'm leaving the room, but not because you tell me to."
Does this sentence *describe* a connection [*Zusammenhang*] between my action and his order; or does it make the connection? (PI §487)

---

[26] "What is your aim in philosophy? – To show the fly out of the fly-bottle" (PI §309).

"You said, 'It'll stop soon'. – Were you thinking of the noise or of your pain?" If he answers "I was thinking of the piano-tuning" – is he stating that the link [*Verbindung*] existed, or is he making it by means of these words? – Can't I say *both*? If what he said was true, didn't the link exist – and is he not for all that making one which did not exist?" (PI §682)[27]

Wittgenstein's urge to say *both* that a connection is being reported *and* that it is being made, that it preexists and is being established, expresses the generality and the relation of manifestation that life-activity statements express. As Wittgenstein says: "Certainly such a link exists [between thinking of someone and that person]. Only not as you imagine it: namely by means of a mental *mechanism*" (PI §689).[28] We are driven to psychology, positing the existence of a mysterious "psychical thing" *because* we are deploying the wrong logical form to describe our life-activities, the language-games partially constitutive of our form of life.

IV Style: Picturing the "Wider Context"

The concept of *style*, along with the perception and attribution of style, belong to the master metaphors by which Wittgenstein explicates the logical features of our life-activities, "the logical" of our life-structurings: in the Nachlass he explicitly defines style as "the expression of a general human necessity."[29] The recurrent images and analogies he uses themselves exhibit the same elements of "the logical" that characterize the logical form of life-activity judgments: a peculiar generality, the relation of manifestation, a fittingness that provides a kind of unity, necessity, and normativity.

---

[27] Wittgenstein considers multiple instances of this general puzzle, e.g.: "I draw a head. You ask 'Whom is that supposed to represent?' – I: 'It's supposed to be N.' – You: 'But it doesn't look like him; if anything, it's rather like M.' – When I said it represented N., was I making a connection [*Zusammenhang*] or reporting one? And what connection was there?" (PI §683).

[28] The logical features of generality and manifestation also elucidate passages in which an interlocutory voice in *Philosophical Investigations* considers a rule (sometimes troped as a signpost) detached from the "wider context" of the life-activity in which it is embedded such that its normatively correct application or execution requires a time-specific "act of understanding," i.e., a mental mechanism; rather, Wittgenstein admonishes, "The arrow points only in the application that a living being makes of it" (cf. PI §§ 85–87, 431–432, 454).

[29] Wittgenstein, Bergen Nachlass (MS 183 28). Original: "Stil ist der Ausdruck einer allgemein menschlichen Notwendigkeit. Das gilt vom Schreibstil wie vom Baustil (und jedem anderen). Stil ist die allgemeine Notwendigkeit sub specie aeternitatis gesehen."

Whereas the wayward philosopher posits psychical mechanisms or independent justifying grounds for the connections or context (*Zusammenhang*) constitutive of our life-activities, Wittgenstein offers an alternative picture, repeatedly drawing upon the analogy of physiognomy – understanding facial expressions – and understanding artistic styles, especially in painting and music.[30] He often brings the two guiding images together in multiple passages across works:

The reinterpretation of a facial expression can be compared to the reinterpretation of a chord in music, when we hear it as a modulation first into this, then into that, key. (PI §536)

Though – one would like to say – every word can have a different character in different contexts, at the same time there is a single character it always has: a face. It looks at us, after all. – But a face in a painting looks at us too. (PPF §38)

A theme has a facial expression [*Gesichtsausdruck*] no less than a face does. (RPPI §434; cf. CV 59)

These are apt and instructive analogies because they emphasize the peculiar features of "the logical" that we have explored.

Descriptions of a facial expression or a style can be seen to exhibit the same logical form and logical features as generic sentences and the relation of generality discussed above: there will be vagueness, boundary cases, gaps, aberrations, and family resemblances in applying the predicates that do not refute the description of the facial expression or the style.[31]

---

[30] On facial perception in relation to aesthetic perception, see Bernie Rhie, "Wittgenstein on the Face of a Work of Art," *nonsite* 3 (October 2011) (my thanks to Toril Moi for this reference). On physiognomy and "experiencing the meaning of a word," see Carolina Scotto, "'Meaning is a Physiognomy': Wittgenstein on Seeing Words and Faces," *Nordic Wittgenstein Review* 8: 115–150 (2019).

[31] Wittgenstein varies the language of family resemblance in the Nachlass: "The melodies of Beethoven's early works have (already) a different racial face [*Rassegesicht*] than e.g. Mozart's melodies. One could draw the type of face that would correspond to the races. And indeed the race of Beethoven is stouter, more coarse-limbed, with a rounder or more quadrangular face, the race of Mozart with finer, more slender and yet pudgier forms and that of Haydn large and slim in the mode of some Austrian aristocrats. Or am I letting myself be seduced by a picture that I have of the figures of these men. I think not" (Bergen Nachlass MS 183 99; cf. CV 22; RPPI §243). Original: "Die Melodien der frühen Beethovenschen Werke haben (schon) ein anderes Rassegesicht als z.B. die Melodien Mozarts. Man könnte den Gesichtstypus zeichnen der den Rassen entspräche. Und zwar ist die Rasse Beethovens gedrungener, grobgliedriger, mit runderem oder viereckigerem Gesicht, die Rasse Mozarts mit feineren schlankeren und doch rundlichen Formen und die Haydns groß und schlank von der Art mancher österreichischer Aristokraten. Oder lasse ich mich da von dem Bild verführen das ich von den Gestalten dieser Männer habe. Ich glaube nicht."

Attributing a facial expression (compare: "he looks sad/morose/crestfallen/ disappointed") or attributing authorship or historical periodization to a painting based on stylistic features does not operate by fixed calculi or necessary and sufficient characteristics. Wittgenstein explicitly finds this "flexibility" common to expression in physiognomy and artistic style:

> Such words as "pompous" and "stately" could be expressed by faces. Doing this, our descriptions would be much more flexible and various than they are as expressed by adjectives. If I say of a piece of Schubert that it is melancholy, that is like giving it a face ... I could instead use gestures or dancing. In fact, if we want to be exact, we do use a gesture or a facial expression. (LC 10)

Understanding a facial expression or a style involves familiarity with the larger, potentially open-ended context: knowing what other gestures/ actions belong to the overall expression of an emotion, for example, or knowing how to continue or recognize a style in a new artwork, or even in a new aesthetic medium.[32] The constituents of a facial expression, a style, a form of life can outrun the discursive resources available to describe it beyond the demonstrative "like this" and "not like that," which is why language-games serve for Wittgenstein primarily as tools for drawing comparisons. This phenomenon Wittgenstein calls "imponderable self-evidence" (*unwägbare Evidenz*) that "includes subtleties of glance, of gesture, of tone," the "fine shades of behavior" that might not be describable, though "If I were a very talented painter I might conceivably represent the genuine and the simulated glance in pictures" (PPF §§358–360, cf. §210 and RPPI §§243, 919).

Similarly, the logical relation of manifestation is at work in these analogical cases as well: the face manifests an emotion, an artwork manifests a style:

> "We see emotion." – As opposed to what? – We do not see facial contortions and make inferences from them (like a doctor framing a diagnosis) to joy, grief, boredom. We describe a face immediately as sad, radiant, bored, even when we are unable to give any other description to the features. Grief, one would like to say, is personified in the face. (Z §225)

In describing how one recognizes emotion expressed *in* the face, he comes close to explicitly defining the unique logical relation of manifestation at work in life-activity judgments: "'I noticed that he was out of

---

[32] Sometimes Wittgenstein expresses this as "being at home" with the phenomenon (e.g., sign, symbol) (Z §234).

humor.' Is this a report about his behavior or his state of mind? ... Both; not side-by-side, however, but about the one via the other" (PPF §29).

An individuated style and an individuated facial expression exhibit the same kind of unity, necessity, and normativity that we saw in judgments applied to the activities of living organisms above. While there is no set of necessary and sufficient features constitutive of a given style or facial expression, there is a unity and the attitude that a certain kind of necessity attends such unity, making it the unity it is, and making it the appropriate unity for the life-activities, in a wider sense, in which it lives. We ascertain these aspects – "the logical" in a face, in a painting, say – often through comparison with other faces, other artworks. For example, the concept of *grief,* encompassing a complex life-activity, is likewise manifested in a wide variety of mental states, attitudes, actions, gestures, and so on, that are nonetheless unified by a kind of necessity (the fittingness of the recurrent pattern) that allows us to speak of a single unified phenomenon: "'Grief' describes a pattern which recurs, with different variations, in the tapestry of life. If a man's bodily expression of sorrow and of joy alternated, say with the ticking of a clock, here we should not have the characteristic course of the pattern of sorrow or of the pattern of joy" (PPF §2).[33]

Style also exhibits its affinity with the kind of unity and necessity attending "the logical" structurings of our life-activities in this passage from Wittgenstein's Nachlass:

Take a theme, like Haydn's (Saint Anthony Chorale), take a part of one of Brahms's Variations [on a theme by Haydn], which corresponds to the first part of the theme and pose the task of constructing the second part of the Variations in the style of its first part. That is a problem of the type of mathematical problems. If the solution is found, for instance how Brahms gives it, then one has no doubt: – this is the solution.

With this way [or "path," *Weg*] we are in agreement. And yet it is clear here that easily there can be different ways, we could be in agreement with each of them, we could call each of them consistent [*konsequent*].[34]

---

[33] Cf. Wittgenstein speaking about "the primary and mutually independent symbols of friendliness [in a dog: "friendly eyes, friendly mouth, the wagging of the dog's tail"]: I mean: they are parts of the phenomena that are called friendliness" (Z §506). "It amounts to this: that only of a living human being and what resembles (behaves like) a living human being can one say: it has sensations; it sees; is blind; hears; is deaf; is conscious or unconscious" (PI §281); see also LWPP II §84.

[34] Wittgenstein, Bergen Nachlass (MS 124 55; cf. MS 161 61r–61v). Original: "Nimm ein Thema, wie das Haydensche (Chorāle St. Antoni), nimm den Teil einer der Brahmsche Variationen, der dem ersten Teil des Themas entspricht und stell die Aufgabe den

The normative correctness of "the solution" lies in the recognizable generality, unity, and necessity of a given style, that nonetheless is open-ended – allowing unthought-of variations and changes – in its possible, conceivable, particular manifestations and instantiations.

These logical features – the relation of manifestation, particular kind of generality, unity, necessity, and normativity – illuminate a picture that recurs in *Philosophical Investigations* in extended sections that are concerned with rule-following and private language, which we can see now as explorations of those minimal "logical" components at work in the text: orderings, sequencing, criteria of sameness, of identity. In various passages, Wittgenstein describes certain psychological attitudes like expecting, remembering, and imagining, where the object that eventually fulfills the attitude as it were determines the content of the original attitude, where at issue is the connection (*Zusammenhang*) between mental state or concept on the one hand, and connections or applications to reality on the other. For instance, he asks, "The red which you imagine is surely not the same (not the same thing) as the red which you see in front of you; so how can you say that it is what you imagined?" (PI §443),[35] and concludes "It is in language that an expectation and its fulfillment make contact" (PI §445).[36] The wayward philosopher might

---

zweiten Teil der Variation im Stil ihres ersten Teiles zu konstruieren. Das ist ein Problem von der Art mathematischer Probleme. Ist die Lösung gefunden, etwa wie Brahms sie gibt, so zweifelt man nicht; – dies ist die Lösung.
Mit diesem Weg sind wir einverstanden. Und doch ist es hier klar, dass es leicht verschiedene Wege geben kann, kann mit deren jedem wir einverstanden sein können, deren jeden wir konsequent nennen könnten."

[35] Or:

I see someone aiming a gun and say "I expect a bang." The shot is fired. – What! – was what you expected? So did that bang somehow already exist in your expectation? Or is it just that your expectation agrees in some respect with what occurred; that that noise was not contained in your expectation, and merely supervened as an accidental property when the expectation was being fulfilled? – But no, if the noise had not occurred, my expectation would not have been fulfilled; the noise fulfilled it; it was not an accompaniment of the fulfillment like a second guest accompanying the one I expected. Was the feature of the event that was not also in the expectation something accidental, an extra provided by fate? – But then what was *not* an extra? Did something of the shot already occur in my expectation? – Then what *was* extra? For wasn't I expecting the whole shot.

"The bang was not as loud as I had expected." – "Then was there a louder bang in your expectation?" (PI §442)

[36] In *Lectures & Conversations* he similarly concludes: "The criterion for it being the one that was in your mind [when I said a certain expression] is that when I tell you, you agree" (LC 37). Relatedly: "If I make a gesture, and you are good imitators, these gestures will have

be tempted to read this as, or merely as, a psychological remark about mental states or an empirical sociological remark about the authority of linguistic practices. We are now in a position to understand this as a *logical*, not a psychological or empirical remark. This is not the blank denial of an inner state or episode: recall PI §304 within the private-language argument where an interlocutor's voice accuses Wittgenstein of concluding "that the sensation itself is a Nothing" and the responding voice says: "Not at all. It is not a Something, but not a Nothing either!"[37] And we can how hear this apparent contradiction as Wittgenstein's endeavoring to express the specific generality and relation of manifestation at work in judgments of our form of life. Rather we can think of understanding what color concepts mean, how they apply in normal circumstances as part of the life-activity, the time-general logic of understanding a language.[38] And we can conceive of that understanding of language as ultimately manifested by, its instantiations normatively exemplified in, its bearers' agreeing in applications of concepts, executions of orders, and so on. The "not something but not nothing," the "reporting" that is also a "making," reflect the manifestation of the generality in the particular that is characteristic of "the logical" at work in *Philosophical Investigations* and that perhaps is quite different from that "which we should ordinarily call reasoning" (Cavell). These acts of agreement between speakers as reciprocal bearers of the same language-game manifest the activities of our "tapestry of life," which provides the "wider context" within which human expression lives.

There is a striking analogy to this line of thinking in Wittgenstein's discussion of the difference in painting style, between a historical portrait and genre painting:

---

to be similar, but different; the shape of the fingers, etc., is different. The criterion for its being this gesture will be the clicking of it in you. You say: 'Now this.' To say what's similar is impossible (to say). Each one makes a gesture immediately and says: 'That's the one'" (LC 39; cf. PI §610).

[37] But cf. the exchange in *Zettel*: "But I do have a real *feeling* of joy!" Yes, when you are glad you really are glad. And of course joy is not joyful behavior, nor yet a feeling round the corners of the mouth and the eyes.

"'But "joy" surely designates an inward thing.' No. 'Joy' designates nothing at all. Neither any inward nor any outward thing" (Z §487). I read this passage as Wittgenstein's refusal to reductively hypostatize the complex, multidimensional phenomena of joy into merely inward sensation or outward behavior.

[38] Cf. Matthias Haase, "The Representation of Language," in *Language, Form(s) of Life, and Logic: Investigations After Wittgenstein*, ed. Christian Martin (Berlin: De Gruyter, 2018), 219–249.

If we compare a proposition to a picture, we must consider whether we are comparing it to a portrait (a historical representation) or to a genre-picture. And both comparisons make sense.

When I look at a genre-picture, it "tells" me something, even though I don't believe (imagine) for a moment that the people I see in it really exist, or that there have really been people in that situation. For suppose I ask: "*What* does it tell me, then?" (PI §522)

The genre painting doesn't portray something determinate, but it doesn't portray nothing either. The portrait (presumably) refers to an individual, that is, a determinate person. The genre painting displays a kind of generality. They are two different language-games: painting things in the world (referring to a determinate) and painting a kind of thing, a kind of generality or form whose application can or cannot be fulfilled by – manifested in – a determinate object in reality, even if that determinate object is deficient in some respects vis-à-vis the form. And these pictorial-stylistic analogies are *logical remarks* on the criss-crossing of language-games that must be disambiguated in order to understand the logical grammar of *proposition*.

These analogies serve then to try to bring the reader to see meaning and understanding neither as merely mental states, processes and psychic mechanisms, nor merely behaviorist bodily movements, but to recognize these phenomena as activities with the logical features that have been identified: this is the "wider context" within which "the logical" in our life-structurings becomes perspicuous:

I see a picture which represents a smiling face. What do I do if I take the smile now as a kind one, now as malicious? Don't I often imagine it with a spatial and temporal context of kindness or malice? Thus I might, when looking at the picture, imagine it to be of a smiler smiling down on a child at play, or again on the suffering of an enemy.

This is in no way altered by the fact that I can also take the apparently genial situation and interpret it differently by putting it into a *wider context*. – If no special circumstances reverse my interpretation, I shall conceive a particular smile as kind, call it a "kind" one, react accordingly. (PI §539, my emphasis)

And similarly, the wider context of a composer's style can alter the recognition ("interpretation") of the emotion expressed in their music: "I hear a melody completely differently after I have become familiar with its composer's style. Previously I might have described it as happy, for example, but now I sense that it is the expression of great suffering. Now I describe it differently, group it with quite different things"

(LWPP I §774).[39] These analogies suggest that such wider contexts are constitutive of and corrections to the narrower descriptions of the phenomena. Just as inner states and episodes and outer behavior should not be metaphysically separated or hypostatized per se (although under specific, say, skeptical circumstances one might speak of the one or the other), but rather comprise logically complex human unities, so too these unities are themselves constitutive parts of larger life-activities.

---

[39] Cf. "we cannot imagine the man who had this name, this face, this handwriting, not to have produced *these* works, but perhaps quite different ones instead (those of another great man) ... It might be like this: I hear that someone is painting a picture 'Beethoven writing the Ninth Symphony.' I could easily imagine the kind of thing such a picture would show us. But suppose someone wanted to represent what Goethe would have looked like writing the Ninth Symphony? Here I could imagine nothing that would not be embarrassing and ridiculous" (PPF §§50–51).

Cf. "Does the theme point to nothing beyond itself? Oh yes! But that means: – The impression it makes on me is connected with things in its surroundings – e.g. with the existence of the German language & of its intonation, but that means with the whole field of our language-games.

If I say e.g.: it's as if here a conclusion were being drawn, or, as if here something were being confirmed, or, as if *this* were a reply to what came earlier, – then the way I understand it clearly presupposes familiarity with conclusions, confirmations, replies, etc. ... And yet again there *is* a paradigm other than the theme: namely the rhythm of our language, of our thinking & feeling. And furthermore the theme is a *new* part of our language, it becomes incorporated in it; we learn a new *gesture*" (CV 59).

And in multiple passages in his later writings concerning aesthetic phenomena and their description Wittgenstein extends the "wider context" to include forms of life, cultures, historical periods. For example:

For how can it be explained what 'expressive playing' is? Certainly not by anything that accompanies the playing. – What is needed for the explanation. One might say: a culture. – If someone is brought up in a particular culture – and then reacts to music in such-and-such a way, you can teach him the use of the phrase 'expressive playing.'(Z §164)

The words we call expressions of aesthetic judgment play a very complicated role, but a very definite role, in what we call a culture of a period. To describe a culture. What we now call a cultured taste perhaps didn't exist in the Middle Ages. An entirely different game is played in different ages.

What belongs to a language-game is a whole culture. In describing musical taste you have to describe whether children give concerts, whether women do or whether men only give them, etc. etc. In aristocratic circles in Vienna people had [such and such] a taste, then it come into bourgeois circles and women joined choirs, etc. This is an example of tradition in music. (LC 25–26)

In order to get clear about aesthetic words you have to describe ways of living. We think we have to talk about aesthetic judgments like "This is beautiful," but we find that if we have to talk about aesthetic judgments we don't find these words at all, but a word used something like a gesture, accompanying a complicated activity. (LC 35)

As above, the logically complex human phenomenon of *grief*, which can extend over years and be manifested in a multitude of phenomena, ranging from occurrent episodes of sorrow, through habitual gestures, tone of voice, practices and activities, and so on, can be seen to constitute a unified life-activity of creatures like us, for whom the elements sufficiently cohere into the logical unity and necessity attending the human life-form. "It amounts to this: only of a living human being and what resembles (behaves like) a living human being can one say: it has sensations; it sees; is blind; hears; is deaf; is conscious or unconscious" (PI §281).

The antepenultimate page of *Philosophical Investigations* recapitulates some of the themes of this chapter in the juxtaposition of the concept of *natural history* and the concept of *style*:

If concept formation can be explained by facts of nature, shouldn't we be interested, not in grammar, but rather in what is its basis in nature? – We are, indeed, also interested in the correspondence between concepts and very general facts of nature. (Such facts as mostly do not strike us because of their generality.) But our interest is not thereby thrown back upon these possible causes of concept formation; we are not doing natural science; nor yet natural history – since we can also invent fictitious natural history for our purposes.

I am not saying: if such-and-such facts of nature were different, people would have different concepts (in the sense of a hypothesis). Rather: if anyone believes that certain concepts are absolutely the correct ones, and that having different ones would mean not realizing something that we realize – then let him imagine certain very general facts of nature to be different from what we are used to, and the formation of concepts different from the usual ones will become intelligible to him.

Compare a concept with a style of painting. For is even our style of painting arbitrary? Can we choose one at pleasure? (The Egyptian, for instance.) Or is it just a matter of pretty and ugly? (PPF §§365–367)[40]

---

[40] An example of the imaginative variation of "very general facts of human nature," including the role of the will, to arrive at alternative forms of life, alternative structurings of our life-activities:

> "But a contradiction in mathematics cannot comport with the application of mathematics. It [the contradiction], when it is consistently used, i.e., used to create arbitrary results, makes the application of mathematics into a farce, or a kind of superfluous ceremony. Its effect is like that of non-rigid benchmarks [*Maßstäbe*] that through expanding and compressing allow diverse measuring results." But was measuring by pacing off not measuring? And if people worked with benchmarks made of dough, should that be called false per se?
>
> Couldn't one easily think of reasons why a certain expansibility of benchmarks would be desirable?

Wittgenstein is clear: his investigations are not, or not only, empirical, not natural science, not yet natural history, because we can vary in our minds "certain very general facts of nature" and imagine different forms of life described in different life-activity judgments: different ways of counting, measuring, different kinds of activities with different kinds of language-game embedded within them. He repeats his caution: his purpose in doing so is not to create or test hypotheses about concept formation. Rather his is a *philosophical*, a *logical* investigation to make perspicuous how "the logical" of our lives is arranged, described, understood. Like the style of painting, or music.

In his Nachlass, Wittgenstein writes:

We are speaking thus about patterns in the tapestry of life. [...]
Imagine to yourself that it is really a matter of patterns on a long band.
The band is moving past me and I say at one time "this is the pattern S," at another time "that is the pattern V," sometimes for a certain period of time I don't know which it is: sometimes at the end I say "it was neither of the two."
How could one teach me to recognize these patterns? One shows me simple examples, then more complicated [examples] of both types. It is almost how I learn to distinguish the style of two composers.
But why does one draw this border with the patterns that is hard to comprehend? Because it is of importance in our life.[41]

"But is it not correct always to produce benchmarks out of harder, more immutable material? Of course it is correct; if one wants it that way." (Bergen Nachlass, MS 124 70–71)

Original:
"Aber ein Widerspruch in der Mathematik verträgt sich doch nicht mit der Anwendung der Mathematik. Er macht, wenn er konsequent, d.h. zum Erzeugen beliebiger Resultate verwendet wird, die Anwendung der Mathematik zu einer Farce, oder einer Art überflüssiger Zeremonie. Seine Wirkung ist etwa die, unstarrer Maßstäbe, die durch Dehnen und Zusammendrücken verschiedene Messungsresultate zulassen." Aber war das Messen durch Abschreiten kein Messen? Und wenn die Menschen mit Maßstäben aus Teig arbeiten, wäre das an sich schon falsch zu nennen?

Könnte man sich nicht leicht Gründe denken, weshalb eine gewisse Dehnbarkeit der Maßstäbe erwünscht sein könnte?
"Aber ist es nicht richtig, die Maßstäbe aus immer härterem, unveränderlicherem Material herzustellen? Gewiss ist es richtig; wenn man es so will."

[41] Wittgenstein, Bergen Nachlass (MS 169 68v–69v). Original:
Wir reden also über Muster im Lebensteppich ...
Denk Dir es handelte sich wirklich um Muster auf einem langen Band.
Das Band zieht an mir vorbei und ich sage einmal "dies ist das Muster S," einmal "das ist das Muster V," Manchmal weiß ich für einige Zeit nicht, welches es ist; manchmal sage ich am Ende "Es war keins von beiden."

The presentation and comparison of elementary language-games as a method in the *Philosophical Investigations* is akin to training one to recognize composers' styles, because artistic styles share the logical features distinctive of the patterns that comprise the tapestry of our shared life.[42]

> Wie könnte man mich lernen, diese Muster zu erkennen? Man zeigt mir einfache Beispiele, dann auch komplizierte von beiden Arten. Es ist beinahe, wie ich den Stil zweier Komponisten unterscheiden lerne.
> Warum zieht man aber bei den Mustern diese schwer fassliche Grenze? Weil sie in unserm Leben von Wichtigkeit ist.

[42] My thanks to Kristin Boyce, Juliet Floyd, and John Gibson for generously providing comments on an earlier draft of this chapter.

9 Wittgenstein's Apocalyptic Subjectivity

Ben Ware

Abstract: This chapter moves through three clear stages. First, the initial sections highlight some of the ways that Wittgenstein has been misread by thinkers working in the tradition of continental philosophy and critical theory (including Badiou, Deleuze, and Marcuse); and, exposing some of these misreadings, it makes the case for grasping Wittgenstein not simply a modernist philosopher, but, more specifically, as an exponent of (what the chapter terms) *philosophical modernism*. Second, the chapter tarries with a number of Wittgenstein's controversial remarks on the atomic bomb and (what he calls) the "apocalyptic view of the world," and it brings these remarks into dialogue with the work of a number of other literary and philosophical figures, including Gertrude Stein, Günther Anders, and Theodor Adorno. Third, and finally, although Wittgenstein's remarks on apocalypse appear in his private, postwar notebooks, they nevertheless provide us with a crucial link to his later philosophy, specifically *Philosophical Investigations* and this is what I turn to in the last sections of the chapter. In the *Investigations*, it is not simply the language of the book that we might describe as apocalyptic, but also, and more importantly, the fundamental conception of philosophy that we find therein. This returns us to the view of philosophical modernism previously outlined.

Keywords: Apocalyptic Writing, Critical Theory, Ethics, Misreading, Modernism, Subjectivity, Gertrude Stein, Günther Anders, Theodor Adorno, Gilles Deleuze, Alain Badiou.

I.

Let us begin with a series of questions which continue to preoccupy Wittgenstein scholarship. How are we to conceive of Wittgenstein's relation to modernism? Is modernism an *internal* component of Wittgenstein's philosophical practice, or is it an *external* tradition to which his philosophy in some way relates? What exactly is it that we mean when we speak of Wittgenstein as a modernist figure?

According to Terry Eagleton in a now famous series of remarks: "Frege is a philosopher's philosopher, Bertrand Russell every shopkeeper's image of the sage, and Sartre the media's idea of an intellectual. But Wittgenstein is the philosopher of poets, playwrights, novelists, and composers."[1] For Eagleton, the *Tractatus* belongs to the great wave of early twentieth-century European modernism; and therefore the true coordinates of the text are not Frege or Russell, but rather Joyce, Schoenberg, and Picasso – what Eagleton calls "all those self-ironizing modernists who sought in their own fashion to represent and point to their representing at a stroke."[2]

This view of Wittgenstein's modernism – one which conceives of the relation in essentially *aesthetic* terms – is now very much what I want to call *the standard view*. To the extent that Wittgenstein is thought of as a modernist at all, then it is, as Marjorie Perloff puts it, because his "way of tackling philosophical problems is best called *aesthetic*": aesthetic in its creative use of "exempla, apposite images, parataxis, and sudden leaps of faith."[3] To adapt a remark from Stanley Cavell's 1971 study *The World Viewed*, we might thus say that what makes Wittgenstein a modernist is that his "philosophy exists in the condition of art."[4]

And of course, all of this, in one respect, is true – absolutely and vitally true. No understanding of either the *Tractatus* or the *Investigations* can proceed without taking seriously the literary and aesthetic dimensions of the works. As early as the wartime *Notebooks*, Wittgenstein describes his problem as one of finding the right form of expression for his thoughts. "My difficulty," he remarks in 1915, is only "an enormous difficulty of expression." In a later letter to Ludwig von Ficker, Wittgenstein famously writes (about his "Logisch-Philosophische Abhandlung") that "the work is strictly philosophical and at the same

---

[1] Terry Eagleton, "Introduction to Wittgenstein," in *Wittgenstein: The Terry Eagleton Script / The Derek Jarman Film* (London: BFI Publishing, 1993), 5.
[2] Terry Eagleton, "My Wittgenstein," in *The Eagleton Reader* (Oxford: Blackwell, 1998), 336.
[3] Marjorie Perloff, *Wittgenstein's Ladder: Poetic Language and the Strangeness of the Ordinary* (Chicago, IL: University of Chicago Press, 1996), 15.
[4] See Stanley Cavell, *The World Viewed: Reflections on the Ontology of Film* (Cambridge, MA: Harvard University Press, 1979), 14.

time literary: but there's no gassing in it."[5] The literary dimensions of the *Tractatus* are also emphasized by Frege:

> The pleasure of reading your book can ... in no way arise through the ... content, but ... only through the form, in which is revealed something of the individuality of the author. [The book] thereby becomes an artistic rather than a scientific achievement; that which is said ... takes a back seat to how it is said.[6]

Frege's comments are now well known; but it will be useful here to briefly pause and compare his insightful, though ultimately unsympathetic, remarks on the artistic elements of the *Tractatus* with those of a number of more recent European philosophers and theoreticians – figures who one might expect to be much more open and sympathetic to the literary and aesthetic dimensions of Wittgenstein's work.

II.

In a series of interviews conducted in 1989, the French philosopher Gilles Deleuze is asked for his thoughts on Wittgenstein. Initially reluctant to engage the topic, Deleuze finally opens up to his interlocutor Claire Parnet:

> For me [Wittgenstein] is a philosophical catastrophe. ...[His work marks] a regression of all philosophy, a massive regression. The Wittgenstein matter is very, very sad. They [the Wittgensteinians] impose a system of terror ... under the pretext of doing something new. It is poverty instituted as grandeur. ...
>
> There isn't a word to describe this danger. It seems, especially since all Wittgensteinians are mean and destructive, if they win there could be an assassination of philosophy. They are philosophical assassins.[7]

What is perhaps most striking about Deleuze's remarks, is not simply their dismissive (even contemptuous) tone, but the fact that they come from a philosopher who is elsewhere utterly committed to the "mobile

---

[5] Letter: Ludwig Wittgenstein to Ludwig von Ficker (October, 1919), cited in Ludwig Wittgenstein, *Prototractatus*, ed. B. F. McGuinness, T. Nyberg, and G. H. von Wright, trans. D. F. Pears and B. F. McGuinness (London: Routledge & Kegan Paul, 1971), 14, n. 2.

[6] Letter: Gottlob Frege to Ludwig Wittgenstein (September 16, 1919), in *Loneliness* (Boston University Studies in the Philosophy of Religion, 19), ed. Leroy S. Rouner (Notre Dame, IN: University of Notre Dame Press, 1998), 91.

[7] *Gilles Deleuze From A to Z*, Dir. Pierre-André Boutang, trans. Charles J. Stivale (Semiotext(e) Foreign Agents, 2012). The film comprises a series of interviews with Deleuze, in which each letter of the alphabet evokes a word: From A ("Animal") to Z ("Zigzag"). The letter W, for Deleuze, evokes "Wittgenstein."

relations" between philosophy and literature; to what he calls "the smooth space" which allows for philosophy-becoming-literature and literature- and art-becoming-philosophy.[8] In their 1991 text *What Is Philosophy?*, Deleuze and his collaborator Félix Guattari, refer to figures such as Kierkegaard and Nietzsche as "hybrid geniuses" who "use all the resources of their "athleticism" to install themselves within [a space of] difference, like acrobats torn apart in a perpetual show of strength."[9] Wittgenstein, however, surely *the* great inheritor of Kierkegaardian and Nietzschean philosophical acrobatics in the twentieth century, is completely absent from the Deleuze–Guattari picture.

In many respects, Deleuze's interview comments reprise a view of Wittgenstein's philosophy put forward, several decades earlier, by members of the Frankfurt School. Theodor Adorno, for example, in his *Hegel: Three Studies*, cites the final proposition of the *Tractatus* – "Whereof one cannot speak, thereof one must be silent" (7) – and takes it, reductively, as an example of "extreme positivism" which, in his words, "spills over" into a "gesture of reverent authoritarian authenticity."[10] Herbert Marcuse's 1964 study *One Dimensional Man*, moves in a similar direction. According to Marcuse, Wittgenstein's later work "militates against intellectual non-conformity", "reaffirms the prevailing universe of discourse and behaviour", and, in its demand for absolute clarity, functions like the philosophical equivalent of a Stalinist politburo:

The intellectual is called on the carpet. What do you mean when you say...? Don't you conceal something? You talk a language which is suspect. You don't talk like the rest of us, like the man in the street, but rather like a foreigner who does not belong here. We have to cut you down to size, expose your tricks, purge you.[11]

There is, of course, no mention here of Wittgenstein's own émigré ("foreigner") status and a life spent not "belonging"; no mention of the fact that his philosophy issues no decrees, but, much like Marcuse's own,

---

[8] Gilles Deleuze, *Difference and Repetition*, trans. Paul Patton (New York: Colombia University Press, 1994), xvi; Gilles Deleuze and Félix Guattari, *"Treatise on Nomadology War Machine,"* A Thousand Plateaus: Capitalism and Schizophrenia, trans. Brian Massumi (London: The Athlone Press, 1988), 351–423.

[9] Gilles Deleuze and Félix Guattari, *What Is Philosophy?* trans. Graham Burchell and Hugh Tomlinson (London: Verso, 1994), 67.

[10] Theodor Adorno, *Hegel: Three Studies*, trans. Shierry Weber Nicholsen (Cambridge, MA: MIT Press, 1993), 101.

[11] Herbert Marcuse, *One Dimensional Man: Studies in the Ideology of Advanced Industrial Society* (London: Routledge & Kegan Paul, 1991), 196.

is thoroughly committed to a liberatory battle against the bewitchment of the intellect; no mention of the fact that rather than a bureaucratic leveling of language and discourse, what Wittgenstein *actually* calls for – explicitly at one point, and elsewhere implicitly – is for philosophy to be written *only* as a kind of poetic or creative composition: "I think I summed up my attitude to philosophy when I said: philosophy ought to be written only as a poetic composition" (CV 1980, 24). As he puts it again, several years later: "If, rather than the more correct way of thinking, I want to teach a new movement of thought, my purpose is a 're-evaluation of values' and [with this] I come to Nietzsche as well as to the opinion that the philosopher should be a poet."[12]

It would thus seem that Wittgenstein is not entirely misguided in his pessimistic prediction that his work would not be understood. Writing in the Preface to the *Investigations*, he remarks that although his work *might* "bring light" into one brain or another, this is not very likely. "My type of thinking is not wanted in this present age," he comments to a friend, echoing Nietzsche: "I have to swim so strongly against the tide. Perhaps in a hundred years people will really want what I am writing."[13]

III.

The only recent continental philosopher to pay any real attention to the literary and aesthetic dimensions of Wittgenstein's writing has been Alain Badiou. Taking his cue from the French psychoanalyst Jacques Lacan, Badiou reads Wittgenstein as a prototypical "antiphilosopher": a figure who, in the tradition of Kierkegaard, Nietzsche, and Lacan himself, exposes the "dishonesty" of conventional modes of philosophizing, acting, in Badiou's words, as an "awakener" of his audience.[14] Badiou highlights the early Wittgenstein's "art of writing," his "abstract literary audacity"; and he suggests that the text to which the *Tractatus* should be

---

[12] Wittgenstein's *Nachlass* (23 March, 1938) item 120, 145r. This remark is translated by Wolfgang Huemer and quoted by David Schalkwyk in his essay "Wittgenstein's 'Imperfect Garden': The Ladders and Labyrinths of Philosophy as Dichtung," in *The Literary Wittgenstein*, ed. John Gibson and Wolfgang Huemer (London: Routledge, 2004), 73, fn. 7.

[13] M. O'C. Drury, "Some Notes on Conversations with Wittgenstein," in *Ludwig Wittgenstein: Personal Recollections*, ed. Rush Rhees (Oxford: Blackwell, 1981) 94.

[14] Alain Badiou, *Wittgenstein's Antiphilosophy*, trans. Bruno Bosteels (London: Verso, 2011), 49, 67.

compared is Mallarmé's *A Throw of the Dice Will Never Abolish Chance*. According to Badiou:

> The affirmative and hierarchical unfolding of propositions, the metaphorical tension combined with a mathematising rigour, the latent irony of the figures, the absolute self-sufficiency and yet the reference to an "overcoming" of the Book: all these features bring together the two projects.[15]

While Badiou is certainly correct to highlight what we might call the "Mallarméan side" of Wittgenstein – the side of him concerned with syntax, precision, and structure – there are nevertheless two key problems with his overall account. First, like Eagleton and Perloff, Badiou conceives of Wittgenstein's modernism primarily in aesthetic terms: his antiphilosophical *act* is, Badiou's says, "archi-aesthetic" (or "chiefly aesthetic"). In this respect, his approach to Wittgenstein's modernism is very much in line with what I'm calling the standard approach. Second, there is a problem with Badiou's notion of antiphilosophy: a concept which does not simply refer to philosophy which is divested of its theoretical pretentions, but one which, in the context of his account of Wittgenstein, crucially entails an ineffabilist dimension:

> The antiphilosophical act consists in letting what there is show itself, insofar as "what there is" is precisely that which no proposition can say. If Wittgenstein's antiphilosophical act can legitimately be declared archi-aesthetic, it is because this "letting be" has the non-propositional form of pure showing. ... It is thus a question of firmly establishing the laws of the sayable (of the thinkable), in order for the unsayable (the unthinkable, which is ultimately given only in art) to be *situated* as the "upper limit" of the sayable itself.[16]

The problem here is that while Badiou praises Wittgenstein's break with traditional, theory-producing modes of philosophy, the aspect of his work that he deems *most significant* is his so-called "theory of saying and showing." "Antiphilosophy," as Badiou puts it, paraphrasing *Tractatus* 4.14, "must set limits to what can be thought; and, in so doing, to what cannot be thought."[17] On its own terms, then, Badiou's notion of antiphilosophy, when applied to the early Wittgenstein, would appear to be at best contradictory: it rehearses the standard, doctrinal reading of the *Tractatus*, while simultaneously claiming that the book does not advance doctrines and theories and is instead committed solely to the idea of philosophy *as an act*.

---

[15] Ibid., 156.   [16] Ibid., 80.   [17] Ibid.

IV.

Where, then, might we turn for an understanding of Wittgenstein's relation to modernism – one which avoids conceiving of the matter in exclusively aesthetic terms (the standard approach), and one which, at the same time, sidesteps the pitfalls of Badiou's notion of modernist antiphilosophy? Here I'd like to suggest that understanding Wittgenstein as a modernist figure requires us, first of all, to begin with a different understanding of modernism itself: one which treats it not (or not *chiefly*) as an aesthetic category, nor indeed as a chronological one, but rather as a *philosophical concept*.

One twentieth-century thinker who makes an explicit case for modernism as having its conceptual roots firmly planted in philosophy is the art critic Clement Greenberg. At the beginning of his 1959 essay "Modernist Painting," Greenberg makes the following claim: "Western civilization is not the first civilization to turn around and question its own foundations, but it is the one that has gone furthest in doing so. I identify modernism with the intensification, almost exacerbation, of this self-critical tendency that began with the philosopher Kant. Because he was the first to criticize the means of criticism itself, I conceive of Kant as the first real modernist."[18] Applying this assessment to art, Greenberg continues: "The essence of modernist art lies ... in the use of the characteristic methods of a discipline to criticize the discipline itself, not in order to subvert it but in order to entrench it more firmly in its area of competence."[19] For Greenberg, the essence of modernism therefore lies in the activity of radical self-criticism and the movement toward absolute self-referential autonomy. Within the domain of art, this involves the elimination of anything extrinsic to the medium of art itself; for example, freedom from sculptural properties like tactility and literary ones like narrative. As Greenberg points out: successful modernist art draws attention to the materiality of the paint, the shape and size of the canvas, and, most importantly, the "ineluctable flatness"[20] of the picture's surface.

Whilst all of this sounds rather radical, it is in fact undergirded by a kind of historical gradualism and by a commitment to the past of art as *the* standard of artistic quality. Greenberg resists explicitly and

---

[18] Clement Greenberg, 'Modernist Painting,' in *The Collected Essays and Criticism Vol. 4: Modernism with a Vengeance, 1957–1969*, ed. John O'Brian (Chicago, IL: The University of Chicago Press, 1995), 85.
[19] Ibid.   [20] Ibid., 87.

repeatedly the idea that modernism operates as a site of break, rupture, or negation. Indeed, as he puts it:

> Nothing could be further from the authentic art of our time [i.e., modernist art] than the idea of a rupture of continuity. Art *is* – among other things – continuity, and is unthinkable without it. Lacking the past of art, and the need and compulsion to maintain its standards of excellence, modernist art would lack both substance and justification.[21]

One could of course say a great deal more about this idea of modernism as inheriting and continuing the past – not least because it becomes a key component in Michael Fried and Stanley Cavell's thinking about modernism. Suffice to say here, however, that it's *against* this idea of modernism (at least in part) that I wish to articulate my own view of *philosophical modernism*: a view which comprises three intimately connected strands – (i) the temporal, (ii) the methodological, and (iii) the formal. These three strands can be elucidated as follows.

(i) Temporal Strand

Philosophical modernism is characterized by an affirmation of the *new* and a *conscious awareness* of one's own philosophical enterprise *as new*. It makes its claim on the present through a rejection of the old – understood as past forms, past ideas, past ways of seeing – in the name of a commitment to a philosophically, aesthetically, ethically, or politically transformed future. This emphasis upon the new is, however, far from unproblematic: (i) it seems to preserve a secret tie to be past, being dependent upon that which it seeks to overturn; and (ii) to the extent that the new is *endlessly* announced, it cannot avoid succumbing to the logic of *the same*. Nevertheless, it is still the new upon which philosophical modernism insists.

Example i:

> I myself still find my way of philosophizing new, & it keeps striking me so afresh, & that is why I have to repeat myself so often. It will have become part of the flesh & blood of a new generation. (CV 1998, 3)

(ii) Methodological Strand

Philosophical modernism finds its truth not in the production of philosophical doctrines and theses, but rather in and through the activity of *negation*. While such negation can take numerous forms it is always, in

---

[21] Ibid., 93.

my view, closely connected to what Walter Benjamin calls "the destructive character." According to Benjamin, "the destructive character knows only one watchword: make room. And only one activity: clearing away. ... Not always by brute force; sometimes by the most refined means. ... What exists is reduced to rubble – not for the sake of the rubble, but for that of the way leading through it."[22] Here, then, negation is not to be equated with *unqualified destructiveness*; rather, destruction is always invested with a positive, transformative force.

Example ii:

Where does this investigation get its importance from, given that it seems only to destroy everything interesting: that is, all that is great and important? (As it were, all the buildings, leaving behind only bits of stone and rubble.) But what we are destroying are only houses of cards, and we are clearing up the ground of language on which they stood. (PI §118)

(iii) Formal Strand

Philosophical modernism strives to find new *forms* for the expression of philosophical thought – an activity which requires opening up a space *outside* the discursive universe of traditional philosophy. In this respect, philosophical modernism places particular emphasis not just on what is said, but on *how* it is said and the *impact* of what is said on the reader. The reader's emotional and affective engagement with the text is thus, we might say, already anticipated by the text itself. The aim of philosophical modernism – as a specific kind of writing – is not (or not chiefly) to bring the reader to new forms of knowledge, but rather to bring them to see that, in Rilke's phrase, they "must change their life." In this respect, formal experimentation and ingenuity is closely tied to ethics.

Example iii:

My propositions are elucidatory in this way: he who understands me finally recognizes them as [nonsense], when he has climbed out through them, on them, over them. (He must so to speak throw away the ladder, after he has climbed up on it.)

He must surmount these propositions; then he sees the world rightly. (TLP 6.54)

---

[22] Walter Benjamin, 'The Destructive Character,' in *Selected Writings Volume 2, Part 2 1931–1934*, trans. Rodney Livingstone et al., ed. Michael W. Jennings et al. (Cambridge, MA: Belknap Press, 2005), 541–542.

In what follows, I want to suggest one way in which Wittgenstein can be grasped as a *philosophical modernist* in the way just outlined. Focusing specifically on the second, methodological strand – which I associate with negation and Benjamin's "destructive character" – I will argue that Wittgenstein's later work can be understood as *apocalyptic*, not simply in tone, but also, and more importantly, in terms of its *philosophical method*. This method can be viewed under a changed aspect once it is considered in light of a number of cultural and political remarks which Wittgenstein makes in his private notebooks of the 1930s and 1940s.

V.

Modernism as a philosophical project is, we might say, apocalyptic through and through. One only need consider the vast number of things that it pronounces dead and buried: God, man, meaning, metaphysics, the subject, history, nature, art, and, of course, philosophy itself. Regarding philosophy's preoccupation with its *own* end, Badiou remarks that

> the great declarations concerning the death of philosophy in general, and of metaphysics in particular, are most probably a rhetorical means of introducing a new way, or a new goal, into philosophy itself. The best means of saying: I am a new philosopher, is probably to say: philosophy is finished, philosophy is dead.... So there is a possibility that the development of philosophy must always be in the form of resurrection. The old philosophy, like the old man, is dead, but this death is in fact the birth of the new man, the new philosopher.[23]

Announcing the end of philosophy is thus a means of clearing the ground, of allowing a new mode of thought – or a new *style of thought* – to emerge (out of the ruins of the old). However, because the theme of the end *continues* to play out, it comes to figure (to use a phrase from Freud) as a kind of *repetition compulsion*. But this compulsion to repeat also turns out to be a vital source of modernist philosophy's creative drive: the theme of the end is what returns, but the variations on this theme are themselves endless. To give just three examples: Hegel's understanding of his own thought as bringing the history of philosophy to an end;[24] Wittgenstein's belief that the *Tractatus* had finally "solved"

---

[23] Alain Badiou, *Philosophy for Militants*, trans. Bruno Bosteels (London: Verso, 2012), 6.
[24] See, for example, G. W. F. Hegel, *Lectures on the History of Philosophy*, vol. 3, trans. E. S. Haldane and Francis H. Simon (London: Routledge & Kegan Paul, 1955), III, 551–552. "The strife of the finite self-consciousness with the absolute self-consciousness, which

"the problems of philosophy," finding them to consist in a "misunderstanding of the logic of our language" (TLP 27); and Heidegger's view that (i) philosophy is metaphysics, (ii) the end of philosophy means the completion of metaphysics, and (iii) "the development of philosophy into the independent sciences ... is the legitimate completion of philosophy."[25]

Philosophical modernism is not, however, only concerned with the end(s) of philosophy, but also with *the end as such*. Thought is, we might say, both haunted and fascinated by the possibility of extinction, wipeout and, ultimately, its own negation. But here, once again, repetition yields difference. In his late essay "The End of All Things" (1794), Kant argues that the notion of an absolute end – the end as *total discontinuity* – is both horrifying and attractive: "frighteningly sublime", as he puts it (8:327).[26] While such an end cannot, strictly speaking, be thought (it implies "an end of all time," which is something about which we are "obviously able to form no concept"), it is certainly not meaningless; indeed, it is "woven in a wonderous way into universal human reason." The moral perfection which our rational natures must aspire to cannot be realized within time, marked as it is by a constant alteration of one's (moral and physical) state (8:335). This leads to the idea of a *final end*, which (at the same time) is the beginning of a duration in which beings as *supersensible* no longer stand under conditions of time and in which their ultimate moral end can thus be attained (8:327/8:335). The idea of *a final end*, then, is what gives worth to the world of rational beings; without it, as Kant writes, "creation itself appears purposeless ... like a play having no resolution and affording no cognition of any rational aim" (8:331).

Moving forward almost a century, we encounter an extinction fable placed at the very beginning of Nietzsche's oeuvre, in his 1873 essay *Über Wahrheit und Lüge im außermoralischen Sinne* [On Truth and Lie in an Extramoral Sense]. The fable reads as follows:

Once upon a time, in some out of the way corner of that universe which is dispersed into numberless twinkling solar systems, there was a star upon which

---

last seemed to the other to lie outside of itself, *now comes to an end*. ... Now, indeed, [the history of philosophy] seems to have reached its goal. ... At this point I bring this history of Philosophy to a close."

[25] Martin Heidegger, "The End of Thinking and the Task of Philosophy," in *Martin Heidegger: Basic Writings*, ed. David Farrell Krell (London: Routledge, 1993), 432–434.

[26] Immanuel Kant, *Religion and Rational Theology*, trans. Allen W. Wood and George Di Giovanni (Cambridge: Cambridge University Press, 1996), 221. All referencing in the body of the text follows the standard conventions for citing Kant's works.

clever beasts invented knowing. That was the most arrogant and mendacious minute of "world history," but nevertheless, it was only a minute. After nature had drawn a few breaths, the star cooled and congealed, and the clever beasts had to die. – One might invent such a fable, and yet he still would not have adequately illustrated how miserable, how shadowy and transient, how aimless and arbitrary the human intellect looks within nature. There were eternities during which it did not exist. And when it is all over with the human intellect, nothing will have happened.[27]

While Kant invites us to entertain an apocalyptic thought experiment in order to arrive at a moral sense of the world, here Nietzsche presents us with a much more disquieting picture of the end: from the emergence of human existence through to its final extinction "nothing will have happened." But perhaps it is possible to move beyond a purely nihilistic reading of this fable and to see it as a kind of provocation, a call to further thought. Faced with the prospect of a final end – an extinction without revelation – how should we assess our egological obsession with "knowing"? In what direction has the "knowledge-drive" taken us and with what consequences? Perhaps we can read the fable as a reminder that, given the inevitability of our species extinction, a transvaluation of our economic, ecological, and political values – the creation of new *passions for life* – is now more urgent than ever before.

VI.

Throughout his notebooks of the 1930s and 1940s, Wittgenstein makes numerous remarks which, in different ways, evoke the sense of an ending. In 1931, for example, when thinking about his work in philosophy, he says to himself: "I destroy, I destroy, I destroy" (CV 1980, 21). In the same year, he comments that "[i]f my name lives on then only as the *Terminus ad quem* of great occidental philosophy. Somewhat like the name of the one who burnt down the library of Alexandria."[28] In the *Big Typescript*, he comments that "*all* that philosophy can do is to *destroy* idols ...[a]nd that means not creating a new one"; and, moreover, that philosophy itself, at least in part, consists in destroying "certain prejudices that are based on our particular way of looking at things."[29]

---

[27] Friedrich Nietzsche, "On Truth and Lie in an Extra-moral Sense," in *Philosophy and Truth: Selections from Nietzsche's Notebooks of the Early 1870s*, trans. Daniel Breazeale (New York: Humanity Books, 1979), 79.
[28] *Philosophical Occasions: 1912–1951* (Indianapolis, IN: Hackett, 1993), 73.
[29] *The Big Typescript*, TS. 213 (Malden, MA: Blackwell Publications, 2005), 413.

In 1946, however, Wittgenstein makes an altogether more startling claim: one that is, seemingly, less a comment on his own philosophical practice and more a piece of social, political, and cultural critique

> The hysterical fear of the atom bomb the public now has, or at least expresses, is almost a sign that here for once a really salutary discovery has been made. At least the fear gives the impression of being fear in the face of a really effective bitter medicine. I cannot rid myself of the thought: if there were not something good here, the philistines would not be making an outcry. But perhaps this too is a childish idea. For all I can mean really is that the bomb creates the prospect of the end, the destruction of a ghastly evil, of disgusting soapy water science and certainly that is not an unpleasant thought; but who is to say what would come after such a destruction? The people now making speeches against the production of the bomb are undoubtedly the dregs of the intelligentsia, but even that does not prove beyond question that what they abominate is to be welcomed. (CV 1980, 48–49)

What then should we make of these remarks, written almost exactly one year after the bombings of the Japanese cities of Hiroshima and Nagasaki – events which left between 129,000 and 226,000 people dead, many of them civilians? We might begin by placing Wittgenstein's comments alongside other modernist responses to the bomb, notably Gertrude Stein's fragment "Reflection on the Atomic Bomb," also written in 1946:

> They asked me what I thought of the atomic bomb. I said I had not been able to take any interest in it.
>   ... I never could take any interest in the atomic bomb, I just couldn't any more than in everybody's secret weapon. That it has to be secret makes it dull and meaningless. Sure it will destroy a lot and kill a lot, but it's the living that are interesting not the way of killing them, because if there were not a lot left living how could there be any interest in destruction. Alright, that is the way I feel about it. They think they are interested about the atomic bomb but they really are not not any more than I am. Really not. They may be a little scared, I am not so scared, there is so much to be scared of so what is the use of bothering to be scared, and if you are not scared the atomic bomb is not interesting.[30]

If Stein is radically *uninterested* in the bomb (a striking example, perhaps, of modernist boredom, intellectual coldness, and subjective withdrawal), then Wittgenstein appears deeply *invested* in it; and for what would seem

---

[30] Gertrude Stein, "Reflections on the Atomic Bomb" (1946), *Yale Poetry Review* (1947), [https://www.writing.upenn.edu/~afilreis/88/stein-atom-bomb.html (accessed April 4, 2020).]

to be two connected reasons. First, the bomb offers the prospect of an "end" and, specifically, the termination of what he calls "soapy water" scientism; and second, the bomb might be thought of as a welcome invention *precisely because* those opposing it (including the likes of Russell and Einstein) are, in Wittgenstein's words, "philistines," the "dregs of the intelligentsia." While Wittgenstein is quick to acknowledge that the latter is perhaps a "childish idea" (he is simply welcoming what his intellectual opponents are against), his general remarks about the bomb need to be understood in relation to a number of other statements that he makes during the same period. The following remark from 1947 is here especially important:

The truly apocalyptic view of the world is that things do *not* repeat themselves. It is not e.g. absurd to believe that the scientific & technological age is the beginning of the end for humanity, that the idea of Great Progress is a bedazzlement, along with the idea that the truth will ultimately be known; that there is nothing good or desirable about scientific knowledge & that humanity, in seeking it, is falling into a trap. It is by no means clear that this is not how things are. (CV 1998, 64)

This passage, I would suggest, needs to be read dialectically. The truly apocalyptic view is one which sees humanity marching directly toward its end; but this end emerges *only* as a possibility once the belief in *total and uninterrupted scientific progress* comes to hold sway. Put another way: the apocalyptic threat arises as the direct consequence of a certain kind of *apocalyptic blindness* ("bedazzlement"), itself a product of the technological-scientific worldview. Humankind has fallen into a trap, mistaking technological progress for human progress and failing to see the reality of the apocalyptic danger that it itself has created. On this point, Wittgenstein comes strikingly close to the view put forward by Theodor Adorno and Max Horkheimer in the opening pages of: "The fully enlightened earth radiates disaster triumphant."[31]

Taken together Wittgenstein's two remarks thus present a distinctly apocalyptic outlook: (i) we are faced with the prospect of an end ("the bomb"); but (ii) this end also reveals or unveils (*apo*, "away" + *kalupto*, "cover") an important truth about reality: what appears at first blush as human "progress" (technological-scientific advancement), turns out in fact to be the very motor of world annihilation. Consequently, it might be necessary, as Wittgenstein suggests, for the end of a world – the world

---

[31] Theodor Adorno and Max Horkheimer, *Dialectic of Enlightenment*, trans. John Cumming (London: Verso, 1997), 3.

of frenzied technoscience – in order to prevent an even more catastrophic end – the total destruction of our existing forms of (ecological, human, and non-human) life.[32]

VII.

It will be useful here to bring Wittgenstein's thoughts into dialogue with those of the German-Jewish philosopher Günther Anders. A contemporary of Marcuse, Hans Jonas, and Hannah Arendt (to whom he was married from 1929 to 1937), Anders devoted much of his work in 1950s and early 1960s to exploring the relation between technology and catastrophe, especially the threat of nuclear annihilation. Writing in the aftermath of Hiroshima and Nagasaki, Anders argues that we have become "inverted Utopians": "while ordinary Utopians are unable to actually produce what they are able to visualise, we are unable to visualise what we are actually producing."[33] This Promethean gap – our capacity to produce as opposed to our power to imagine – defines the moral situation facing us today.[34] Our society is, according to Anders, a society of machines and technological devices; and it through these that the great "dream of omnipotence has at long last come true."[35] This dream, however, turns out to be the very nightmare from which we cannot awake, precisely because "we are [now] in a position to inflict *absolute destruction* on each other."[36] With these new "apocalyptic powers," we enter what Ander's calls "The Last Age":

On August 6, 1945, the day of Hiroshima, a New Age began: the age in which at any given moment we have the power to transform any given place on our planet, and even our planet itself, into a Hiroshima. On that day we became, at least "modo negativo," omnipotent; but since, on the other hand, we can be wiped out at any given moment, we also became totally impotent. However long this age may last, even if it should last forever, it is "The Last Age": for there is no

---

[32] For a reading of Wittgenstein's later work in relation to ideas of utopia and alternate futures, see Ben Ware, "Right in Front of Our Eyes: Aspect Perception, Ethics and the Utopian Imagination in Wittgenstein's *Philosophical Investigations*," in *Living Wrong Life Rightly: Modernism, Ethics and the Political Imagination* (London: Palgrave, 2017), 7–36.
[33] Günther Anders, "Theses for the Atomic Age," *The Massachusetts Review* 3 (2): 493–505 (Spring, 1962); 496.
[34] Ibid.
[35] Günther Anders, "Reflections on the H Bomb," *Dissent* 3 (2): 146–155 (Spring, 1956); 146.
[36] Ibid. (added emphasis)

possibility that it's "differentia specifica," the possibility of our self-extinction, can ever end – but by the end itself. . . .

Thus the basic moral question of former times must be radically reformulated: instead of asking "*How* should we live?," we now must ask "*Will* we live?"[37]

Surviving the threat of extinction will entail, at least in part, expanding our capacity for fear and anxiety and cultivating *a renewed sense of the apocalyptic*. As Anders puts it: "Our imperative: 'Expand the capacity of your imagination,' means, in concreto: 'Increase your capacity of fear.' Therefore: don't fear fear, have the courage to be frightened, and to frighten others, too. Frighten thy neighbour as yourself. This fear, of course, must be of a special kind: 1) a fearless fear, since it excludes fearing those who might drive us towards cowardice; 2) a stirring fear, since it should drive us into the streets instead of under cover; 3) a loving fear, not fear *of* the danger ahead but fear *for* the generations to come."[38] We thus need to become *enlightened doomsayers*.[39] Anders distils this doomsaying message into a wonderful short parable which retells the biblical story of Noah:

One day, he [Noah] clothed himself in sackcloth and covered his head with ashes. Only a man who was mourning [the death of] a beloved child or his wife was allowed to do this. Clothed in the garb of truth, bearer of sorrow, he went back to the city, resolved to turn the curiosity, spitefulness, and superstition of its inhabitants to his advantage. Soon he had gathered around him a small curious crowd, and questions began to be asked. He was asked if someone had died and who the dead person was. Noah replied to them that many had died, and then, to the great amusement of his listeners, said that they themselves were the dead of whom he spoke. When he was asked when this catastrophe had taken place, he replied to them: "Tomorrow." Profiting from their attention and confusion, Noah drew himself up to his full height and said these words: "The day after tomorrow, the flood will be something that has been. And when the flood will have been, *everything that is will never have existed*. When the flood will have carried off everything that is, everything that will have been, it will be too late to remember, for there will no longer be anyone alive. And so there will no longer be any difference between the dead and those who mourn them. *If I have come before you, it is in order to reverse time, to mourn tomorrow's dead today*. The day after tomorrow it will be too late." With this he went back whence he had come, took off the sackcloth [that he wore], cleaned his face of the ashes that covered it, and went to

---

[37] Anders, "Theses for the Atomic Age," 493.   [38] Ibid., 498.

[39] The phrase is from Jean-Pierre Dupuy, one of Anders's most sophisticated readers. See, for example, Jean-Pierre Dupuy, "The Precautionary Principle and Enlightened Doomsaying: Rational Choice before the Apocalypse," *Occasion: Interdisciplinary Studies in the Humanities* 1 (1): 1–13 (October 5, 2009).

his workshop. That evening a carpenter knocked on his door and said to him: "Let me help you build an ark, *so that it may become false*." Later a roofer joined them, saying: "It is raining over the mountains, let me help you, so that it may become false."[40]

For Anders's Noah, then, the catastrophe is at once both, the catastrophe is at once both *necessary*, fated to occur, and a *contingent accident*, one that need not happen. The way out of this paradox, based on a new understanding of the relation between future and past, requires us to act *as if* the catastrophe has already happened – or is fated to happen – in order to prevent it from becoming true. By acting *as if* the catastrophe has already taken place, we are able to project ourselves into the postapocalyptic situation and ask ourselves what we could and should have done otherwise.[41] "Let me help you build an ark, so that it may become false."

There is an important distinction to be drawn here between Anders and Wittgenstein, as well as a crucial point of connection. In Anders's case, the prophecy of catastrophe is made in order to prevent it from becoming true: whilst we are living in the "Time of the End," we must "do everything in our power to make The End Time *endless*," to prevent it from becoming "The End *of* Time." His position is thus apocalyptic (since it believes in the possibility of The End of Time), but also *anti*-apocalyptic (in the sense that it fights against man-made apocalypse).[42] Wittgenstein, by contrast, would seem (at least in his notebooks) to believe that (i) the catastrophe is already in train ("the scientific and technological age is the beginning of the end for humanity") and (ii) it is only "the *prospect*" of a final end that allows us to imagine a future beyond the "infinite misery" of capitalist "progress" in which "peace is the last thing that will ... find a home" (CV 1994, 72). It is therefore the threat of extinction itself which promises to reconnect us with our basic humanity; and it is here that the key connection with Anders becomes clear. Both philosophers are conscious of themselves as writing in *a moment of danger*; and both, in different ways, encourage "an alteration in the mode of life of human beings"[43] – one grounded in a certain kind of ethical-imaginative leap. While their work is directed towards the realization of a more humane

---

[40] Cited in Jean-Pierre Dupuy, *The Mark of the Sacred*, trans. M. B. DeBevoise (Stanford, CA: Stanford University Press, 2013), 203.

[41] Ibid., 204. See also, Jean-Pierre Dupuy, *A Short Treatise on the Metaphysics of Tsunamis*, trans. M. B. DeBevoise (East Lansing, MI: Michigan State University Press, 2015), chapter 1. For a critique of Dupuy's theory of "enlightened catastrophism," see Ben Ware, Nothing but the End to Come: "Extinction Fragments," *e-flux journal* (September, 2020).

[42] Anders, "Theses for the Atomic Age," 494.   [43] The phrase is from RFM.

world – a world that fully accords with human needs and potentials – it would nevertheless be correct to say that both are *pessimists*, albeit of a distinctly dialectical type.[44] As Anders writes: "If some, paralyzed by the gloomy likelihood of the catastrophe, have already lost courage, they still have a chance to prove their love of man by heeding the cynical maxim: 'Let's go on working as though we had the right to hope. Our despair is none of our business.'"[45] Wittgenstein, similarly, in a telling encounter with his friend Rush Rhees, appears to endorse *tragic hope* in the face of pseudoscientific optimism:

> Walking home ... Wittgenstein remarked that when someone said he was optimistic *because* the law of historical development showed that things were bound to get better, this was nothing he could admire. On the other hand, if someone says: "By the look of them, things are getting worse, and I can find no evidence to suggest that they will improve. And yet in spite of this, I believe things will get better!" – I can admire that.[46]

VIII.

Although Wittgenstein's remarks on apocalypse appear in his private notebooks, they nevertheless provide us with a crucial link to his later philosophy. The epigraph of the *Investigations*, drawn from Nestroy, warns readers that "progress ... always looks much greater than it really is"; while the book's Preface speaks of "the darkness of this time" – a reference, no doubt, to the catastrophic period, 1936-1945, during which the book was composed. In the body of the *Investigations*, we hear of machines "bending, breaking off [and] melting" (PI §193); exploding boilers (466); and people who see "the cross piece of a window as a swastika" (420). But it is not simply the language of the book that we might describe as apocalyptic, but also, and more importantly, the fundamental conception of philosophy that we find therein. This is expressed very clearly in the metaphilosophical remarks at §§89–133. Here Wittgenstein carries out a kind of apocalyptic-anti-apocalyptic

---

[44] For an exploration of the idea of dialectical pessimism, see Ben Ware, "Excremental Happiness: From Neurotic Hedonism to Dialectical Pessimism," *College Literature: A Journal of Critical Literary Studies* 45 (2): 198–221 (2018).
[45] Anders, "Theses for the Atomic Age," 505.
[46] *Recollections of Wittgenstein*, ed. Rush Rhees (Oxford: Oxford University Press, 1984), 201–202.

move: he strives to bring to an end not philosophy as such, but rather philosophy as *a discourse of the end*[47] – that is, philosophy which takes as its goal "crystalline purity" (107), "perfect order" (98), "complete exactness" (91); philosophy which serves to prescribe and insist that "this is how things *must* be":

> We want to say that there can't be any vagueness in logic. The idea now absorbs us that the ideal "must" occur in reality. ...
>
> The ideal, as we conceive of it, is unshakable. You can't step outside it. ...
>
> When we believe that we have to find that order, the ideal, in our actual language, we become dissatisfied with what are ordinarily called "sentences," "words," "signs." The sentence and the word that logic deals with are supposed to be something pure and clear-cut. And now we rack our brains over the nature of the *real* sign. ...
>
> The more closely we examine actual language, the greater becomes the conflict between it and our requirement. (For the crystalline purity of logic was, of course, not something I had discovered: it was a requirement.) (PI §§101, 103, 105, 107)

Where then does this striving after the ideal of perfect order and crystalline purity come from? It would seem to be a perfect example of an issue which Wittgenstein highlights in the *Blue Book*: "Philosophers constantly see the method of science before their eyes, and are irresistibly tempted to ask and answer questions in the way science does. This tendency is the real source of metaphysics, and leads the philosopher into complete darkness" (BB 18). Being held captive by a picture of the "the ideal" is, Wittgenstein says, akin to having "a pair of glasses on our nose through which we see whatever we look at. It never occurs to us to take them off" (103). But perhaps the answer is not the *removal* of the glasses absolutely (there can, after all, be no pure and unmediated act of seeing), but rather a radical *perspectival shift*: one that allows us to see what has been there all along, right in front of our eyes. Here, once again, we encounter the end of one world (or, in this case, the end of one particularly regime of seeing) and the opening up of a new one: a world of unknown familiarity.

---

[47] On this point, see also Simon Glendinning, "Wittgenstein's Apocalyptic Librarian," in *Wittgenstein and the Future of Philosophy: A Reassessment After 50 Years*, ed. Rudolph Haller and Klaus Puhl (Vienna: OBV & HPT, 2002), 61–70. I would, however, question Glendinning's rather too simple contention that the later work "teaches us how to bring philosophy to an end."

This brings us to the second sense of apocalyptic in the later Wittgenstein: the revelatory and indeed *the ethical* moment signposted at §129:

> The aspects of things that are most important for us are hidden because of their simplicity and familiarity. (One is unable to notice something because it is always before one's eyes.) The real foundations of their inquiry do not strike people at all. Unless that fact has at some time struck them. And this means: we fail to be struck by what, once seen, is most striking and most powerful.

Here philosophy is being presented as an activity with which involves relearning how to "look" at the world. Its aim, according to Wittgenstein, is to loosen the grip of fixed ways of seeing; to destabilise routinized habits of thought and perception; and bring us to the point from which it is possible to view the everyday through a dialectical optic.

This change in how we see can have a number of far-reaching consequences. For instance, by striving to see things otherwise, we also, in the words of the critic Fredric Jameson, initiate a "reawakening of the imagination of possible and alternate futures, a reawakening of that historicity which our current system – offering itself as the end of history – necessarily represses and paralyses." Understood in this way, seeing language, self, and the world otherwise becomes inseparable from the imaginative activity of seeing the future otherwise. In our own apocalyptic moment – a period of ecocidal acceleration, deadly plagues, and inter-imperialist war – nothing, we might argue, could now be more urgent.

Index

Acker, Kathy 28
Acknowledgment 16, 18, 40, 144, 161, 170, 175
Acknowledgment and No Approach 49–51
Adorno, Theodor 106–109, 207
Aesthetics 38, 62, 79, 104, 109–110, 115, 129, 154, 156–157, 169
Altieri, Charles 4
Anders, Günther 211
Antihumanism 106
Antin, David 29
Aspect-perception 30, 79, 104, 115, 117, 122, 124
Austen, Jane 144
Austin, J. L. 44, 85, 93

Badiou, Alain 199, 203
Baraka, Amiri 38–39
Bernhard, Thomas 24–25
Bernstein, Charles 159
Big Data 66–67
Blasing, Mutlu Konuk 161
Bloom, Harold 105

Calvino, Italo 18
Carter, Angela 22
Cavell, Stanley 17, 43, 45, 77, 85–86, 91, 96, 113–114, 134, 145, 159, 169, 175
Celan, Paul 163–167
Chodat, Robert 135
Churchland, Paul 67
Coetzee, J. M. 36
Collini, Stefan 97
Crary, Alice 110–111
Criticism 1, 41–43, 45–47, 51–52, 54, 56–59, 61–62, 64, 67, 71, 76, 78–80, 82, 86, 97, 99, 102, 109, 114, 134, 145, 147, 162, 200
Culler, Jonathan 92, 154

Davis, Lydia 29–30
Deleuze, Gilles 195
DeLillo, Don 23
Descartes, René 94
Descombes, Vincent 64
Diamond, Cora 141, 145
Duck-rabbit 117

Eldridge, Richard 134, 138
Ellmann, Richard 120
Empson, William 92, 97, 99–103

Felski, Rita 105, 122
Fiction 17, 23, 35, 78, 126–127, 129–131, 135, 139–140, 143–145
Fish, Stanley 150
Floyd, Juliet 170
Formalism 162
Frege, Gottlob 17, 21, 156, 173, 178–179, 195–196
Furey, Michael 119

Gass, William 21, 32
Gibson, John 130, 145
Greenberg, Clement 201
Guyer, Paul 79

Hanfling, Oswald 94
Harrison, Bernard 130, 145
Heidegger, Martin 204
Hempfer, Klaus 154
Hermeneutics of suspicion 104–105, 121–122, 124
Historicism 92
Hölderlin, Friedrich 156
Horkheimer, Max 207
Huemer, Wolfgang 158
Humanism 101, 104, 106, 122, 161

Immanent critique 178, 201
Irvin, Sherri 161, 164

Jameson, Fredric 82
Janik, Allan 17

Kant, Immanuel 114, 205
King Lear 46–49
Koethe, John 151–152, 155
Kramnick, Jonathan 69

L=A=N=G=U=A=G=E poetry 159
Laugier, Sandra 84, 91
Leavis, F. R. 42
Lebensform See Wittgenstein, forms of life
Lerner, Ben 30–31
Levine, Caroline 162, 165
Literary studies 43, 46, 56, 62–63, 66, 69, 73, 81, 86, 92, 104–105, 109, 119, 122, 124, 129, 135, 146–147, 159
Logic 17, 20, 65, 73, 86, 101, 139, 170, 176, 179, 181–182, 188, 201, 204, 212
Lyric, nature of 147–151

Maddy, Penelope 171
Marcuse, Herbert 197
Meaning 23, 36, 55, 60, 75, 86, 92, 98–99, 104, 138, 144, 159, 180
  autonomy of 119
  form, and 59
  hidden 122
  logic, and 189
  meaningfulness, and 65, 101
  meaning-making 136
  textual 123
  use, as 37, 84, 97, 132
Modernism 108, 151, 155, 194, 198–204
Moi, Toril 64, 80, 86
Moretti, Franco 66–67, 71–72
Mosley, Nicholas 31

Nabokov, Vladimir 22
Narrative 24, 68, 72, 75, 126, 132, 135, 140–141, 143, 149, 153, 163, 165, 200
Nelson, Ingrid 162
Nelson, Maggie 27, 39
Neuroaesthetics 69
Neuroscience 77, 79
Nietzsche, Friedrich 128, 198, 204

OED 97
Ong, Yi-Ping 139

Perloff, Marjorie 27, 159
Phenomenology 47, 50, 54, 59, 61
Plato 128
Poetic meaning 153, 161–163
Pynchon, Thomas 20

Ramazani, Jahan 153

Said, Edward W. 124
Schalkwyk, David 132, 139, 145
Sebald, W. G. 32–35
Seeing-as 116–117
Seeley, William P. 68
Standish, Paul 90
Starr, G. Gabrielle 68
Stein, Gertrude 206
Stewart, Susan 161
Style 183–193
Subjectivity 45, 48, 53–54, 57, 59, 91, 148, 151–152, 158, 160

Veblen, Thorstein 69

Wallace, David Foster 36–38
Waters, William 161, 164
Wittgenstein
  Culture and Value 126, 155
  Forms of Life 38, 82, 85, 88, 90, 92, 103, 160, 162, 171–172, 176, 179–180, 182, 190, 192
  grammatical investigation, philosophy as 141
  Lectures on Aesthetics 63, 79–80, 109, 112–113, 115, 117, 119
  On Certainty 28–29, 73, 150
  Philosophical Investigations 18, 24, 27, 29, 32–33, 35–36, 44, 46, 49, 57, 59, 82, 84–86, 99, 109, 115–116, 118, 126, 130–131, 134–135, 139, 156, 158, 168–169, 171, 174, 179–180, 183, 187–188, 191, 193, 208
  Poetry, philosophy as 16
  Private language, on 30–31, 35–37, 88, 151, 187
  Remarks on the Philosophy of Psychology 115
  Tractatus 17, 19–20, 22, 24, 26–28, 35–36, 38, 40, 156, 158, 169, 195–199, 203
Woolf, Virginia 141–143